Pepita Aris

The Sauce Book

McGRAW-HILL BOOK COMPANY
New York   St. Louis   San Francisco   Mexico

Acknowledgements

*All photographs supplied by The Anthony Blake
Photo Library*

*Our thanks to Wedgwood, who supplied the
"Contessa" sauceboats on the cover, and to Lawleys of
London, who provided the silver spoons.*

A Phoebe Phillips Editions Book

ISBN 0-07-002189-9

1 2 3 4 5 6 7 8 9   8 7 6 5 4

**Library of Congress Cataloging in
Publication Data**
Aris, Pepita.
   The sauce book.

   1. Sauces.   I. Title.
TX819.A1A74   1984   641.8'14   84-5717
ISBN 0-07-002189-9

CONTENTS

INTRODUCTION

In *The Sauce Book* I have collected together in one place more than 400 sauces from all over the world. The traditional sauces of England and America are here, with familiar names from Europe and the Middle East. Lesser-known recipes ring the changes on food cooked in familiar ways. There are some Indian and Oriental ideas too, including sauces such as curries that are cooked with the dish instead of separately.

Sauces range from quick dips to ones that virtually form a meal with rice, to classic sauces served in a sauceboat; and styles vary from wholesome nut sauces to the minimal elegance of *nouvelle cuisine*. Some recipes are new, others go back to the 18th century. All in all, they cover every type of dish and every occasion. The very important introductory sections include basic recipes as well as vital advice about ingredients and methods, and I have given the exact meaning of many traditional cooking terms.

The majority of sauces can be prepared in very little time and can therefore be made while the main course cooks. They are also a boon for the non-cook – someone who must prepare meals every day, but professes to lack time or skill. Quickly assembled food from the freezer or microwave oven can be transformed by a baste or last-minute gravy, adding flavor as well as eye appeal.

Simple or sophisticated, traditional or original, a sauce adds individuality to any dish. Because it is the cook's own contribution to the dish it gives character to plainly cooked food; it can also make the same basic ingredients appear very different on different occasions. If you are cooking an ambitious dish, the right sauce will complement it. On the other hand, a well-judged sauce can transform nothing much into something rather special.

To be successful a sauce need not be complicated. What can be nicer than lemon juice on smoked salmon or melted, seasoned butter poured over fresh, hot asparagus? It is careful matching and appropriateness that count – with, sometimes, a talent for the unexpected.

Sauces are well known as the foundation of classic cooking. This culinary tradition has been handed down through the centuries by professional cooks, but is equally important in domestic cooking. Each generation experiments, emphasizing some aspects and disregarding others; it makes changes and contributes new ideas. But the basic recipes for the great established sauces – brown gravies, tomato sauce and creamy wine sauce among them – are acknowledged by amateurs and professionals alike, who think they are well worth the time and effort involved.

I have taken a thoughtful look at this classical repertoire and the famous French sauces: which are the most useful and how can they best be tackled on the occasions when you want to show your very best? How do you cope, within the limits imposed by modern life, with the traditions created by professionals without regard to time or cost? To answer these questions, I have included tips and hints collected from a great many well-known chefs.

There are no recipes for pickling and chutneys, because they need a period to mature before they can be eaten and so do not answer the immediate need of any meal. They are also always made in large quantities. The quick relishes here can all be eaten within 24 hours, though a few can also be stored successfully.

Time and cost have been the guide when choosing sauces that might also be classed as soups or stews; these recipes require comparatively modest amounts of meat and don't need casseroling. I have included several glazes and bastes which moisturize food and add taste, and some garnishes that are eaten like sauces.

Author's Note

The Sauce Book is easy to use and recipes are alphabetical within each section. Remember that many sauces have 2 or 3 names or are well known in their original language as well as English. If you do not see a favorite recipe immediately, look in the index which lists alternatives, as well as main ingredients. The charts at the end highlight suitable sauces for any type of dish you may have on hand. They cannot include every possibility, but are there as a quick and easy reference. The introduction to each recipe recommends specific dishes with which the sauce can be served. Again they are by no means exclusive, but are suggestions to start you off. Some recipes, Béchamel for example, are so adaptable that they will go with almost everything.

Obtaining the right ingredients is often a problem. You may not have all the necessary spices and bottled sauces in your cupboard all the time – even those that are readily available. Fresh ingredients are sometimes in the markets, sometimes not. In many recipes, therefore, I have given you a choice – both the ingredient you are most likely to have on hand and the one that is traditional or which I prefer.

When shopping for ingredients it is worth bearing in mind the recipe's origin – don't try to imitate a tomato sauce that is normally made with very ripe southern tomatoes by replacing them with chilly, flavorless, midwinter northern ones; the sauce will not be a success. Use canned tomatoes instead. Similarly, *shoyu* – light soy sauce – is often used in Japanese recipes. If you cannot find it in a Chinese specialty store, use ordinary Chinese soy as a substitute and only failing this the dark, heavy Japanese soy sauce.

Modern equipment saves time and I have a hearty respect for the pressure cooker with its capacity to blend flavors. The microwave oven is marvelously useful, too, but I don't believe that the cooking process improves the flavor in the same way, so a sauce will help here. Food processors slice and chop so effortlessly that salads have been transformed and purées are light work. A blender is a boon. It would be a pity, however, to reduce every sauce to the same smooth purée, just because this is what it does so well; irregularity in texture can add variety and charm.

Equipment needed for sauces is modest: a small, heavy-based saucepan, a wooden spoon with a corner that will reach to the base of the saucepan side, a short, sharp vegetable knife, a potato peeler and sieve and, if possible, a grater with two sizes of hole. A rack to keep meat above the roasting pan will help create good meat drippings, and I love my hand-held electric mixer.

Small touches are important for sauces: hot plates are essential for a hot sauce. Chilling reduces flavor, so a sauce served at room temperature needs less acid and seasoning than the same sauce thoroughly chilled. Seasoning is crucial – and the cook is the right judge. Taste the sauce yourself before serving and season to please yourself. For this reason I have not given quantities for salt and pepper.

Bear in mind that the final consistency of the sauce depends on the type of heat used for cooking as well as on the recipe ingredients: a double boiler is essential in some recipes where ingredients will curdle if cooked over direct heat. If a sauce is for coating food, but appears too thin, boil a little to reduce it; if a pouring sauce seems too thick, add a little of the appropriate broth, milk or wine and heat gently.

I have taken 1 cup as my standard measure, though many sauces make only approximately this amount. This quantity will serve 4 people, allowing 4 tblsp each; increasing the quantities to serve 6 or 8 is not difficult. It is, however, impractical to make some recipes in small quantities, and therefore I have also included information on reheating and freezing, and using leftover sauces imaginatively.

If you are multiplying a recipe, remember that a sauce will take longer to reduce when the volume is larger. It is also true that many spices and herbs are very persistent and will often flavor a much larger quantity of liquid than is given. Do not, then, simply double the original quantity of seasonings such as nutmeg and cayenne. Use the original quantity, then taste and think again: only add more if needed.

Nothing is so frustrating as not being able to recreate past successes. When you find a particularly successful combination of sauce and dish, make a note of it in the margin for next time – and you will eventually create your own sauce book.

Hot Savory Sauces

In this, the longest chapter, you will find creamy elegant sauces for fish or delicate vegetables, or a hearty tomato sauce for a pizza topping or a pasta supper dish. There are nouvelle cuisine purées for dramatic display and frothy butter sauces. The classic rich gravies of French cuisine for party roasts, steaks and game are given, plus background information and many tips from good cooks. There are different types of curry sauce for rice as well as glazes and bastes from America or the Far East for grilled meats, kabobs or microwave cookery, tangy fruit sauces, instant dips and mouth-searing spice mixtures — plus extra tips for adding even more variety to basic recipes.

CLASSIC WHITE SAUCES

At the base of most satin-smooth white French sauces there is the **roux**, a cooked paste of butter and flour that will absorb many times its own volume of liquid without forming lumps. The traditional French roux is equal weights of butter and flour, but the American system is equal volumes – which makes the sauce slightly more buttery and therefore richer and I prefer this. There is also less danger of the roux burning.

Choose a small, heavy-based pan for sauce-making: small means a small surface area and consequently less skin forming on top; heavy-based reduces the risk of burning. Melt the butter over low heat – don't let it color – and add the flour. Stir to a paste with a wooden spoon and cook gently. For a white sauce cook for 1 minute, for more robust sauces you can cook for 2 minutes, until the paste is pale fawn, or for a brown roux for 5–10 minutes until it is dark. It is not unusual to fry onions in the butter first and cook the flour with them: this is still a roux.

Warm the liquid; basic proportions are 2 tblsp butter and 2 tblsp flour to 1 cup liquid for a sauce of pouring consistency. Stir in the liquid slowly off the heat, then cook on a low heat, stirring steadily around the sides and across the bottom of the pan, for 5 minutes until thick and glossy. Some cooks use a balloon or sauce whisk for this – the reason being that whisking is the best cure for any lumps.

In the U.S. the basic "white sauce" is simply milk, butter and flour, plus salt and pepper. The French are more sophisticated and flavor the milk. For a classic **Béchamel** (page 24) flavor the milk with a bay leaf or bouquet garni, vegetables such as carrot, celery, onion and mushroom peelings or stems, seasonings including nutmeg, and perhaps meat, such as small amounts of veal or ham. These are infused in the hot liquid for 30 minutes, so it absorbs some of their flavors. Nowadays modern miracles called bouillon cubes can be used discreetly instead of some or all of these flavorings. A tiny knob of a chicken, vegetable, or pale beef cube (about a quarter) will help your sauce, simply because it contains small amounts of monosodium glutamate, the tastebud-waker. (Some vegetarian cubes are made without MSG.)

Béchamel is one of the great foundation sauces – the French call them *sauces mères* or "mother sauces" – and a great many other things may be added to it to make new sauces.

For **Velouté** (page 74), the second white foundation sauce, a hot liquid other than milk is used. This may be specially prepared broth (chicken, veal or fish), but just as often it is the hot liquid used to cook the food which the sauce will accompany.

Both Béchamel and Velouté are good-tempered sauces – they can be made ahead and stored in the refrigerator (with the tops covered with plastic wrap or a butter wrapper) and will freeze for 3 months, so they are worth making in larger quantities. Freeze in 1 cup packs, leaving ½ in headspace. Thaw overnight if possible, then reheat in a double boiler to avoid any scorching.

If you have cooked something delicious in a liquid, you may well want to turn this into a sauce in the same pan. If the flavor and quantity are right, thickening the liquid is simple. Easiest to use is **beurre manié**, or "kneaded butter." Some people keep a supply ready-made in the refrigerator – it keeps for months. To make, use butter at room temperature and mash it with an equal volume of flour until a smooth paste is formed. Take the liquid for thickening off the heat and drop in pea-sized pieces of beurre manié. Bring back to a boil, stirring, and cook until thickened. The coating of fat around each flour grain ensures that it will expand without forming unattractive lumps.

To thicken a liquid without adding extra fat, which will be there already if you have fried meat, use **arrowroot** or **cornstarch**. Arrowroot gives by far the better texture to the sauce, but cornstarch is more stable. The basic proportions are 1 tblsp to 1 cup liquid. Make a paste with 2 tblsp water, then stir in some hot liquid from the pan. Return to the pan and cook for 1–2 minutes, stirring, until thickened.

If you want to thicken a liquid but cannot boil it without the risk of curdling (if it has egg yolks, yogurt or cream and lemon juice in it), you can use what the French call **fécule**. This is potato flour, which thickens without being boiled; its modern equivalent is a spoonful or so of instant potato.

A richer way of thickening a well-flavored pale liquid is with a **liaison**. Egg yolks, usually combined with cream, are beaten with a little of the hot liquid, and this is returned to the rest of the liquid and stirred gently over low heat until thickened.

Classic proportions are 2 large egg yolks plus ¼ cup heavy or light cream to 1 cup liquid. The French foundation sauce made this way is Allemande (page 20) and this is used as a base for other delicious things. Once made, egg-thickened sauces must be treated with great caution to avoid curdling and only reheated in a double boiler.

With the coming of the new wave of French cooking, lighter (but not necessarily more slimming) sauces are again in fashion. Heated cream, whisked butter and vegetable purées are their thickeners. A smaller quantity of well-reduced, flavorful liquid may be offered, instead of a larger quantity of a thickened one. A liquid that is reduced increases in flavor as it decreases in quantity. To **reduce**, bring to a rolling boil over high heat and continue boiling: 1 cup will reduce by half in about 8 minutes. Larger quantities (of broth, for example) are best boiled in two wide pans to increase the surface area for evaporation.

The **consistency** of a sauce – and the number it will serve – varies according to use; in general 4 tblsp per person. A pouring sauce, served in a sauceboat, should be just thick enough to glaze the back of a spoon; allow 2 tblsp flour to 1 cup liquid. This is right for a soup base, too. To coat food portions, allow 3 tblsp flour to 1 cup liquid. This sauce will just coat the back of a spoon. If a thicker sauce is needed, you can always boil slightly to reduce it. Remember that sauces get thicker as they cool, so they rarely need correcting for using cold. A very thick sauce is sometimes needed for a base for soufflés or croquettes; this is called a **panada**. Use ¼ cup flour to 1 cup liquid.

The flavor of a sauce lies in the liquid used to make it. The English-speaking peoples don't honor vegetables much with their own sauce, but the simplest of white roux sauces uses the vegetable liquid to make velouté in which to serve them. Cook the vegetables in the minimum of water with a discreet amount of a bouillon cube.

Onion, cauliflower and asparagus water are all worth saving as simple stocks; I cook the trimmings from cauliflower (20 minutes) and asparagus (30 minutes) again in the same water as used for the fresh vegetable. Real vegetable stock – a selection of older vegetables, omitting cabbage and its relatives – simmered for hours is not worth the fuel cost.

A French habit is to cook vegetables in a **blanc à legumes**, a lemony "white vegetable stock" which helps preserve the color of white or pale vegetables. Mix 2 tblsp flour with 1 tblsp lemon juice; add 1 quart water and 1 tsp salt. Boil for 2 minutes then strain. I use this for cooking white vegetables such as leeks, but mainly for those tiresome roots like Jerusalem artichokes and salsify that discolor so easily. Scrub and cook them in their skins then peel. Use the liquid for a simple Velouté.

Next in the hierarchy comes court bouillon or "short-time stock," so called because it takes only 30 minutes to make, unlike meat-based stocks. A **simple court bouillon** can be used for poaching anything. I use 8 crushed black peppercorns, 1 crumbled bay leaf, 1 sliced onion, 3 parsley stalks, snapped in several places (not the sprigs – these darken the liquid so keep them for the garnish) and 2 tblsp white wine vinegar to 2 quarts water. Add salt according to the circumstances.

Use this court bouillon for cooking hams and pickled beef tongue, after blanching or soaking as directed. Cook a beef tongue for up to ¾ –1 hour per pound, a large ham for 15 minutes per pound, and a smaller one for 20 minutes per pound. Cool the meat in the stock.

Ham and tongue stocks can be used for sauce-making, but need great discretion, as their saltiness is just as likely to ruin the sauce as it is to make it. Taste before adding: they should never make up more than a quarter of any liquid. Do not use them in association with bouillon cubes or condensed or dry-packaged soups, and hold off salting the sauce until the final seasoning.

If you need the court bouillon to poach a fish, but are not intending to make a sauce from the liquid afterwards, the simple version (given above) will do admirably.

To make real Court Bouillon for Fish (page 12), suitable for use as the base of a sauce, fish trimmings are needed. Poach the fish in it then reduce the liquid to make the sauce. Another option is to omit the trimmings, and flavor the liquid used for poaching in another way. For **quick fish stock**, poach your fish directly in ½ cup milk plus the same volume of dry white vermouth or white wine, with the addition of ½ chopped onion, ½ crumbled bay leaf and 4 crushed black peppercorns. Strain after cooking and make Velouté (page 74).

Quicker but more expensive, you can substitute canned or bottled clam juice (or clam and tomato) for fish stock.

Court Bouillon for Fish

This quantity will poach a medium-sized whole fish; make the court bouillon up to 24 hours ahead and start with it cold. For poaching fillets or steaks for 4, half the court bouillon is enough, and it can be used hot. Go late in the day to the fish merchant or you will not get any trimmings. The reduced liquid can be used to make sauce for the fish, or for soup, and its quality really depends on what, and how much, fish trimmings you put in it at the beginning.

Makes 2½ cups

½–2 lb fish heads, skin and bones (flat fish give the best flavor), or a small whole flounder (cut up) plus trimmings as available, or, if desperate, frozen fish fillets
1 large onion, sliced
1 carrot, sliced
½ celery stalk
3–4 parsley stalks, snapped in several places
8 black peppercorns, crushed
2 tsp white wine vinegar or lemon juice
¾ cup dry white vermouth or dry white wine
½ tsp salt (optional)

Put all the ingredients in a large kettle, add water to cover and bring to a boil, skimming occasionally with a slotted spoon. Lower the heat and simmer, uncovered, for 20–30 minutes (no more or the bones could make the stock bitter). Strain immediately. Use the liquid hot for poaching fillets or steaks, but use cold to poach a large fish.

After cooking, boil in the open pan to reduce by half. This well-flavored fish stock (correctly called a **fish fumet**), can be used to make Velouté (page 74) or Allemande (page 20) to serve with the fish. Alternatively, fiercely boil the liquid in which the fish was cooked until reduced to a few syrupy spoonfuls, called **fish glaze**, then add this to a made sauce just before serving.

Use court bouillon and its reduced versions within 2 days if not freezing. They can all be frozen for 1 month.

The best way to make **chicken stock** is to poach a roaster chicken in a pan not much bigger than itself, together with 1 sliced carrot, 1 sliced onion, 1 celery stalk, 1 bay leaf, 6 crushed black peppercorns, 3–4 parsley stalks, snapped in several places, a strip of lemon rind, ½ cup dry white wine or hard cider and enough water to cover. Cook for 1–1½ hours. To be truthful, I usually include a chicken bouillon cube for good luck.

Strain and measure the liquid, then boil to reduce and concentrate it, but do not reduce below 2 cups, or the flavor of the bouillon cube may dominate. The meat from a chicken cooked like this, packed in its own reduced stock and ready to make a complete meal is a convenient freezer pack.

Chicken Giblet Stock

The easiest of chicken stocks; other birds, such as turkey, duck and pheasant can be used the same way. These, however, all produce a dark stock, and this is emphasized by frying the vegetables (and carcasses if using) first. A light chicken stock is generally more useful.

Makes 2½ cups

Raw chicken neck, gizzard and heart, plus any scraps of skin (but not the liver)
Chicken carcass and bones, cooked or raw, broken up (optional)
1 carrot, sliced
5 celery stalks, chopped
1 onion, sliced
1 clove
1 bouquet garni, fresh or dried
1 thin strip of lemon rind
6 black peppercorns, crushed
2–3 parsley stalks, snapped in several places
1 chicken bouillon cube

Put all the ingredients in a large kettle and cover with about 5 cups of water. Bring to a boil, skimming off any scum. Simmer, covered, for 1½ hours, or 30 minutes in a pressure cooker on high. The final quantity of stock will depend on speed and length of boiling. Strain and leave until cold, then remove the fat from the surface. The stock can be stored in the refrigerator, covered with fat, for 4 days and frozen (without fat) for 3 months.

Right: *Orange Cream is used for this turkey dish, presented in nouvelle cuisine style, garnished with orange sections, orange julienne and concassé tomato.*

CLASSIC BROWN SAUCES

The simplest of all brown sauces is the few spoon-fuls of juice that exude from meat during cooking. Skimmed of fat, this is called **jus** in French. The meat juice can be transferred to a tall pitcher and allowed to go cold. It will then separate into a layer of fat (**drippings**), which can be lifted off, and the delicious brown **meat jelly** beneath.

More often, the meat liquid is transformed into a quick sauce in the pan in which the meat is fried. A few tablespoons of wine are added, from half to equal the liquid already present, and the pan is **deglazed**. This means the liquid is stirred to pick up all the meat drippings, the thicker patches in the liquid and any little crusty bits clinging to the sides and bottom of the pan. At the same time the liquid is boiled to reduce the amount and concentrate its flavor. This gives a rich sauce, just enough to "glaze" the meat.

For more sophisticated brown sauces, a **stock** is essential. For brown beef stock, bones are needed and are fried first in the pan until brown to give a good color to the stock. Put the onion skins in too, to help the color. For the best stocks a quantity of beef shank is also included. Flavoring vegetables and herbs are added, and water to cover. The stock needs to simmer for a long time, usually about 4 hours. A kettle of minimum 5 quart capacity is necessary; a tall one is traditional. With the minimum heat possible the liquid should barely simmer, never boil, so that a gentle transfer of flavors takes place from the ingredients to the cooking liquid. Electric burners are ideal for this; with gas, a heat diffuser could be used under the pot.

Stocks are not particularly expensive to make, nor are they time-consuming, because the stockpot does all the work. With good organiza-tion, the stock can cook while you are doing some-thing else in the house! Most stocks keep in the refrigerator for 4 days and in the freezer for 3 months. Well reduced, they are even more useful and take up little space.

Brown Bone Stock

First class stock makes first class sauce: the French call this fond brun, the "brown base" of a good sauce. It needs some organization, but takes up very little time. Reduced, the stock makes a luscious Meat Glaze (page 56).

Makes 7 cups

¼ cup good beef drippings or butter
¼ cup chopped bacon or 2 tblsp chopped cooked ham (optional)
3 lb beef shank or neck bone, with meaty scraps attached and preferably marrow inside, sawn into manageable pieces
½ lb beef shank (if the bones are not meaty), chopped
2 large onions, quartered but not peeled
2 large carrots, roughly chopped
1 large leek, white part only, thickly sliced, or 2 celery stalks, chopped
½ tsp salt
2 over-ripe tomatoes, roughly chopped (optional)
A few mushroom stems, chopped
8 black peppercorns
1 bay leaf
1 bouquet garni, dried or fresh
2–3 parsley stalks, snapped in several places

Heat the oven to 475°. Melt the drippings or butter in a roasting pan on top of the stove and fry the bacon, if using, until it gives off fat. Put in the bones, chopped beef, ham, if using, onions, car-rots and leek or celery. Turn them in the fat and cook in the oven for 45 minutes, turning regularly, until well browned.

Transfer the bones and vegetables to a large stockpot. Add 1 cup water to the roasting pan and bring to a boil, scraping around to deglaze the pan. Pour onto the bones and add 3 quarts water.

Bring to a boil, skimming the surface of any scum. Sprinkle in the salt, wait a moment and skim again. Add the tomatoes, if using, mush-room stems, peppercorns, bay leaf, bouquet garni and parsley stalks. Partially cover and simmer very gently for 3 hours or until reduced to about 7 cups. Strain the stock, then leave to get cold. Remove the hard fat before use. The stock can also be reduced to make Meat Glaze (page 56). Both are the base of many delicious sauces.

The stock will store, covered, in the refrigerator for up to 4 days if covered by fat. Freeze (without fat) in 1 cup packs (leaving ½ in headspace) for up to 3 months. Alternatively, freeze in an ice cube tray, then bag the cubes.

A wide range of ingredients can be used to make stocks. Generally **household stocks** can make use of meat bones left from the table or unwanted in cooking, older birds and carcasses and older vegetables, as well as vegetable trimmings. The main thing is to bear in mind the purpose of the stock and make it appropriate to the dish. If you are making stock ahead, label it with any special ingredients.

Light Stock

Adapt this general-purpose stock to what is available.

Makes about 6 cups

2 lb leftover meat bones, cooked or uncooked, with gristle
  and fat removed
Giblets of 1 chicken
1 large onion, sliced
1 large carrot, sliced
2 celery stalks, or a bunch of celery leaves
1 bay leaf
2–3 parsley stalks, snapped in several places
1 bouquet garni, dried or fresh

Put all the ingredients in a stockpot and cover generously with water. Bring to a boil, then turn down to the barest simmer. Cover and cook for about 2½ hours.

Strain the stock and leave until cold, then remove any fat before use. When ready to use, taste and fortify it as necessary with a tiny piece of light beef or chicken bouillon cube. If it is to be reduced as part of a sauce, remember this adds salt.

Covered, the stock can be stored for 4 days in the refrigerator; freeze (leave ½ in headspace) in 1 cup packs, for 3 months.

If a recipe requires **beef stock**, you have a number of choices. The classic French beef stock usually contains a proportion of veal: my Brown Bone Stock (opposite) is a practical version. Alternatively, use Light Stock or good canned broth or consommé. A dark bouillon cube could also be used for a brown sauce.

Once made, a good stock is often further reduced, and for this reason it is important not to oversalt it initially. In good restaurants the process of **reduction** is often repeated several times. A sauce – itself made with reduced stock – is often left to simmer for ¾–1 hour after making, to concentrate it further. So start with over twice the volume of liquid ultimately needed but, for obvious reasons, calculate the thickening agents according to the final volume. And always salt to taste last, just before serving. Provided this is practical in terms of timing, it gives the finest results.

For a dinner party, you can make the sauce well ahead, then stand it, still in its saucepan, in – not over – a **bain marie**, or water bath – a roasting pan or large saucepan of hot water. Try to keep the water at simmering or below, half off the heat, and let the sauce boil away gently until the right quantity and consistency is reached.

Meat glaze, or *glace de viande* (page 56) is the most famous of the reduced sauces. Good stock is boiled until it is reduced to about one-tenth of what it was – a few syrupy tablespoonfuls. So good is its flavor that 1–2 tblsp can be used, with the same quantity of wine, to deglaze a pan for a quick sauce. The same small quantities are often added to other sauces – usually the classic brown ones – to give them character. Meat glaze can also be added to sauces like Béarnaise. Canned broth or consommé can be reduced in the same way and substituted (but not stock based on a bouillon cube).

Since most cooks need more stock for soups and sauces than they can possibly make, short cuts are essential. **Canned consommé** will pass for Brown Bone Stock in most circumstances. However, if a lighter stock is needed, you may find consommé's brown color a disadvantage. It is worth testing several brands to find the one that is closest to the real thing. Put them in different pans and boil hard to reduce to about one-third of the volume; the stock basis will become apparent and you can eliminate the least acceptable. Be careful when recipes require the liquid to be reduced considerably. Some canned consommés and

broths and their double concentrates taste very artificial when much reduced – don't drive them beyond their own natural limit.

Bouillon cubes on the market are now available in "lamb" and "fish" flavors as well as light and dark beef cubes, chicken and vegetable. To test them, make up with one-quarter of the water specified and sip. Generally speaking you get what you pay for – the best cubes do cost more. A small nugget of cube, one-quarter or less, can be used to bolster many sauces. As cubes usually contain a little monosodium glutamate they will enhance the flavors already present without introducing much in the way of a new flavor.

A **quick bouillon from a cube** can be made by mixing about 2 cups water with a cube, according to the manufacturer's instructions. Add 3 tblsp each chopped onion and carrot and 1 tblsp chopped celery, plus ½ cup dry white wine or vermouth, 2 parsley stalks, snapped in several places, ½ bay leaf, crumbled, and a sprig of fresh thyme or tiny pinch of dried thyme. Simmer for 20–30 minutes or until reduced to 2 cups and strain. Add 1 tblsp tomato paste if wished.

Brown roux – flour cooked until colored in butter – is at the base of most great sauces. Onions are often browned in the fat first and the flour is then sprinkled in. It is essential that the flour colors to a good nut brown; stirring over low heat, this can take from 5–10 minutes.

Most **fats** can be used for a brown roux, though if part of the initial process involves searing meat over high heat, don't use butter alone: it burns easily at high temperatures. Use half butter, for its special flavor, and half oil. For sauce to accompany a particular meat dish, however, you may well do best to use the fat of the animal concerned. Trim excess fat from the meat and **render** it: chop it very small then cook it gently until it turns liquid with very crisp little pieces of fat (throw them away or use as a soup garnish). Strain the fat while hot and use it for frying. **Drippings**, the meat fat left from roasts, which has cooled and separated from its juice, are also excellent. Keep the fat from different meats separately (and never fry in fat from sausages which is horrible). Once cold, fats will store in the refrigerator for up to 2 months.

Left: *Beef Stock Gravy, based on a rich bone stock and duxelles, makes a rich accompaniment to a veal chop, Belgian endive and a stuffed tomato.*

Many classic sauces are based on rendered salt pork or bacon, as this lends special flavor to a dish. If neither is available, include ½ slice of cooked ham, finely chopped, in the sauce with the vegetables.

Bacon or ham are always included in a classic **mirepoix**. This dice of vegetables is fried as the base of a sauce, and it is always freshly made. For frying use 3 tblsp meat drippings or 2 tblsp butter plus 1 tblsp oil with 1 tblsp chopped cooked ham. Or, easiest of all, use 2 oz bacon, cut into matchstick strips, fried with ½ tblsp butter just to start the bacon giving off its own fat. In the fat gently fry 1 chopped onion, 1 chopped garlic clove, 1 chopped carrot, ½ crumbled bay leaf and a sprig of fresh thyme or pinch of dried thyme until the onion is soft. You are then ready to proceed with the sauce, often by adding flour to make roux.

A similar chopped, fried mixture is **duxelles**, based on mushrooms. This can be used as a sauce base, but may also be prepared ahead and a spoonful added to a sauce toward the end of cooking. Duxelles will add a mushroom flavor, but also, because the mixture contains a natural stimulant to the taste buds (the same one as in monosodium glutamate), it automatically enhances the other flavors in the sauce.

To make duxelles, fry 1 tblsp chopped onion in 1 tblsp each butter and oil, with ½ cup chopped mushroom stems. (Recipes often specify mushroom stems for economy: these are usually trimmed away, leaving the caps for something more decorative. If you have no stems use chopped mushrooms.) Stir over medium heat until the onion has softened and all the moisture has evaporated. Nutmeg and parsley are the traditional flavorings for this mixture. Keep, covered, in the refrigerator for up to 5 days, or freeze, well wrapped, for 1 month. Add a spoonful to a made Velouté (page 74) or a brown sauce.

Accenting the flavor can be achieved by any combination of small additions. For an elaborately made sauce these will not be necessary; for a quickly made one, you may well come to bless these small tricks. The golden rule is to taste before and after seasoning.

If a sauce seems to lack definition and character, try 1 tblsp lemon juice, and possibly a small pinch of cayenne pepper or a few drops of hot pepper sauce, per 1 cup. If a sauce seems strong or too aggressive, or if you have overdone the bouillon cube and it is unpleasantly salty or too crude, 2 tsp.

brandy or a medium Madeira wine, with a tiny pinch of sugar, will soften it. Most sauces are made more lively by the addition of wine – red or white. Boil ¼ cup wine in a small pan until reduced to 1 tblsp and stir this in. If the sauce is a hearty one, vinegar may be used instead of wine – 1 tblsp red or white, well reduced – plus a tiny pinch of sugar if needed. Other possibilities are 1 tsp Dijon-style mustard, 1 tsp Worcestershire sauce or onion juice (from grated onion), and flavorings like nutmeg (tiniest amount) and celery salt. Always add less spice or herbs than you think you may need and work upwards – you can always add more afterwards.

The most famous flour-thickened sauce is **Espagnole** (page 45). A good-quality brown stock is needed as its base. The sauce is then prepared in the traditional way by frying vegetables and making the roux. Once the stock has been added the sauce is left to simmer slowly and reduce from one-half to one-third of its original volume. This concentrates the flavors wonderfully and gives it a character that no instant sauce can match.

Reduction is at the heart of almost all the classic brown sauces. Once made, Espagnole can be reduced to about one-third to become Demi Glace (page 40), which is then used to strengthen other sauces. Many other brown sauces use Espagnole as their base; almost invariably the volume is again reduced – concentrating the flavor – to make room for the new ingredients. During the next period of gentle simmering, additional flavoring ingredients are often added; these usually give the sauce its name and character. Avoid the temptation to take a "short cut" by using less liquid in the first place and putting all the ingredients in together. The extra 20 minutes of slow simmering are the key to the sauce's fine flavor, while the succession of additions maintains a balance.

Degreasing before seasoning is very important. This is true of modest sauces, as well as the grander ones, but is even more crucial when a sauce has been made in several stages, each possibly involving fried additions. A small ice cube or 1 tblsp cold water dropped into the liquid will cause fat to rise to the surface and float. Skim with a spoon if there is a lot of fat, then draw strips of paper towel over the surface, picking up the floating circles of fat, until there are none left. Taste, season and serve.

THE BUTTER SAUCES

Think of the easiest sauce you can imagine – just golden **melted butter**, with a little salt or lemon juice added. From freshly cooked asparagus and shellfish to hard-cooked eggs, this melted salted butter, called **beurre fondu** in France, is often as good a sauce as you can get.

If you want to give butter more character, you can cook it first. **Clarified or drawn butter** has all the impurities (salt, water, etc.) removed and will therefore reach a much higher temperature than ordinary butter without burning; also there will be no black specks, which spoil the appearance of a sauce. For ½ cup clarified butter, put ¾ cup butter in a small, heavy-based pan and heat until the foaming subsides. Skim off the floating froth. The butter will separate into a clear yellow oil and a milky residue. Pour off the oil; this will solidify and can be kept in the refrigerator for many weeks (add the residue to the soup pot).

Clarified butter can be heated until golden-brown in color and nutty tasting – called Beurre Noisette (page 26) or "nutty butter" – or until dark brown (not black) for "black butter" or Beurre Noir (page 26). Slightly heightened with seasonings and lemon juice, these quick hot butters add moisture and character to food.

In a **softened butter sauce**, the butter is only half melted, so that it still has bulk, as well as an attractive lightness. Some of the nouvelle cuisine sauces rely entirely on softened butter for volume (see Foaming Wine Sauce, page 48). Butter is often lightly whisked into classic sauces in tiny pieces at the end of a recipe. Do not overbeat the sauce, and do not stir or reheat it afterwards, or it could separate.

A **hot emulsion sauce** is made by whisking cold butter with egg yolks in a warm atmosphere. The two form an emulsion – rather like a warm mayonnaise. The most famous are Hollandaise (page 52) just sharpened with lemon juice, and Béarnaise (page 24), with reduced wine vinegar.

Having curdled Hollandaise a great many times, I have come to the conclusion that the right equipment is indispensable. A **bain marie** – a saucepan standing in a pan of warm water – is no longer practical for many sauces, because modern fuel sources are too hot, even at their lowest. The temperature of the water in a bain marie should be three-quarters of the way to boiling, but with modern ranges it inevitably creeps up higher; the water boils and the sauce is spoiled. If you have a really slow electric hob it may be practical, but with gas it is impossible.

I find it best to use a **double boiler** to make all slow sauces safely and to reheat them. This can be simply a bowl resting securely on a saucepan, with two-thirds inside it. Put 1 inch warm water in the pan. It is essential the bowl does not touch the water. A small pan suspended, by rim and handle if necessary, in a larger one is even more useful, because there are occasions when you want to start a sauce over direct heat and then continue in a double boiler, and a heatproof top container saves dish washing. To check, stand the top container beside the bottom one and make sure it will be suspended at least 2 inches above the bottom of the lower pan; if not, it risks touching the water below and so won't do the job properly. When making the sauce, keep the water in the bottom below boiling, turning off the heat if necessary.

A **hand-held electric beater** is a godsend for sauces. The old-fashioned balloon whisk and the rotary beater are efficient but give aching wrists. Hand whisking is also the best way to remove lumps in any flour-based sauce.

With the right equipment, Hollandaise and its derivatives can be made with ease – provided you don't hurry. I find the classic method of making it easier than scraping out a blender at the end. Use cold butter – it has the volume already – and add very little at a time. Rewarming Hollandaise can be risky (always use a double boiler). However, it can be kept warm in a small, wide-necked Thermos.

TOMATO AND PUREED SAUCES

The oldest sauces in the world, reaching back to ancient Egypt and classical Greece, are purées, which were thickened by stirring in bread crumbs or ground nuts or sometimes sieved hard-cooked egg yolks, and then beaten until amalgamated. These sauces still survive from medieval Europe, in the Middle East and around the Mediterranean.

Another Mediterranean tradition and forerunner of the French mirepoix (page 17) is **soffritto**. When making a *ragù*, or sauce, the Italian housewife will start by frying a mixture of onions and garlic, the basis of whatever is to follow. This is *soffritto*, called *sofrito* in Spain and *refogado* in Portugal. It is such a standard way of making a sauce in Latin America and countries bordering the Mediterranean that recipe books may simply list *soffritto* as an ingredient. Other vegetables such as carrots or celery may also be included, and, of course, tomatoes.

Introduced to Europe in the early 16th century, the first yellow tomatoes were a limited success. It was only when red ones arrived from America that **tomato sauce** really started its career, being enthusiastically adopted in southern Italy. It wasn't known outside the Mediterranean area, however, until the Marseilles volunteers took it to Paris during the French Revolution – France's national anthem and tomato sauce arrived in the capital at the same time. A sauce of infinite variety, it can be served cooked or raw, with wine, sherry or Madeira added, with cream or chilies, or with a wide choice of herbs – even including mint. It can be coarse, or smoothly puréed.

If the skin and seeds remain in the sauce, they may spoil its appearance, while the tomato juices dilute its flavor – all the taste of a tomato is in its red flesh. This can be used separately and is called **concassé tomatoes** in French (literally "chopped"). Pour boiling water over each tomato, in turn, in a cup; count to 10, then peel off the skin, quarter the tomato and discard seeds and juice. Then chop the flesh.

The new wave of cooking has brought other **puréed** vegetable sauces to the fore. Puréed fresh peas with a little added cream (sauce Clamart) and fluffy, light onion or carrot purées, to which red **fruit** such as raspberries and black currants are added, have come to supplement the heavier flour-thickened sauces, and partially replace them. These colorful puréed sauces are often poured on the plate, rather than over the food, to be used as the colored background to the display of nouvelle cuisine food. They are very different in feel to the traditional fruit sauces of Eastern Europe and America, which have always accompanied fatty meat.

AGRODOLCE

The Italians like sour-sweet sauces with game. Invented for hare and venison, this sauce does wonders for broiled turkey drumsticks or braised rabbit.

Serves 6

2 tblsp brown sugar
¼ cup currants
4 (1 oz) squares semisweet chocolate, grated
1 tblsp chopped candied orange peel
1 tblsp chopped candied lemon peel
1 cup red wine vinegar
1 tblsp capers
1 tblsp pine nuts or chopped blanched almonds

Combine the first 7 ingredients in a saucepan and soak for 2 hours. Simmer for 10 minutes, then stir in the nuts before serving.

ALLEMANDE

Par excellence the dinner party sauce: the egg yolks and cream add richness to a Velouté, while the roux base means that disaster is less likely while your attention is on other things. It used to be called "sauce parisienne," and dishes which it accompanies are often called "à la parisienne." The greatest of French chefs, Carême renamed it "sauce allemande" (German sauce) nearly 200 years ago, half as a joke, to contrast it with France's great brown sauce, "sauce espagnole" (Spanish sauce).

Made with fish stock, the sauce is worthy of sole or sea bass; made with chicken stock it is excellent with poached chicken, eggs and such vegetables as asparagus, lima beans, salsify and carrots.

Makes 1½ cups

2 tblsp butter
6 mushroom stems or 2 button mushrooms, finely chopped
2 tblsp flour
1 cup well-flavored fish stock (page 11) or chicken stock (page 12), hot
2 large egg yolks
4–6 tblsp heavy cream
Salt and ground white pepper

Melt the butter in a small, heavy-based saucepan over low heat and fry the mushrooms for 2 minutes. Sprinkle with the flour and cook gently, stirring, for 1 minute.

Off the heat, stir in one-third of the stock until smooth, then add the remainder. Cook for 5 minutes, stirring. (This can be done ahead.)

Strain the sauce into the top pan of a double boiler, pressing the mushrooms well. Beat the egg yolks and cream together, then stir in a little hot sauce. Add to the remaining sauce in the double boiler. Set over simmering – not boiling – water and stir gently until thickened; the sauce must not boil. Check the seasonings before serving.

ALMOND SAUCE

This simple Spanish sauce for poached chicken is thickened with almonds and egg yolks. In Spain the yolks may well be hard-cooked then sieved, though I use raw ones. At the other end of the Mediterranean crushed garlic and more lemon juice are included, while the yolks are replaced by ½ tsp turmeric.

Makes 1½ cups

½–¾ cup roughly chopped, blanched almonds, or ground almonds (less good)
1 tblsp butter
1 cup chicken stock (page 12)
2 large egg yolks
Salt and freshly ground black pepper
1 tsp lemon juice (optional)

Fry the almonds in the butter until just colored, then purée in the blender with a little stock. Return the purée to the pan and stir in most of the remaining stock; heat gently. Mix the remaining stock with the egg yolks and stir in. Over the lowest possible heat, bring to simmering, stirring all the time. Taste and season, adding lemon juice if needed.

AMERICAINE

It was a fashionable dinner party controversy in the 1960s whether this sauce for lobster was invented in the U.S. or in Armorique (the old name for Brittany). It was given its name by Pierre Fraisse, a chef in Paris but native of Languedoc, who had spent some years in America; he based it on an earlier Mediterranean dish. An easy tomato and brandy sauce, it can be made with other shellfish and even white fish; and mixed with a modest quantity of seafood makes a good pasta sauce.

Shellfish or fish to be served in the sauce should initially be tossed in the fat to color and stiffen, then cooked with the tomato while it reduces. Remove them before adding the shells. Reheat the seafood in the sauce after thickening.

Serves 4
Shells of lobster or shrimp (optional)
2 tblsp olive oil
1/4 cup butter
2 onions, chopped
1 clove garlic, crushed or finely chopped
1 cup dry white wine if using shellfish, or half fish stock
   (page 11) and half white wine if using fish
1/4 cup brandy
1 bay leaf
1 lb ripe tomatoes, roughly chopped
2 tblsp finely chopped parsley
2 tblsp finely chopped fresh tarragon, or 1/2–3/4 tsp dried
   tarragon
Salt and freshly ground black pepper
2 tblsp tomato paste
1 tblsp lemon juice
1/8 tsp cayenne
1 tblsp flour
2 tblsp heavy cream

Cook the shells, if using, in the oil and 3 tblsp of the butter for 5 minutes. Remove and reserve. Add the onions and garlic to the fat and fry gently until transparent. Pour in the wine or stock mixture and brandy and add the bay leaf. Simmer for 10 minutes.

Add the tomatoes with 1 tblsp each parsley and fresh tarragon (or all the dried tarragon). Season and simmer for 15 minutes or until the tomatoes are reduced. Add the shells and simmer for a further 10 minutes.

Press through a sieve, or use a food processor if there are no shells. Add the tomato paste, lemon juice and cayenne (and any shellfish coral). Mash the remaining butter with the flour to make a paste. Drop in tiny pieces into the sauce and bring back to a boil, stirring. Stir in the cream and garnish with the remaining fresh herbs.

ANCHOVY HOT BUTTER

For steaks and lamb chops.

Serves 4
1¾ oz canned anchovies, drained
1/4 cup light cream
1 clove garlic, minced or finely chopped
1/2 cup tawny port
Butter and juices from frying
1/4 cup cold butter, diced small
1 tblsp chopped fresh basil leaves, or pinch of dried basil
Freshly ground black pepper

Blot the anchovies with paper towel to remove all oil. Purée in the blender with the cream and garlic. Scrape out.

Add the port to the pan in which the steaks or chops were sautéed and bring to a boil, stirring to incorporate the sediment in the pan. Boil until reduced to 4 tblsp. Add the anchovy cream and boil again until reduced to about 6 tblsp. Off the heat quickly whisk in the butter, piece by piece, then stir in the basil. Taste and season with pepper. Serve at once; do not reheat.

APRICOT GLAZE

This is the classic glaze for a country ham, which is boiled and then finished in the oven, or baked. The glaze is also good on ham steaks and lamb chops broiled or cooked in a microwave oven. See also Orange Glaze (page 61).

Glazes 4–6 lb ham

3 tblsp apricot jam, avoiding fruit lumps
1 tblsp brown sugar
1 tsp mustard powder or pinch of ground cloves
2 tsp lemon juice

Melt the jam with the brown sugar in a small pan until liquid, then stir in the mustard or cloves and lemon juice. Sieve if wished – I find I can paint the meat with a pastry brush avoiding any fruit bits, leaving them in the pan.

APRICOT AND LAMB TAGINE

Called "tagines" in Morocco and "khoresh" in Persian cooking, these fruit and meat mixtures are popular all over North Africa. Serve with couscous or rice.

Serves 4

1 medium-size onion
¼ cup butter
1 lb lean boneless lamb
Salt and freshly ground black pepper
½ tsp ground cinnamon
2 tblsp raisins
⅔ cup dried apricots, soaked for 30 minutes in boiling water to cover and roughly chopped

Fry the onion in the butter until soft and golden. Slice the lamb into small thin strips and add to the onion. Fry, turning, until brown on all sides. Season and sprinkle with the cinnamon.

Add the raisins and apricots with their soaking liquid. Add more water to cover if necessary. Cook gently, covered, for 1 hour or until the lamb is tender and the sauce well reduced.

AURORE

Any white sauce such as Béchamel (page 24) or Velouté (page 74) can be made "dawn-colored" with tomato paste (or ketchup). This creamy sauce goes well with fried sole or flounder, poached chicken and hot hard-cooked eggs (to be served as an appetizer or light supper dish), as well as pale vegetables like salsify.

Makes 1 cup

2 tsp butter
2 tsp flour
1 cup heavy cream
¼ chicken bouillon cube
1 tblsp tomato paste
1 tsp grated onion (optional)
Pinch of cayenne (optional)
Salt and ground white pepper

In the top pan of a double boiler over direct heat melt the butter and sprinkle in the flour. Cook, stirring, for 1 minute. Place over the bottom pan containing simmering water and add the cream. Cook, stirring occasionally, until thick.

Crumble in the bouillon cube and add the tomato paste. Taste and season; the onion and cayenne will make the sauce less bashful.

BARBECUE BASTE WITH GINGER AND SOY

I have given a series of basting sauces because they are so useful for quick grills and for giving some character to frozen chicken portions. They also do wonders for the appearance and flavor of microwave-cooked meat and poultry: use the baste to coat the food when you first put it in, then baste once when turning the food. The molasses version of this recipe goes well with pork; if possible marinate the meat in the baste for 4 hours before cooking. Without the molasses the baste is good with white fish steaks such as cod.

Serves 4

1 clove garlic, crushed, with salt if necessary
2 tblsp finely chopped white part of scallion (for fish only)
¼ cup olive oil
¼ cup soy sauce
1 tblsp molasses (for meat only)
½ tsp prepared mustard
2 slices fresh ginger root, finely chopped, or pinch of ground ginger
2 tblsp dry sherry wine
Salt and freshly ground black pepper

Mix all the ingredients together, and use as a baste.

BARBECUE BASTE, ORIENTAL-STYLE

Marinate pork or lamb, then use the sauce for basting. This barbecue baste is best suited to small pieces of meat or kabobs, as the ground seeds become bitter if overcooked. See also Chinese Sparerib Sauce (page 33).

Serves 4

¼ cup olive oil
2 tblsp grated onion with juice
2 tsp coriander seeds, ground
2 tsp cumin seeds, ground
3 tblsp soy sauce
2 tblsp lemon juice
1 tsp sugar
¼ tsp ground ginger
Freshly ground black pepper

Mix all the ingredients together, adding pepper to taste. Marinate the meat for 4 hours, then use to baste the meat while grilling.

BARBECUE HOT BASTE

Use to baste fatty meat, like country-style spareribs, or rather bland ones like chicken portions from the freezer.

Serves 4

1 clove garlic, crushed, with salt if necessary
⅓ cup firmly packed brown sugar
2 tblsp olive oil
¼ cup tomato ketchup
2 tblsp Worcestershire sauce
1 tblsp prepared mustard
1 tblsp red wine vinegar
½ tsp chili powder, or ¼–½ tsp hot pepper sauce

Mix all the ingredients together and use as a baste.

BARBECUE MUSTARD BASTE

This is an excellent baste for cheering up lamb chops or for chicken and turkey drumsticks (slash the latter well). See Mustard Glaze (page 60) for another version.

Serves 4

¼ cup olive oil
2 tblsp tomato ketchup
1 tblsp prepared English mustard
1 tblsp Dijon-style mustard
1 tsp sugar
Anchovy paste to taste
Pinch of paprika
Salt and freshly ground black pepper

Mix all the ingredients together. Use to marinate meat or poultry for 4 hours, then use as a basting sauce.

BARBECUE RED BASTE

Though they normally make a welcome contribution to taste, chopped herbs and ground spices are not always successful in bastes for grilling. The heat of the barbecue first dries then toasts them, making them bitter, and useless as flavor-makers. (There is not the same problem in the microwave, where there is no radiant heat.) Butter is another danger. Best for flavor, it has a low flash point at which it becomes bitter; use it with another fat or oil or with moisturizing tomato paste. Butter, chopped herbs and spices are all best used for meat or poultry that is cooked slowly, or far from the heat source, and are not suitable for food that takes more than about 5–6 minutes each side.

Makes 10 tblsp

2 tblsp butter
2 tblsp margarine
¼ cup paprika
2 tblsp tomato paste
Finely grated rind and juice of 1 lemon
⅛ tsp dried mixed herbs
½ tsp celery salt
½ tsp cayenne
Freshly ground black pepper

Beat the butter and margarine together until soft. Beat in the paprika then the tomato paste and the other ingredients and use for basting.

BEARNAISE

First choice to accompany roast fillet of beef or broiled sirloin steak, this sauce is a derivative of Hollandaise and honors the most popular of all French kings, Henri IV, a native of Béarn. It is a 19th century sauce, invented at a restaurant named after the king in St Germain outside Paris.

Makes 1 cup

2 tblsp coarsely chopped fresh tarragon
2 tblsp coarsely chopped fresh chervil (optional)
2 tblsp tarragon vinegar
½ cup dry white wine
1 tblsp finely chopped shallots or white part of scallion
1 tsp black peppercorns, coarsely crushed
3 large egg yolks
Salt
¾ cup butter, diced small

Put the first 6 ingredients into a small pan and boil until reduced to 2 tblsp. Set aside. Put the yolks, 1 tblsp cold water and a pinch of salt in the top of a double boiler over simmering – not boiling – water: the water must not touch the top pan. Whisk the yolks until combined, then strain in the reduced wine.

Whisk in the first piece of butter. When it has been absorbed, add the next. Continue whisking and adding butter, being careful to whisk over the bottom and around the sides of the pan regularly. When all the butter has been absorbed and the sauce is thick and fluffy, check the seasonings and serve.

For roast lamb or filet mignon add 1 tblsp tomato paste with the reduced wine – this is **Sauce Choron**.

BECHAMEL

This is the classic French sauce, from which so many others are derived. The process can be speeded up, but the finished sauce will lack subtlety. Béchamel is most used for boiled vegetables, cheese dishes and gratins.

Makes 1 cup

1 cup milk
½ small onion, finely chopped
2 in length of carrot, finely chopped
1 bay leaf, crumbled
6 black peppercorns, crushed
Tiny pinch of freshly grated nutmeg
1 tblsp finely chopped cooked ham
2 tblsp butter
2 tblsp flour
Salt and ground white pepper

Place the milk in a saucepan. Add the next 6 ingredients and bring slowly to a boil; simmer 1 minute. Cover and leave to infuse (off the heat) for 30 minutes.

In a small, heavy-based saucepan melt the butter over low heat – it must not sizzle. Sprinkle in the flour and cook gently, stirring with a wooden spoon, for 1 minute to make a white roux; do not let it color. Remove from the heat. Scald the milk – bring it almost back to a boil. Off the heat, strain about one-third of the hot milk onto the roux. Stir until smooth, then strain in the remaining milk, pressing the vegetables well. Bring to a boil and cook gently, stirring, for 1 minute. Before serving taste and add salt and pepper.

1 tblsp lemon juice or a pinch of cayenne will add liveliness to the sauce. Up to ¼ cup more butter can be whisked into the finished sauce, in small pieces, to add richness and gloss: serve immediately. Alternatively, the sauce can be enriched with up to ½ cup heavy cream. It is safe to boil the sauce after the addition of the cream if necessary; check the seasonings again before serving, and point up with lemon juice or cayenne if needed.

If making the sauce ahead, cover the surface with plastic wrap or a butter wrapper to prevent a skin forming. I find it easier to make double quantities; store the leftover sauce in the refrigerator for 2–3 days or freeze in 1 cup packs (leaving ½ in headspace) for up to 3 months. Thaw overnight if possible, and always reheat in a double boiler to prevent scorching. Béchamel can be used whenever a white sauce is needed.

BÉCHAMEL 2

Excellent when you have ready-flavored milk on hand, for instance from poaching fish, or only a small amount of homemade stock (or even strained soup). This sauce is quick – and very good indeed when made with half home-made chicken stock (page 12) and half cream.

Makes 1 cup

1¼ cups milk, or half stock and half milk, light or heavy cream
1 bay leaf
¼ chicken or fish bouillon cube
2 tblsp butter
2 tblsp flour
Salt and ground white pepper
Tiny pinch of grated nutmeg
1 tblsp lemon juice

Warm the liquid with the bay leaf, and dissolve the bouillon cube piece in it. Melt the butter in a small, heavy-based saucepan over low heat. Sprinkle in the flour and cook gently, stirring, for 1 minute.

Off the heat stir in one-third of the liquid until smooth, then add the remainder. Cook gently, stirring, for 5 minutes. Fish out the bay leaf with the spoon and discard. Season with salt, pepper and nutmeg and add the lemon juice; this gives a sauce of pouring consistency.

If cream was not used, the sauce can be enriched by whisking in up to ¼ cup butter, in little pieces, or 6 tblsp heavy cream.

BEEF STOCK GRAVY

Simple to make, this gravy depends on the flavor of the stock used. In France, where it is replacing the richer Espagnole, it is called "jus lié" thickened meat juice. It goes well with any meat, game or poultry.

Makes 1 cup

1 tblsp arrowroot
1 cup canned consommé or broth, or Brown Bone Stock (page 14), warm
Salt and freshly ground black pepper
2 tblsp sherry, Madeira or red wine, or 1 tblsp lemon juice (to finish)

Mix the arrowroot with 2 tblsp cold water, then stir a little hot consommé or broth or stock into the paste. Return to the pan and cook, stirring, for 1 minute or until thick enough to coat the back of the spoon. Check the seasoning. Add the sherry, wine or lemon juice just before serving; a spoonful of duxelles (page 17) could also be added. Do not reheat from cold or boil continuously, or it could go thin again – because liquids thickened with arrowroot are not always stable.

BERCY

Bercy, on the eastern side of Paris, is famous for its two great wine depots – so wine is the keynote of this sauce. The fish version, given here, is more useful than the meat one, made with beef marrow. Serve with fried or poached turbot, fried sole or flounder.

Makes 1 cup

1 shallot, finely chopped, or 1 tblsp chopped white part of scallion
4 black peppercorns, crushed
¾ cup dry white wine or dry white vermouth
1 × Velouté (page 74), made with fish poaching liquid and mushrooms, or Béchamel 2 (left), made with ½ fish poaching liquid and ½ light or heavy cream
Poaching liquid from the fish
1 tsp lemon juice (optional)
Salt and ground white pepper
¼ cup heavy cream (for Velouté), or 1 tblsp butter (for Béchamel)
1 tblsp finely chopped parsley

Put the shallot or scallion, peppercorns and wine or vermouth in a small pan and boil until reduced to 2–3 tblsp. Dish up the fish and keep warm. Quickly make the Velouté or Béchamel, using part of the fish poaching liquid. Add the reduced wine to Velouté, then strain the sauce, or strain the reduced wine into a Béchamel.

If liked, pour any remaining poaching liquid into a pan and boil fiercely until reduced to 2–3 tblsp **fish glaze**. Add to the sauce; alternatively, taste the sauce and add the lemon juice if needed. Season to taste.

For Velouté stir in the cream and heat through. For Béchamel whisk in the butter in little pieces and do not reheat. Add the chopped parsley and serve at once.

BEURRE BLANC

White butter sauce has been taken up by nouvelle cuisine cooks because of its lightness. Traditionally served with pike, it also goes well with broiled lobster and positively flavored fish such as skate and mackerel, and with cauliflower, asparagus and leeks.

Makes ¾ cup

1 small shallot, finely chopped, or 1 tblsp finely chopped
    white part of scallion
3 tblsp white wine vinegar
3 tblsp white wine
¾ cup cold, lightly salted butter, cut into small pieces
Salt and ground white pepper

Put the shallot or scallion, vinegar and wine into the top pan of a double boiler over direct heat. Boil until reduced to about 1 tblsp.

Set the pan over the bottom pan containing lightly simmering – not boiling – water: it must not touch the water. Whisk in a piece of butter and, when it has been absorbed, add the next. Continue until all the butter is incorporated. Season to taste and serve immediately.

The sauce congeals when cold. Any left over can be used as a flavored butter, or small lumps can be beaten into a Béchamel or Velouté before serving to enrich them.

BEURRE NOIR

Butter acquires a new and attractive taste when heated. Although the French name means "black butter," it should never be cooked beyond dark brown or it will burn and be uneatable. Throw it away if you miscalculate, and start again. Always use clarified butter. Serve with fish like fried skate and mackerel. When chopped capers are included, it is the classic accompaniment to brains.

Makes 6 tblsp

½ cup butter
Salt and freshly ground black pepper
1 tsp lemon juice
1 tsp finely chopped parsley (optional)
1 tblsp chopped capers (optional)

To clarify the butter, heat it in a small, heavy-based saucepan until foaming subsides, then skim the surface. Let it stand for 1 minute, then pour off the oil slowly into a cup, leaving the milky sediment behind. Pour this away (into the soup pot or onto potatoes) and clean out the pan with paper towels. Return the clarified butter to the pan – there will be about 6 tblsp.

Heat the butter until it turns dark brown, then immediately remove from the heat. Season to taste and add the lemon juice, and parsley and capers if wished.

BEURRE NOISETTE

Gently heated butter acquires a nutty taste and color, hence the French name for this sauce, "hazelnut butter." Serve it with fried chicken, asparagus or broccoli; it is also excellent with fried fish. The lemon juice is sometimes replaced by white wine vinegar.

Makes 6 tblsp

6 tblsp clarified butter (see previous recipe)
Salt and freshly ground black pepper
1 tsp lemon juice

Heat the clarified butter in a small heavy-based saucepan until it colors to golden brown. Season to taste and add the lemon juice.

My **Browned Butter** is not a true variant of Beurre Noisette, just a quicker and more convenient substitute – ideal as a speedy sauce for broiled fish. You do not need to clarify the butter first, because it is heated only to the point when the color change starts. Heat ¼ cup butter until just beginning to color, then stir in 2 tblsp meat jelly from a roast or Meat Glaze 2 (page 57). Add 1 tblsp malt vinegar, a tiny pinch of sugar and a few drops of Worcestershire sauce. Season to taste.

BIGARADE

To make this classic sauce for roast duck, bitter or Seville oranges, called "bigarades" in French, are needed. These are in season after Christmas. Lemon juice can be added if you have only sweet oranges. Bigarade can also be served with turkey, hot, boiled ham, goose or any game. See also Maltaise (page 55).

Makes 1 cup

1 tblsp butter
1 tblsp flour
1½ cups duck stock or good stock, hot
2 Seville oranges, or 2 sweet oranges plus 1 tblsp lemon juice
Duck or meat juices from the roasting pan
1 tblsp Grand Marnier or Triple Sec
Salt and freshly ground black pepper

Melt the butter in a small, heavy-based pan and sprinkle with the flour. Cook, stirring, for about 4 minutes or until colored. Off the heat stir in one-third of the stock until smooth. Add the remainder and bring to a boil, stirring. Leave over low heat to reduce gently.

Meanwhile, with a potato peeler, pare the rind thinly from the oranges. Cut the rind into fine julienne strips, matchstick length. Boil them for 5 minutes, drain well and add to the sauce.

Squeeze the oranges, and add the juice, with lemon juice if using, to the sauce. Skim the meat juices well of all fat and add to the sauce. Boil gently if necessary to reduce to the right consistency. Stir in the orange liqueur and season to taste.

BLACK CURRANT SAUCE

Serve this nouvelle cuisine sauce across a plate, garnished with very thin slices of rare-roast duck breast and a spray of black currants. It also goes well with goose.

Serves 4

½ lb (1 pint) black currants, fresh or frozen
1 cup red wine
⅛ tsp ground cinnamon
1 tblsp lemon juice
Pinch of grated nutmeg

Cook the first 3 ingredients together until reduced by half. Purée in a blender or food processor, then sieve for a smooth sauce. Taste and add the lemon juice and nutmeg. Add any skimmed meat juices from cooking before serving.

BOLOGNESE

Most famous of all spaghetti sauces, it is known as "ragu" in Bologna, the gastronomic capital of Italy, where it is as likely to be the filling for lasagne, as it is a pouring sauce. Tomato is not the dominant flavor of the sauce. See also Sugo (page 70).

Serves 4–6

3 tblsp olive oil
3 tblsp butter
¼ lb unsmoked bacon or pancetta, finely chopped
1 medium-size onion, chopped
1 clove garlic, crushed or finely chopped
1 medium-size carrot, finely chopped
1 celery stalk, finely chopped
½ lb lean ground beef
¼ lb chicken livers, trimmed of membrane and green patches and roughly chopped
½ cup dry white wine
16 oz canned tomatoes
½ cup good consommé or stock (page 15)
1 bay leaf
Salt and freshly ground black pepper
Tiny pinch of grated nutmeg
¼ cup heavy cream

Heat the olive oil and butter and fry the bacon or pancetta and onion until the bacon gives up all its fat. Add the garlic, carrot and celery and cook for a further 2 minutes, or until the onion is soft.

Add the beef and cook over medium-high heat, stirring, until the beef loses its pinkness. Add the chicken livers and turn until colored well on all sides. Stir in the wine and cook until almost evaporated.

Add the canned tomatoes and juice, chopping them roughly with the spoon. Add the consommé or stock and bay leaf. Season with salt, pepper and nutmeg. Cover and simmer gently for 30 minutes or until thick and well reduced. Stir in the cream, then check the seasonings. Serve with pasta or as part of a pasta dish, serving freshly grated Parmesan or Pecorino cheese separately.

If wished ¼ lb bulk pork sausage meat or more ground beef can be substituted for the livers.

BORDELAISE

From Bordeaux, this glossy, grape-colored sauce is, as you might expect, based on wine. If Espagnole (page 45) is used instead of reduced broth-plus-arrowroot, the sauce is excellent without the traditional beef marrow. Marrow bones can be difficult to buy, so I shop ahead and keep them in my freezer: they store for 3 months. Bordelaise is a classic for hamburgers and other broiled meat, such as kidneys, chops and steaks and it is also served with fried sweetbreads.

Makes 1 cup

1 cup well-reduced canned consommé or broth (page 15), or Brown Bone Stock (page 14), boiled to reduce by half
2 shallots or 1 small onion, finely chopped
1 clove garlic, crushed or finely chopped
1 bay leaf
4 black peppercorns, crushed
1 cup dry red wine, preferably a Cabernet Sauvignon
2 tblsp finely sliced beef marrow, taken from the bone center
1 tblsp arrowroot
Salt

Put the shallots or onion, garlic, bay leaf and peppercorns in a small pan with the wine and boil until reduced by three-quarters. Combine with the reduced consommé or broth or stock and simmer for 20 minutes until further reduced.

Five minutes before the end, bring salted water to a boil in a small pan and soften the marrow slices in it for 2–3 minutes. Drain.

Mix the arrowroot with 2 tblsp cold water. Pour the sauce into a pitcher, then strain back into the pan. Mix a little hot sauce in the arrowroot paste, return to the pan and cook 1 minute.

Add the marrow slices and whisk until disintegrated and the sauce is very glossy. Taste and season. If wished 1 tsp lemon juice and ½ tsp finely chopped parsley can be added.

BOURGUIGNONNE

The classic red wine and mushroom sauce, Bourguignonne, or Burgundy sauce, comes from France's great red wine district. Serve with poached eggs, sweetbreads, brains, chicken or roast or broiled beef. Beef served "à la bourguignonne" is usually a casserole garnished with fried bacon, mushrooms and small, braised onions.

Makes 1 cup

2 shallots or 1 small onion, chopped
3 parsley stalks, snapped in 2 or 3 places
1 bay leaf
2 sprigs fresh thyme, or large pinch of dried thyme
½ cup chopped button mushrooms
1½ cups full-bodied red wine such as a hearty burgundy, a Pinor Noir or Shiraz
1½ tblsp butter
1 tblsp flour
Salt and freshly ground black pepper
Pinch of cayenne

Put the first 5 ingredients in a small, heavy-based pan, pour in the wine and boil gently for 20 minutes, or until reduced by one-third. Strain into another pan.

Mash together the butter and flour; drop tiny pieces into the hot liquid and bring the sauce back to a boil over low heat, stirring all the time. Season to taste, adding cayenne.

BREAD SAUCE

This medieval sauce makes a creamy, traditional accompaniment to roast goose and pheasant, but also goes well with roast lamb, turkey or chicken.

Makes 1 cup

2 cups milk
1 small onion
3 whole cloves
1 cup soft white bread crumbs
Pinch of ground mace, or tiny pinch of grated nutmeg
Salt and ground white pepper
1 tblsp butter
2 tblsp heavy or light cream

Put the milk in a small heavy-based pan. Stud the onion with the cloves and add; this is called a cloûté. Simmer for 20 minutes or until the onion is soft and the milk reduced. Remove the onion with a spoon and discard. Stir the crumbs into the milk. Add the mace or nutmeg and season to taste, then stir in the butter and cream and serve.

BROWN SAUCE

This is a good dark sauce when broiled or fried meat does not provide much liquid, or when you need to reheat any type of meat.

Makes 1–1½ cups
2 tblsp butter
2 slices bacon, cut in matchstick pieces, or 2 tblsp chopped cooked ham
1 small onion, chopped
2 tblsp flour
½ cup chopped mushrooms
1½ cups good stock or canned consommé
1 tsp tomato paste (optional)
2 tblsp red wine (optional)
Salt and freshly ground black pepper

Melt the butter and fry the bacon, if using, until the fat runs. Add the onion and fry for 5 minutes until beginning to color. Sprinkle with the flour and cook for 4–5 minutes, stirring, until brown.

Add the mushrooms and ham, if using, and cook 4 minutes. Off the heat stir in one-third of the stock or consommé until smooth, then add the remainder. Cook gently, stirring occasionally, for 5 minutes. Strain the sauce (use it unstrained for reheating meat), pressing the vegetables well. Add the tomato paste and wine if wished; taste and season.

Sherry, brandy or port can be used instead of the red wine; 2 tsp grainy mustard or 1 tblsp Worcestershire sauce will make it more piquant. A pinch of dried herbs can be cooked in the sauce for the last 5 minutes.

For **Herby Brown Sauce** cook 2–3 fresh herb sprigs – rosemary for lamb or thyme for veal – in the sauce before straining.

BUTTER SAUCES

Hot butter sauces include those under Beurre (page 26), Hollandaise (page 52) and Foaming Wine Sauce (page 48).

BUTTERED ALMOND SAUCE

Sometimes called "almondine sauce" in the U.S., and "amandine" in the Southern States and France, this makes an attractive crispy topping for pan-fried trout, but also adds crunch to chicken, broccoli or cauliflower florets.

Serves 4–6
¼ cup butter
¾ cup flaked blanched almonds (preferably bought whole and flaked before using)
½ tsp salt
Pinch of cayenne
1 tblsp lemon juice (optional)

Melt the butter in a small heavy-based saucepan and fry the almonds, stirring constantly, until they begin to brown. Add the salt, cayenne and lemon juice, if the sauce needs it.

BUTTERED CRUMBS

A classic accompaniment to roast pheasant.

Makes 1 cup
¼ cup butter
1 cup bread crumbs from 1-day-old bread
Salt and freshly ground black pepper

Melt the butter and toss the crumbs until saturated; season. These can be used to stuff birds for roasting, which will help stop the birds drying out while cooking. Or they can be kept warm in the bottom of a low oven, when they will become slightly crisp. Serve separately in a sauceboat.

Mix in 1 chopped, hard-cooked egg and use as a topping for vegetables such as cauliflower: thus it becomes à la **Polonaise**.

CALVADOS CREAM

Calvados, the apple brandy of Normandy in Northern France, is used to make a celebrated sauce for roast pheasant, or fried veal cutlets and pork chops; garnished with fried apple rings the dish becomes à la normande.

Makes 1 cup

2 tblsp butter
2 tblsp flour
¾ cup heavy cream
2 tblsp Calvados or applejack
1 tblsp lemon juice
Salt and ground white pepper

Melt the butter in a small heavy-based pan over gentle heat and sprinkle in the flour. Cook for 1 minute, stirring. Off the heat stir in a little of the cream until smooth. Add the remainder and bring to a boil, stirring. Add the Calvados and lemon juice, and season to taste. Add any meat juices, skimmed of fat, and serve.

CAPER SAUCE

The astringency of capers goes well with ham or lamb, fried fish and all kinds of poached or roast poultry.

Makes 1 cup

2 tblsp capers, roughly chopped
1 × Béchamel (page 24), Velouté (page 74) or Mock Hollandaise (page 58)
Salt and ground white pepper

Stir the capers into the hot sauce and season to taste.

For **Green Caper Sauce**, put 2 tblsp chopped parsley, 1 tblsp chopped fresh chervil, 1 tblsp chopped fresh tarragon and 6 spinach leaves, trimmed of stalks, into a small pan. Add boiling water to cover and boil for 2 minutes. Drain, refresh in a colander under cold running water, then dry on paper towels. Put the herbs and spinach in a blender or food processor with 2 chopped gherkins, the capers and 2 tblsp butter, and blend to a purée. Add this to the hot sauce just before serving.

CARBONARA

A classic for spaghetti, this sauce can also be served with lima beans and small carrots. The obscure Italian name "alla carbonara" means "in the style of the charcoal burners." These poor folk camped out in the woods around Rome, where they could only cook one-pot meals, so their spaghetti sauce contained the local raw ham, with eggs that were cooked in the heat of the pasta.

Serve the original recipe as a luxury appetizer – for each person you need 1 egg, 2 tblsp heavy cream and 2 tblsp chopped Parma or San Daniele ham. The bacon and egg sauce given below is a more useful supper dish for teenagers in a hurry to eat and be gone.

Serves 4

Cooked, hot pasta or vegetables for 4
¾ tblsp butter
¼ lb Canadian bacon, chopped
¼ cup heavy cream
3 medium-size eggs
½ cup grated Parmesan cheese
Salt and freshly ground black pepper

Melt 1 tblsp of the butter in a saucepan and fry the bacon. Add the cream and heat through. In a mixing bowl beat the eggs with half the cheese.

Drain the pasta or vegetables. Melt the remaining butter in the pan, and return the pasta or vegetables. Season and toss, then add the bacon and cream mixture, and the egg and cheese mixture. Toss again: the heat of the food makes the sauce cohere. Serve the remaining Parmesan separately.

CARDINAL SAUCE

The princes of the Church were known for their gourmet eating and the version of Cardinal sauce for fish is Nantua sauce (page 60), made with the shells and flesh of a 1½ lb lobster.

CELERY SAUCE

For roast or poached chicken as well as roast shoulder of lamb, it also goes well with corned beef and, slightly reduced, makes a good sauce for split baked potatoes. Dilute it with a little more chicken stock for celery soup.

Makes 1½ cups

4 celery stalks, sliced and strings removed if they are outside stalks
2 cups chicken stock (page 12), or stock made with a chicken bouillon cube if wished
2 tblsp butter
1 tblsp flour
¼ cup heavy cream
Salt and ground white pepper
Tiny pinch of ground mace or grated nutmeg

Put the celery and stock in a saucepan and simmer for 30 minutes or until the celery is cooked and the stock reduced by over half. Purée the mixture in a blender or food processor.

Melt the butter and sprinkle in the flour. Cook for 1 minute, stirring. Off the heat stir in one-third of the celery mixture until smooth. Add the remaining mixture and cook for 5 minutes, stirring occasionally. Stir in the cream and season to taste, adding the mace or nutmeg.

CHASSEUR

In Central and Eastern Europe mushroom hunting is a national pastime – a passion never shared by the English-speaking peoples. The French name for the sauce means "hunter" – of mushrooms, not game. A party sauce when served with filet mignon or noisettes of lamb, sauce chasseur also goes well with simpler dishes, such as noodles, sautéed chicken, liver and rabbit.

Makes 1 cup

1 cup well-reduced canned consommé or broth (page 15), or Brown Bone Stock (page 14), boiled to reduce by half, hot
2 tblsp butter
1 shallot or ½ onion, finely chopped
1¼ cups chopped button mushrooms

3 tblsp brandy plus 6 tblsp white wine, or ½ cup white wine
1 tblsp arrowroot
1 tblsp tomato paste
2 tsp Worcestershire sauce
1 tblsp Meat Glaze (pages 56–57) or meat jelly from a roast
Salt and freshly ground black pepper
1 tblsp chopped fresh tarragon or parsley

Melt the butter and fry the shallot or onion until soft. Add the mushrooms and cook gently, stirring, for 2–3 minutes. Add the brandy, if using, and wine and boil until reduced by half. Add to the reduced consommé or broth or stock.

Mix the arrowroot with 2 tblsp cold water. Stir in a little hot consommé, then return to the pan. Add the tomato paste, Worcestershire sauce and meat glaze or jelly. Cook gently for 5 minutes, then season to taste. Stir in the chopped herbs.

CHEDDAR CHEESE SAUCE

Easy and indispensable as a pasta sauce – for both noodles and lasagne – and for gratins and fish or vegetables. See also Fondue (page 49), Mornay (page 58) and Soufflé Cheese Sauce (page 69).

Makes 1¼ cups

1 cup grated Cheddar cheese
Pinch of paprika
1 tsp Dijon-style mustard
Small pinch cayenne (optional)
Dash of Worcestershire sauce (optional)
1 tblsp grated onion or onion juice (optional)
1 × Béchamel (page 24) or Velouté (page 74)

Stir the cheese and seasonings into the hot sauce and taste. Add the optional extras; for **onion juice**, put the grated onion (and juices) in a tea strainer or small sieve and press well with a spoon.

CHERRY SAUCE

Good with roast duck or turkey, in the 19th century this was served with hot ham and tongue. Without the seasoning and poultry juices it is an excellent dessert sauce.

Makes 1½ cups

½ lb morello or dark cherries, pitted if wished
2 tblsp sugar (for morellos)
3 cloves
½ cup red wine or port
Pinch of ground cinnamon
1 tblsp cornstarch
Juices from roast poultry, if available
Freshly ground black pepper

Cook the cherries with the sugar, cloves, wine, cinnamon and ½ cup water for about 20 minutes or until soft. Mix the cornstarch to a paste with 2 tblsp water, add a little hot cherry juice. Return to the pan and bring to a boil, stirring. Just before serving stir in the well-skimmed juices from roast poultry. Season to taste.

CHESTNUT SAUCE

Traditional with game, this makes a change with roast turkey or beef. If using fresh chestnuts, prepare 1 lb by slashing each one; cook in boiling water for 20–25 minutes then peel and skin. Mash or chop finely. Canned chestnut purée is less work and gives a smoother sauce; the sauce serves 6–8 people.

Makes 2 cups

3 tblsp butter
1 tblsp chopped onion
1 tblsp chopped carrot
1 tblsp flour
½ cup sherry wine (or port)
1 bouquet garni, fresh or dried
1 bay leaf (omit for fresh bouquet garni)
1 cup unsweetened chestnut purée
Salt and freshly ground black pepper

Melt the butter in a heavy-based pan and fry the onion and carrot until the onion softens. Sprinkle in the flour, stir well and cook gently for 1 minute. Add the sherry or port, bouquet garni and bay leaf and cook gently until well reduced. Remove the herbs.

Stir in the chestnut purée, heat through, taste and season. If port is used, a little sage can be added with the herbs.

CHILI TOMATO SAUCE

This barbecue side sauce can be used for basting meat or fish under the broiler or in the oven. It can also be served with grilled poultry or poached eggs. It is called "salsa ranchero" in Mexico, where it is made with a higher proportion of chilies. If you find you have overdone the chili, try adding a small pinch of sugar: it will modify the hotness.

Makes 1½ cups

2 cloves garlic, crushed or finely chopped
1 medium-size onion, chopped
2 tblsp olive oil or bacon fat
¾ lb tomatoes, skinned, seeded and chopped, or 16 oz canned tomatoes, drained and chopped
2 red chilies, stalks removed, seeded and chopped, or ¼ tsp hot pepper sauce, or ½ tsp Chinese chili sauce, or 1 tsp chili powder, or 1–2 tblsp chili seasoning
½ tsp sugar
2 tblsp vinegar
Salt and freshly ground black pepper

Fry the garlic and onion in the oil or fat over low heat until soft. Add the chopped tomatoes, chilies or chili sauce or powder, sugar and vinegar. Stir well. Simmer, covered, for 15–20 minutes; taste and season.

You can go on making this hotter until your mouth catches fire. Possible additions include a pinch of ground cumin seeds, 1 tblsp grated horseradish or a pinch of cayenne.

CHINESE SPARERIB SAUCE

I find spareribs cooked in the oven and basted frequently with sauce are much more succulent than those that are marinated then grilled. This quantity is sufficient for 2–3 lb spareribs. Use the sauce, too, as a marinade and for basting slices of fresh pork side, chicken portions and turkey drumsticks.

Makes 2 cups

2 cloves garlic, crushed, with salt if necessary
1 tsp salt
2 slices fresh ginger root, finely chopped, or pinch of ground ginger
2 tblsp honey
¼ cup soy sauce
3 tblsp red wine vinegar
1 cup stock
Freshly ground black pepper

Combine all the ingredients and use as a baste.

CIDER SAUCE

Serve with rabbit, broiled or fried ham steaks, or boiled ham and roast pork. It is also excellent for reheating sliced pork or ham; add chopped fresh herbs if available.

Makes 1 cup

1 cup hard cider
1 bay leaf
1 clove
½ cup well-reduced canned consommé or broth (page 15), or homemade stock boiled to reduce by half
2 tsp Worcestershire sauce
1 tblsp tomato ketchup
½ tsp grated onion
1 tblsp arrowroot

Put the cider, bay leaf and clove in a pan and boil until reduced by half. Heat the consommé or broth or stock and add the Worcestershire sauce, ketchup and onion. Mix the arrowroot with 2 tblsp cold water. Stir in a little hot consommé or broth or stock, then return to the pan. Cook for 1 minute, stirring.

Holding back the bay leaf and clove, pour the cider into the brown sauce. Simmer for 5 minutes, then check the seasonings.

CLAM SAUCE

An American classic for pasta, clam sauce can also be served with poached or fried fish. This sauce is made with white wine; the version with tomato sauce called "alla vongole" in Italian is much better known and is under Marinara (page 56).

Makes 1½ cups

3 cloves garlic, crushed or finely chopped
¼ cup butter
¼ cup olive oil
1 cup canned minced clams, drained and juice reserved, or 20 fresh clams, chopped, and liquor reserved
½ cup dry white wine
2 tblsp finely chopped parsley
2 tsp chopped fresh oregano, or pinch of dried oregano
Salt and freshly ground black pepper

Cook the garlic in the butter and oil until soft. Add ½ cup of the reserved clam juice, or the liquor from opening fresh clams, and the wine. Boil until reduced to ½ cup. Add the clams and heat through. Add the herbs and season.

Overleaf: *Serve roast chicken in French style with lemon-flavored Poulette, garnished with quarters of lemon and the grated rind.*

CRAB SAUCE

Appropriately for a pantry sauce, it can be paired with frozen fish fillets. Use the smaller quantity of crab for an appetizer pasta sauce or to dress a fish dish. Use the larger quantity to eke out fish, or add cooked button mushrooms to fill a pastry case for a light main course.

Makes 1½ cups

3–8 oz crabmeat, canned and drained or frozen and thawed
1 × Béchamel (page 24) or Béchamel 2 (page 25), made with ½ milk and ½ fish stock (page 11) or bouillon made from a fish cube, if wished, hot
1 tsp anchovy paste, lemon juice or Worcestershire sauce, or 1 tblsp dry sherry wine
Salt and ground white pepper

Stir the crabmeat into the hot sauce and add the flavoring. Season to taste.

Fresh Crab Sauce is a luxury, as it needs a live crab. Put the crab into lightly salted fast boiling water and boil for 15 minutes for the first 1 pound and 10 minutes for each subsequent pound. Reserve the water and leave the crab until cold. Clean the crab, reserving the shells as well as the crabmeat. Return the shells to the reserved water and boil for a further 30 minutes. Strain the liquor, discarding the shells. Make a fish Velouté (page 74) with the liquor, then add ¼ lb crabmeat, 1 tsp anchovy paste and lemon juice. Season with cayenne.

CREAM CHEESE SAUCE

Serve over pasta and with fried fish or fried chicken breasts.

Makes 1 cup

¼ cup butter
1 cup sliced button mushrooms
1 (8 oz) package cream cheese, or half cream cheese with ½ cup buttermilk
2 tblsp chopped chives
Salt and freshly ground black pepper

Melt the butter and cook the mushrooms, stirring, for 2 minutes. Meanwhile, beat the cheese or cheese and buttermilk in a bowl until smooth. Beat in the chives and seasoning. Stir into the mushrooms and heat until melted.

CREAM SAUCE

Oh so quick and simple: just heat 1 cup cream in a double boiler and flavor with 1 tblsp lemon juice and seasoning: or heat equal quantities of cream and butter together with a piece of mace. Cream sauces go well with poached fish, vegetables, eggs or chicken and with light mousses of all sorts, or use it to dress pasta.

Makes 1 cup

1 shallot, finely chopped, or 1 tblsp finely chopped white part of scallion
1 tblsp lemon juice
Salt and ground white pepper
½ cup butter
½ cup heavy cream

Put the shallot or scallion in a small pan with the lemon juice and 3 tblsp water. Add a little seasoning and boil until the liquid has reduced to about 2 tsp.

Meanwhile, heat the butter in the top of a double boiler over simmering water. Strain in the reduced liquid. Slowly stir in the cream until hot and completely amalgamated. Taste and season.

CREAMY MUSTARD SAUCE

I make this sauce – which is quickly assembled in the pan after frying steaks or pork chops – when kind relations or friends give me pots of assorted mustards as a gift. The mustard makes a thick emulsion so use cream without a thickener. A more conventional white sauce, flavored with mustard and particularly suitable for fish, is given under Velouté (page 74); see also Deviled Cream (page 41).

Serves 4–5

¼ cup white wine
2 tblsp coarse-grained or strong mustard, such as Meaux
2 tblsp mild or creamy mustard, such as Dijon
Pinch of paprika
½ cup light cream
Salt
1 tblsp brandy (optional)

Pour off the juices left from frying the meat and keep the meat warm. Add the wine to the pan and stir to deglaze. Add the mustards and paprika and stir in. Stir in the cream and bring to a boil. Add the juices that collected under the meat. Taste and season, then stir in the brandy, if using, and serve.

A **White Mustard Sauce** can also be made by adding 1 tblsp mild mustard or 1 tsp fiery mustard to any white sauce.

CREOLE SAUCE

From "criolla," the name for the Spanish-speaking inhabitants of the Caribbean and the Gulf of Mexico, Creole cooking is a blend of traditions brought by each new wave of immigrants – Spanish, French and African (often the slave-cooks). Tomatoes and peppers were eaten in this part of the world a century before they were known in Europe, and the name Creole sauce is commonly given to any tomato sauce which contains peppers and in the U.S. also to brown sauces which contain tomato and peppers. Serve with fried meat, poultry or fish, cooking these in the sauce for a few minutes if wished. It can also be used as a pasta sauce.

Makes 1½ cups

1 medium-size onion, finely chopped
1 green pepper, seeded and chopped
2 tblsp vegetable oil
2 tblsp flour
2 medium-size, ripe tomatoes, skinned, seeded and
  chopped
1 cup chicken stock (page 12) or fish stock (page 11)
Pinch of dried thyme
1 tsp lime or lemon juice
1 tsp white wine vinegar
Salt and freshly ground black pepper
Hot pepper sauce (optional)

Fry the onion and green pepper in the oil until the onion is soft. Sprinkle with the flour, stir well and cook for 1 minute. Add the tomatoes. Stir in one-third of the stock until smooth, then add the remainder. Cook gently, stirring, until thickened, then add the thyme, citrus juice and vinegar. Simmer for 5 minutes. Taste and season, adding a few drops of hot pepper sauce (or 1–2 tsp chili seasoning) if wished. Chopped celery and olives can be included as a garnish.

All wine can be used instead of the broth (but omit the vinegar) or half and half wine, sherry, Madeira and tomatoes.

CUP OF COFFEE SAUCE

The Swedish custom of pouring the morning cup of coffee over the lunchtime lamb was popularized in the American Mid-West by the actor Alfred Lunt. Make it an evening cup and also add brandy if you like!

Makes 1 cup

1 cup strong black coffee
2 tsp sugar
2 tblsp heavy cream
¼ cup brandy (optional)
1 tsp cornstarch
Salt and freshly ground black pepper

Roast the leg of lamb (shoulder is too fatty) at 325°. About 30 minutes before the end of roasting, pour over the sugared, creamy coffee, including the brandy if wished. Continue cooking, basting every 10 minutes, until the lamb is cooked.

Remove the lamb to a carving board, and skim the fat from the roasting pan. Mix the cornstarch with 1 tblsp water and stir in. Bring to a boil and season to taste.

Above: *Poivrade provides a dark gravy for game, garnished with pear slices and black currants and a colorful selection of vegetables.*

Right: *The cream and wine of Bercy make a light fricassé with fish, onions and mushrooms. Asparagus tips, new carrots and dill add color.*

CURRY CREAM SAUCE

Lightly flavored, this is a French-style white sauce "à l'indienne," not a true curry. Serve with vegetables such as cauliflower and poached eggs, chicken or fish. It is particularly good with mushrooms and scallops. See also Saffron Cream (page 67).

Makes 1 cup

1 small onion, chopped
2 tblsp butter
1 clove
½ bay leaf, crumbled
6 black peppercorns, crushed
1½ tblsp flour
1 tblsp curry powder (not Madras) or paste
1½ cups mixed milk and salted cauliflower or onion
   water
¼ cup heavy cream
1 tsp lemon juice

In a heavy-based pan fry the onion in the butter with the clove, bay leaf and peppercorns. When the onion is soft, sprinkle in the flour and curry powder or paste and cook for 1 minute, stirring well. Off the heat stir in one-third of the liquid until smooth. Add the remainder and bring to a boil, stirring. Leave to simmer, stirring occasionally, for 20 minutes or until reduced by half.

Sieve the sauce, pressing the onion. Add the cream and heat through. Add the lemon juice, check the seasonings and serve.

If fresh fennel is available, sweat 2 tblsp chopped fennel and 1 chopped garlic clove with the onion, and omit the clove.

CURRY SAUCE

The Hindi word "turcarri" simply means sauce; spicy curries have been part of British cooking for more than 200 years, so it is not surprising they have been adapted to Western ingredients. Up to 1½ lb fried meat, 4 chicken portions or 4–6 hard-cooked eggs (add ½ tsp turmeric for color) can be simmered in the sauce. Without them it will

serve 2, poured over rice. See also Korma Curry Sauce (page 53) and Vindaloo Curry Sauce (page 74).

Serves 4–6

2 onions, chopped
1 clove garlic, crushed or finely chopped
2 tblsp oil
1 small carrot, chopped
1 small parsnip, chopped
2 celery stalks, chopped
1 small green pepper, seeded and chopped (optional)
1 tblsp flour
1 tblsp curry powder
1½ cups stock
1 tblsp tomato paste
¼ cup golden raisins
2 tblsp coarse-cut marmalade or fruit chutney
1 tsp Meaux or coarse-grained mustard
2 tsp coriander seeds, crushed (optional)
2 tblsp roughly chopped, blanched almonds
3 tblsp lemon juice
Salt and freshly ground black pepper
⅛–¼ tsp cayenne (less if using green pepper)

Fry the onions and garlic in the oil until soft. Add the chopped vegetables and cook for 5 minutes, stirring. Sprinkle with the flour and curry powder, stir well and cook for 1 minute.

Add the stock, tomato paste, raisins, marmalade or chutney and the mustard then bring to a boil, stirring. If using, add meat, chicken or eggs; cook gently for 15 minutes. Stir in the coriander seeds, if used, the almonds and lemon juice, season to taste including the cayenne and simmer 5 more minutes. If liked, garnish with chopped parsley and celery leaves or green tops of scallions.

DEMI GLACE

Its French name means "half-glaze" sauce because it is made by reducing Espagnole by half, to a glaze. Described as the final perfection of brown sauce, it is the base for many classic recipes and ideal for party roasts and broiled meat and for game.

Makes 1 cup
1 cup Espagnole (page 45)
½ cup Brown Bone Stock (page 14) or canned consommé
Salt

In a medium-sized heavy-based saucepan simmer the sauce and stock until reduced by one-third – about 30 minutes. Season just before serving. 2 tblsp tomato paste or 2 tblsp sherry wine make good additions. For broiled meat for a party, add up to 6 tblsp Madeira wine.

DEVILED CREAM

This piquant sauce adds spice to broiled or fried veal chops or baked eggs. It is also traditionally used to reheat cooked chicken or turkey.

Makes 1 cup

1 cup heavy cream
½ tsp Chinese chili sauce
1 tblsp Worcestershire sauce, or ½ tsp anchovy paste
1 tsp Dijon-style mustard
½ tsp lemon juice
½ tsp paprika
Pinch of grated nutmeg
Salt and ground white pepper

Heat all the ingredients together gently in a double boiler.

DEVIL SAUCE

So-called because it is hot, in 18th century England a devil sauce was often a paste for flavoring reheated cooked meat, bones or poultry. Make Mustard Glaze (page 60) with hot mustard (not the milder Dijon-style), use as a baste and you will get the idea! See also bastes under Barbecue (pages 22–23). In France sauce "à la diable" is a classic brown sauce made hot with mustard or pepper.

This thin sauce has an unexpected kick the moment after you taste it; the acid in the vinegar brings out the heat in the chilies. Serve with steaks or broiled fish.

Makes 1 cup
2 tblsp butter
3 shallots, finely chopped, or 3 tblsp chopped white part of scallion
1 green chili, seeded and finely chopped, or ½ tsp chili powder
1 tsp freshly grated fresh ginger root
1 tblsp red wine vinegar
1 tblsp currant jelly
1 cup well-flavored stock
½ cup red wine
2 tsp Worcestershire sauce
Pinch of cayenne
Tiny pinch of grated nutmeg

Melt the butter and cook the shallots or scallion, chili, if used, and ginger until the shallots are lightly colored. Add the vinegar and currant jelly and cook until the jelly has melted.

Pour in the stock, red wine and Worcestershire sauce and boil gently for 20 minutes or until reduced by one-third. Strain the sauce and taste. Add the cayenne, nutmeg and chili powder, if using, and serve.

DOLCELATTE

A really quick pasta sauce; it is also good with green and lima beans and new carrots. Gorgonzola cheese can be used in the same way. It is almost as creamy, but has a more positive flavor.

Makes 1½ cups
¼ cup butter
5 oz Dolcelatte cheese, roughly chopped
¾ cup light cream
Salt and freshly ground black pepper
¼ cup grated Parmesan cheese

Melt the butter and stir in the Dolcelatte and cream. Heat through until smooth, season and stir in the Parmesan. Toss with the pasta or vegetables and serve more Parmesan separately.

Overleaf: *A delicious selection of pasta sauces. Clockwise, from the bottom right: Pesto, Bolognese, Tomato Amatriciana, Dolcelatte, Sugo, Marinara made with clams and Tomato Sauce.*

EGG SAUCE

An excellent sauce for cod as well as duller white fish like haddock, this is particularly useful to cheer up fillets from the freezer.

Makes 1 cup

2 tblsp finely chopped parsley
Leaves of ½ bunch of watercress, chopped (optional)
2 tsp horseradish cream or horseradish sauce
2 hard-cooked eggs, chopped
1 × Béchamel (page 24), hot
Salt and ground white pepper
3 tblsp butter or heavy cream

Stir the parsley, watercress, horseradish and eggs into the hot Béchamel. Check the seasonings and whisk in the butter, in little pieces, or the cream just before serving.

EGG AND LEMON SAUCE

This foaming yellow sauce is called "avgolémono" in Greece; it suits poached and fried chicken or fish, according to the stock used.

Makes 1½ cups

2 tsp cornstarch
1 cup chicken stock (page 12) or fish stock (page 11), hot
2 large eggs, separated
Salt and freshly ground black pepper
¼ cup lemon juice

Mix the cornstarch to a paste with 1 tblsp cold water and add a few spoonfuls of hot stock. Return to the pan of stock and cook for 1 minute, stirring.

Beat the egg whites in a medium-sized bowl with a pinch of salt until stiff. Then beat in the egg yolks, one at a time, with the lemon juice. Gradually pour in the hot stock, still beating.

Pour the sauce into the top of a double boiler and heat gently for 1–2 minutes; do not let it boil.

Remove from the heat and beat for 1 minute; taste and season. Serve with fried or poached chicken, poached or baked fish or boiled vegetables but don't drink German-style wine with it – it is far too lemony. The sauce can also be served cold, with fish or chicken, though it will not stay frothy after it is chilled.

EMERGENCY TOMATO SAUCES

A sauce to make from canned tomato juice or from paste, when you have neither fresh nor canned tomatoes. Use it as a very quick pasta sauce or with green beans. It is also useful for layered dishes, for example cod with potatoes, and noodles or lasagne with cheese.

Makes 1 cup

1 tblsp butter
1 tblsp flour
1 cup tomato juice
1 tblsp lemon juice
Salt and freshly ground black pepper

Melt the butter over gentle heat and sprinkle in the flour. Cook, stirring, for 1 minute. Off the heat stir in one-third of the tomato juice until smooth. Add the remaining tomato juice and the lemon juice and cook for 2 minutes. Season and serve.

The following sauce, made from tomato paste, is rather spicier. Heat 2 tblsp oil and fry 1 chopped onion until soft. Off the heat stir in 3 tblsp tomato paste with 3 tblsp water. Add 1 tsp salt, 2 tblsp red wine or malt vinegar and a pinch of cayenne, then stir in a further 1¾ cups water. Simmer for 2 minutes.

ESPAGNOLE

Although the name means "Spanish," Espagnole has been one of the great sauces of French classical cooking since the 18th century, perfect for all meat and game. Many other sauces are derived from it, so make it in quantity and store some in the freezer.

Makes 2 cups

3 tblsp meat drippings, or 2 tblsp butter plus 1 tblsp oil
¼ cup chopped bacon or cooked ham
1 large onion, chopped but not peeled
1 clove garlic, chopped or crushed
1 carrot, chopped
2 celery stalks, chopped
3 tblsp flour
1 quart Brown Bone Stock (page 14) or well-flavored light stock (page 15), warm
2 parsley stalks, snapped in several places
1 bay leaf
1 sprig of fresh thyme or pinch of dried thyme
6 black peppercorns
1 tblsp tomato paste
Salt (only if serving immediately)

Melt the drippings or butter and oil and fry the bacon, if using, until it gives up its fat. Add the onion, garlic, carrot, celery, and ham if using. Fry over medium heat, stirring occasionally, until the onion is golden. Sprinkle with the flour, stir well and cook for 5–10 minutes until a good brown.

Off the heat stir in one-third of the stock. When smooth add the remainder and bring to a boil, stirring. Add the parsley stalks, bay leaf, thyme and peppercorns. Simmer gently for 30 minutes.

Add 1 tblsp cold water to the pan to precipitate the fat, then skim it off with a spoon. Simmer for a further 1 hour, then repeat the skimming. For the last skim, draw strips of paper towel across the surface to pick up floating fat.

Add the tomato paste and continue simmering until reduced to about 2 cups. Strain the sauce, pressing the vegetables well to extract all the juice. Reheat and season with salt just before serving.

Salt is not included in the basic recipe, as Espagnole is the basis of many other sauces and may well be reduced further.

The sauce will store, covered, in the refrigerator for 1 week, but should be reboiled after 4 days. Freeze it, preferably in 1 cup packs, for up to 1 month.

FENNEL AND PERNOD SAUCE

This goes well with fish such as broiled mackerel and mullet, or scallops or mussels.

Makes 1 cup

½ small bulb fresh fennel
3 tblsp butter
1 small onion, finely chopped
6 tblsp dry white wine
1 cup heavy cream
3 medium-size egg yolks
4 tsp Pernod
1 tsp dried tarragon or 2 tsp chopped fresh tarragon

Reserve the fennel fronds for garnishing and chop the bulb. Melt the butter and fry the onion and chopped fennel gently until the onion is soft. Add the wine and boil until reduced to a syrupy liquid. Add the cream and boil again for 1–2 minutes.

Mix the egg yolks with the Pernod and add the tarragon. Stir in a little hot cream. Off the heat stir back into the pan. Heat through, stirring, very gently without boiling. Check the seasonings, and garnish the finished dish with the reserved fennel fronds.

It can be used for a nouvelle cuisine presentation if the sauce is strained before thickening. Pour a small quantity onto each plate and lay the fish on top. Lay thin strips of tomato across the fish and garnish with fennel fronds.

Overleaf, from the left: *Soy Glazed roast duck, Sweet and Sour, Chinese Style over pork, dishes of Hoisin Sauce and Chili Tomato Sauce and ribs cooked in Chinese Sparerib Sauce.*

FINES HERBES

The best of the herb sauces, this white wine sauce for poached chicken, veal, eggs or fish is sophisticated but easy to make. France's "best herbs" are parsley, tarragon, chives and chervil, used in equal quantities. Add them to any sauce – for example Espagnole (page 45) – just before serving and it will become sauce fines herbes. Mushroom peelings, traditionally associated with the herbs, can be included too. If you have no wine, infuse the herbs in part of the stock; add ¼ cup heavy cream to finish.

Makes 1 cup
1 shallot, finely chopped, or 1 tblsp finely chopped white part of scallion
3 tblsp butter
2 tblsp flour
1 cup chicken stock (page 12) or fish stock (page 11), hot
1 tblsp finely chopped parsley
1 tblsp finely chopped fresh tarragon
1 tblsp finely chopped chives
1 tblsp finely chopped fresh chervil (optional)
½ cup dry white wine or dry white vermouth
Salt and ground white pepper

Fry the shallot or scallion gently in the butter in a small, heavy-based pan until soft and golden. Sprinkle with the flour and cook, stirring, for 1 minute. Off the heat stir in one-third of the stock until smooth. Add the remainder and bring to a boil, stirring, then cook for 5 minutes.

Reserve one-third of each herb for finishing and put the remaining herbs in a small pan with the wine or vermouth. Boil until reduced to 2 tblsp then strain this into the sauce. Season to taste and stir in the reserved herbs.

FIVE MINUTE PASTA SAUCE

This quick and easy sauce can also be used as a pizza topping or for reheating cold meat and poultry.

Serves 4
1¾ oz canned anchovies
1 clove garlic, finely chopped
16 oz canned tomatoes
12 ripe olives, pitted
3 tblsp capers
2 tblsp finely chopped parsley

Drain the oil from the anchovies into the saucepan and fry the garlic while you snip up the tomatoes in the can with scissors. Empty into the saucepan and heat while you chop the anchovies and olives. Add these to the pan with the capers. Cook 3 more minutes, sprinkle with parsley and you're there.

FOAMING WINE SAUCE

This vermouth butter sauce is sometimes called "sabayon" by nouvelle cuisine cooks, because its yellow fluffiness imitates the dessert sauce. Serve with fish such as flounder, sole or turbot and light fish, chicken and vegetable mousses, changing the stock if necessary.

Makes ¾ cup
1 cup dry white vermouth, preferably French
5 tblsp reduced fish poaching liquid (page 11)
2 large egg yolks
1 tblsp heavy cream
Salt and ground white pepper
Pinch of cayenne
¾ cup cold butter, diced small

Boil the vermouth to reduce to one-quarter. Add the fish liquid and boil again until reduced to 4 tblsp.

Put the yolks and cream in the top of a double boiler over simmering – not boiling – water: it must not touch the water. Whisk until combined and season with a little salt and pepper. Pour in the hot reduced vermouth mixture and whisk again; add the cayenne.

Whisk in the butter, a piece at a time, waiting for each piece to be absorbed before adding the next. Taste then serve at once.

FONDUE

Wine- or apple-flavored, with a hint of garlic, this is an excellent sauce for poached eggs on spinach or poached onions. It can also be used for dipping French bread.

Makes 1 cup
1 small shallot, finely chopped, or 1 tblsp finely chopped white part of scallion
1 tblsp butter
1 small clove garlic, crushed, with salt if necessary
1 cup hard cider, apple juice or dry white wine, or ¾ cup dry white vermouth
¼ cup chicken stock (page 12)
¾ cup grated Gruyère, Emmenthal or Swiss cheese
Tiny pinch of grated nutmeg
1½ tblsp cornstarch
¼ cup light or heavy cream
Salt and ground white pepper

In a small, heavy-based saucepan fry the shallot or scallion in the butter for 1–2 minutes without coloring. Add the garlic and cook for ½ minute. Add the cider, juice or wine, or vermouth, and stock and boil until reduced to 6 tblsp.

Stir in the cheese and nutmeg. Mix the cornstarch with the cream and add. Stir until melted and thick, then taste and season.

GARLIC FONDUE

This cheese sauce can be served with fried food, such as fish croquettes and with vegetables. If you want to use it as a dipping sauce for French bread, in the traditional Swiss manner, thicken it slightly with an egg yolk.

Makes 2 cups
3 tblsp butter
2 tblsp flour
¾ cup milk or light cream
1 shallot or ½ small onion, finely chopped
1 clove garlic, finely chopped or crushed
½ cup dry white wine or vermouth
1 cup grated Gruyère, Emmenthal or Swiss cheese, or make up ⅓ with grated Parmesan
Salt and ground white pepper

Pinch of grated nutmeg
Pinch of cayenne
1 large egg yolk (optional)

Melt 2 tblsp butter, sprinkle in the flour and cook, stirring, for 1 minute. Off the heat add the milk or cream. Bring to a boil, stirring, then simmer gently for 2 minutes.

Meanwhile, fry the shallot or onion and garlic in the remaining butter until soft. Add the wine or vermouth and boil until reduced to 4 tblsp. Add to the white sauce, with the grated cheese. Stir over low heat until the cheese has melted, and season to taste, adding nutmeg and cayenne. Use immediately, or a skin will develop on top. For a dipping sauce, beat in the egg yolk and heat through before serving, on a table burner if possible.

GOOSEBERRY SAUCE

Served with mackerel in Britain and France, the sharpness of this fruity sauce reduces the oiliness of the fish. Indeed, the French name for these berries is "groseilles aux maquereaux" or "currants for mackerel."

Makes 1 cup
½ lb (1 pint) gooseberries, untrimmed
1 strip thinly pared lemon rind (optional)
1 tblsp sugar

Cook the gooseberries with ¼ cup water, the lemon rind, if wished, and sugar in a small, heavy-based pan over gentle heat, checking they are not burning, until soft and well reduced. Rub through a food mill. Return the purée to the pan and reheat. The sauce can be flavored with a pinch of nutmeg or ginger; up to half the quantity of apple purée can be included.

To make the sauce from 16 oz canned gooseberries, drain them and purée; mix with ½ × milky Béchamel (page 24) and add lemon juice and nutmeg to taste. A little chopped fennel frond looks pretty as a garnish if this sauce is served with fish.

For dessert use, mix the finished sauce with ¼ cup sweet white wine, thickened with 1 tsp arrowroot, if wished. Bring back to a boil, and serve hot or cold.

Rhubarb sauce can be made the same way and eaten with mackerel and with desserts such as sweet dumplings.

GRAPE CREAM

This sauce is also well known under its French name "sauce Véronique." It was called after the baby daughter born to the fish chef of a Paris restaurant on the same day that the sauce was created. Some people like white Malaga grapes: I prefer small, sweet Niagara. The sauce is part of the classic dish sole Véronique and goes well with fried flounder.

Makes 1 cup

About 1 cup fish poaching liquid
5 tblsp dry white wine
1 tsp onion juice, or 2 tsp grated onion
1 tblsp cornstarch
½ cup heavy cream
2 tsp lemon juice
Salt and ground white pepper
6 oz green grapes, seeded if necessary
1 tblsp butter

Dish up the fish and keep warm. Drain the cooking liquid into a small heavy-based pan, add the white wine and onion juice or grated onion and boil fiercely until reduced to ½ cup.

Meanwhile, make a paste with the cornstarch and a little of the cream. Stir in a little hot liquid, then return to the pan with the remaining cream. Bring to a boil, stirring, and cook for 1 minute. Stir in the lemon juice and season to taste. Add the grapes and heat through. Just before serving, whisk in the butter, in little pieces; do not reheat.

GREEN FIELDS SAUCE

Pretty and spring-like, this sauce is excellent with fried veal cutlets, roast veal, ham, cheese soufflé and timbales of fish or chicken. See also Springtime Green Sauce (page 70).

Makes 2 cups

2 tblsp butter
½ lb fresh bulk spinach, stalks removed and washed, or frozen spinach
1 tblsp each chopped parsley, fresh tarragon and chives
½ clove garlic, crushed or finely chopped

1 shallot, finely chopped, or 1 tblsp chopped white part of scallion
1 tblsp flour
1 cup chicken stock (page 12)
Tiny pinch of grated nutmeg
2 large egg yolks
¼ cup heavy cream
Salt and ground white pepper

Melt half the butter in a saucepan and add the spinach and herbs. Cover tightly and cook over low heat, turning from top to bottom regularly, until the spinach has been reduced to a purée, about 10 minutes. Process until smooth.

In another pan fry the garlic and shallot or scallion in the remaining butter until soft. Sprinkle with the flour and stir well. Off the heat stir in one-third of the chicken stock until smooth. Add the remaining stock and bring to a boil. Cook for 1 minute. Add the spinach purée and season with nutmeg. Mix the yolks and cream and add to the pan, stirring over very low heat; do not boil. Season to taste and serve.

GREEN PEPPERCORN SAUCE

Nouvelle cuisine has made green peppercorns fashionable: make this sauce with the poaching liquid that remains when you have cooked chicken or fish. It can be thickened with beurre manié or served, in the modern fashion, much reduced without thickening. It is good with ham as well as with poached chicken or fish.

Makes ½–1 cup

1 cup mixed milk and fish poaching liquid, or well-flavored chicken stock (page 12)
½ cup dry white wine
1 tblsp Dijon-style mustard
¼ cup heavy cream
2 tsp beurre manié, made by mashing together equal quantities of butter and flour (optional)
1 tsp green peppercorns, lightly crushed
Salt

Dish up the chicken or fish and keep warm. Pour the milk, if using, and stock into a heavy-based saucepan and boil to reduce by half (if you intend to thicken it) or to one-third, for an unthickened sauce. In another small pan boil the wine until reduced to 1 tblsp.

Stir the reduced wine, mustard and cream into the broth and heat gently. Thicken, if wished, by stirring in tiny pieces of beurre manié and bring back to a boil; cook for 1 minute. Add the green peppercorns, taste for seasoning and serve.

◆

GUMBO

Gumbo is the Creole name for okra, the many-sided pod that traveled with the slaves from the Gold Coast to the Caribbean in the 18th century. There it was combined with the local vegetables, in particular the tomato, to make a soup or stew, to which it gave a thick, slightly gelatinous consistency. In New Orleans gumbo has a different – and French – tradition and is thickened with filé powder rather than okra. Many ingredients can be the basis of gumbo, including live shellfish. This one is easy to make. A spicy sausage like chorizo can be substituted for the ham; broil it lightly first to get rid of some of the fat, then chop. Serve with rice.

Serves 4–6
¼ cup olive oil
2 chicken quarters or ½ roaster chicken, cut up
1 large onion, finely chopped
1 clove garlic, crushed or finely chopped
2 tsp paprika
1 dried red chili, seeded and chopped, or pinch of cayenne
1 green pepper, seeded and chopped
2 cups frozen and thawed or canned and drained whole kernel corn
½ lb okra, stems trimmed off and split lengthwise into 2 or 3
1 ham bone, or ½ cup ham stock (page 11)
1 cup cubed cooked ham
½ chicken bouillon cube
2 tblsp tomato paste, or 2 tomatoes, skinned, seeded and chopped
1 bay leaf
Salt and freshly ground black pepper

Heat the oil in a large saucepan and fry the chicken pieces, turning, until brown on all sides. Add the onion and garlic and cook gently until soft but not colored. Sprinkle with the paprika and add the chili or cayenne. Add the green pepper, corn and okra. Snug in the ham bone, if using, and add the remaining ingredients. Add water to cover and simmer gently for 45 minutes. Remove all the bones and return the shredded chicken to the pan. Taste and season.

◆

HERB SAUCES

Fines Herbes (page 48) combines four herbs. See also Parsley and Chive Sauces (page 63), Tarragon Sauce (page 72), Sage and Onion Sauce (page 67) and Watercress Sauce (page 75). Mint Jelly and Mint Sauce (page 93) are also eaten with hot food.

◆

HERBY ONION GRAVY

◆

This gravy for roast beef is thickened with vegetables in the nouvelle cuisine style, rather than with flour.

Makes 1½ cups
¾ lb onions, sliced
1 cup bouillon, made with a cube
1 bay leaf
2 tsp chopped chives
2 tsp chopped parsley
Salt and ground white pepper

Cook the onions in the bouillon with the bay leaf for 20 minutes or until soft. Drain off and reserve the liquid. Remove the bay leaf, then purée the onions in a blender or food processor.

Make the onion stock up to 1 cup with more bouillon or water. Bring to a boil, add the onion purée and chopped herbs and cook gently for 5 minutes. Check the seasonings and serve.

HOLLANDAISE

The nearest thing to hot mayonnaise, this is France's tribute to Dutch butter: the name means "Dutch" sauce. It is one of the charming aspects of French cooking that their three great foundation sauces – white, brown and butter – are all attributed to neighboring countries (see Allemande, page 20). For success the sauce must never boil, so cook in a double boiler in which the top pan does not touch the water surface. If it does curdle, remove from the heat and pop in an ice cube; when the sauce congeals around it, take the ice cube out again and continue (see also introduction to this section).

Serve Hollandaise warm with hot asparagus or broccoli, but it is also good with more modest boiled or steamed vegetables; try it with peas, Jerusalem artichokes, even potatoes. It makes a simple appetizer with poached eggs. A classic accompaniment to broiled or hot poached salmon and hot fish mousses, it is also worth making for plainly poached white fish. As a topping for hot canapés it is quite unusual.

Makes ¾ cup

1 tblsp lemon juice
3 large egg yolks
Salt and ground white pepper
¾ cup unsalted butter, diced small

Put the lemon juice, 1 tblsp cold water and the yolks in a pan or bowl over simmering – not boiling – water; season and whisk.

Add 1 cube butter and whisk until absorbed, then add the next; continue adding butter, being careful to whisk over the bottom and around the sides of the bowl continually. When all the butter has been incorporated remove from the heat and whisk for 2 more minutes. Return to the heat and whisk again for 2 minutes. The sauce can be kept warm in a thermos or over barely simmering water.

For white fish 2 tsp Dijon-style mustard or 2 tblsp cubed, blanched cucumber can be whisked in. Hollandaise is also the basis of other sauces.

Hollandaise remains stable as it cools. For topping canapés, use only half the butter given, then broil just before serving to color and heat through. Any leftover sauce can be refrigerated for up to 1 week and whisked, in little pieces, into a Béchamel or Velouté to enrich it before serving.

HOLLANDAISE IN A BLENDER

Makes ¾ cup
¾ cup butter, chopped
3 medium-size egg yolks
1 tblsp lemon juice
Salt and ground white pepper

Pour very hot water into the blender goblet and set aside to warm. Clarify the butter by heating it in a small pan until foaming subsides, then skim the surface. Let it stand for 1 minute, then pour off the oil slowly into a pitcher, leaving the milky sediment behind. Pour this off (into the soup pot or onto potatoes) and clean out the pan with paper towels. Return the clarified butter to the pan and bring to a boil.

Pour the water out of the blender and shake dry. Add the yolks, lemon juice and 1 tblsp boiling water. Season and blend for 10 seconds. With the machine running, pour the hot butter in through the hole in the lid in a thin stream. Blend until thick. Check the seasonings and serve.

KIDNEY AND RED WINE SAUCE

Serve with rice or noodles.

Serves 4

4 slices bacon, chopped
2 tblsp oil
8 lamb kidneys, skinned, cored and roughly chopped
1 onion, chopped
1 clove garlic, chopped
1 tblsp flour
½ cup red wine
½ cup light stock (page 15) or canned consommé
½ tsp prepared English mustard
Salt and freshly ground black pepper

Fry the bacon in the oil until it gives up its fat. Push to one side. Over high heat put in a few kidney pieces and toss until the cut sides are sealed. Push to the side and add more pieces until they are all colored – it is important that they don't bleed liquid into the pan. Add the onion and garlic and fry over a low heat for 5 minutes more.

Sprinkle with the flour, stir well and cook for 1 minute. Stir in the wine, stock or consommé and mustard. Simmer for 10 minutes, then season to taste. Serve immediately.

A LA KING

Brooklyn's most famous sauce honors E. Clarke King II and was created at the Brighton Beach Hotel. Famous for transforming poached chicken into chicken à la King, it is also an excellent sauce for reheating leftover turkey and ham.

Makes 1 cup
¼ cup butter
1 cup thinly sliced mushrooms
1 tsp finely chopped onion
1 tblsp flour
1 cup light cream
¼ chicken bouillon cube
3 medium-size egg yolks
2 tblsp lemon juice
2 tblsp dry sherry wine
¼ cup chopped canned pimiento
Salt and ground white pepper

Melt the butter in the top pan of a double boiler over direct heat and fry the mushrooms and onion for 5 minutes, stirring. Sprinkle with the flour and cook, stirring, for 1 minute. Add three-quarters of the cream and the piece of bouillon cube. Bring to a boil, stirring.

Set on the bottom pan of the double boiler, containing simmering water. Beat the yolks with the remaining cream, stir in a little hot liquid and return to the pan with the lemon juice and sherry. Stir until thickened. Stir in the pimiento and heat through. Taste and season. If reheating cooked meat in the sauce, add it before the egg yolks and heat through before adding the yolks.

KORMA CURRY SAUCE

Made with yogurt or cream, the mild kormas of North India are very attractive to Westerners. The name means "braised" vegetables or meat; ideally the meat – usually lamb – is marinated ahead in the yogurt. You will need 1–1½ lb meat. Fry it before adding to the sauce. Four portions of chicken or ½ lb peeled shrimp could be treated the same way. Serve with rice.

Serves 4
1½ cups blanched almonds, or 1 cup ground almonds plus
     2 drops rose-water
3 tblsp butter
Salt
1 onion, chopped
1 clove garlic, finely chopped
Seeds from 6 cardamom pods (husks discarded)
1 tsp coriander seeds
1 tsp cumin seeds
6 black peppercorns
2 tsp turmeric
¼ tsp ground cloves
1 small red or green chili, stalk removed and seeded, or
     ½ tsp chili powder
1 in piece fresh ginger root, chopped, or ½ tsp ground
     ginger
1 cup chicken stock (page 12)
1 cup plain yogurt, homemade if possible (page 106), or
     heavy cream (for a richer sauce)
Juice of 1 lemon

Fry the whole almonds, if using, in 1 tblsp of the butter until golden. Sprinkle with salt, then grind in a blender or food processor and reserve. Wipe out the pan with paper towels.

Fry the onion and garlic in the remaining butter until soft but not colored. Grind, blend or crush in a mortar all 3 types of seed and the peppercorns with the turmeric and ground cloves. Add to the pan with the chili or chili powder and ginger. Stir in the chicken stock and almonds (or ground almonds and rose-water if using). Simmer for 20 minutes minimum – sautéed lamb pieces, chicken or shrimp can be added at this stage.

Stir in the yogurt or cream and lemon juice, season to taste and cook 5 more minutes.

LEMONY CHICKEN SAUCE

Admirable for couscous or pasta, this is called "hamud" in Egypt and served with rice. Chicken giblets are traditionally used. See also Poulette (page 64).

Serves 4

1–2 chicken portions, or chicken giblets plus 1 uncooked chicken carcass with plenty of meat scraps
1 chicken bouillon cube
1 large potato, diced small
2 celery stalks, with leaves reserved
2 leeks, white parts only, cut in rings
1 small turnip, diced
2 small zucchini, unpeeled but thinly sliced
2 cloves garlic, chopped
Strip of finely pared lemon rind
Juice of 1–2 lemons
Freshly ground black pepper
2 tblsp finely chopped parsley

Put the first 9 ingredients (except the celery leaves) in a saucepan and cover with 1 quart water. Bring to a boil and skim if using giblets. Cover and simmer gently for 1½ hours; or cook in a pressure cooker on high for 30 minutes. The potato and leek should disintegrate into the sauce.

Shred the chicken and return to the sauce. Discard the bones, skin and lemon rind. Add lemon juice to taste and season. Sprinkle with the celery leaves and parsley.

LENTIL SAUCE

Serve with couscous, pasta or brown rice.

Makes 2 cups

1 onion, chopped
2 cloves garlic, crushed or chopped
2 tblsp olive oil
1 cup split red lentils
16 oz canned tomatoes
1 small green pepper, seeded and chopped, or 1 tblsp paprika

1 bay leaf
½ cup red wine
½ chicken bouillon cube
1 tblsp tomato paste
1 tblsp red wine vinegar
Pinch of dried mixed herbs
Salt and freshly ground black pepper

Fry the onion and garlic gently in the oil until soft. Add the lentils, tomatoes with their juice, green pepper, if using, bay leaf, red wine and bouillon cube. Break up the tomatoes with the spoon, add water to cover and simmer for 20–30 minutes or until the lentils are soft. Remove the bay leaf. Add the tomato paste, vinegar, mixed herbs and paprika, if using. Season to taste and serve.

LIGHT GRAVY

Made in the pan while meat or poultry is roasting, this light sauce has no flour.

Makes ½ cup

1 large onion, chopped
2 celery stalks, chopped
2 cloves garlic, chopped
½ bay leaf
Fat and meat drippings in the pan
½ cup light stock (page 15) or chicken stock (page 12)
2 tblsp medium-dry sherry wine
Salt and freshly ground black pepper

About 45 minutes before roasting ends, add the onion, celery, garlic and bay leaf to the pan and toss them in the meat fat. If the meat is very lean, add up to ½ cup water and stir. Check regularly that the pan is not drying out.

Remove the roast to a warm place. Add the stock to the pan, place over low heat and stir to deglaze the pan; boil for 2 minutes to reduce a little. Add the sherry, taste and season. Strain the liquid, pressing the vegetables well to extract the juice, and serve.

LYONNAISE

The name of the French industrial city of Lyon on a recipe indicates that it contains fried onions. Serve this sauce with fried meat, liver or poultry. It is also excellent for reheating leftover turkey or pork.

Makes 1 cup
2 medium-size onions, finely chopped
3 tblsp butter
½ cup dry white wine (optional)
¼ cup white wine vinegar
2 tblsp flour
1 cup canned consommé or broth
2 tblsp Meat Glaze (pages 56–57) or meat jelly from a roast
Salt and freshly ground black pepper
1 tblsp chopped parsley

Fry the onions in the butter until golden brown. In another pan boil the wine (if using) and the vinegar until reduced by half.

Sprinkle the flour on the onions and cook, stirring, for 5–10 minutes until a good brown. Off the heat add one-third of the consommé or broth, then stir in the remainder, with the reduced vinegar mixture. Cook gently for 15 minutes, then add the meat glaze or jelly. Taste and season, then stir in the parsley.

This sauce is usually strained when served with white meat like chicken or roast turkey. I prefer it unstrained with lamb liver, and the onion adds character when heating leftover meat such as pork and turkey. For economy the wine can be omitted.

MADEIRA SAUCE

A classic sauce for broiled kidneys, roast fillet of beef and all game; the better the brown sauce you start with, the better the end result. I use Sercial Madeira, which is on the dry side; game can take a slightly sweeter one like Bual.

Makes 1 cup
⅔ cup Madeira wine
1 cup Brown Sauce (page 29), Espagnole (page 45) or Demi Glace (page 40)
Salt

If you have been frying or roasting meat, pour off the fat in the pan and pour in ½ cup of the Madeira. Stir to deglaze and boil 1–2 minutes. If you are broiling boil to reduce. Add to the brown sauce.

Simmer the brown sauce very gently for about 20 minutes or until reduced by one-quarter. Add the remaining Madeira and season to taste.

If you are using Espagnole or Demi Glace, the sauce can be enriched with butter; whisk in 1 tblsp in tiny pieces. Serve immediately; do not reheat.

For **Quick Madeira Sauce**, deglaze the pan with ½ cup Madeira; stir in 2 tblsp Demi Glace (page 40) or Meat Glaze (page 57).

MALTAISE

The name of this hot emulsion sauce comes from the Maltese orange or blood orange, which grows in Italy, Southern Spain and presumably in Malta. When blood oranges are not available a little tomato paste can be added to sweet orange juice to correct the color. Serve the sauce with hot asparagus, broccoli or mussels on the half shell.

Makes 1 cup
1–2 blood oranges, or other sweet oranges
1 × Hollandaise (page 52)

Grate the rind off 1 orange and squeeze them both. Add the rind and juice to taste to the warm Hollandaise.

For **Maltaise Butter**, beat the grated rind of ½ orange, 1 tsp orange juice and 1 tsp tomato paste into ¼ cup softened butter; this is excellent with lamb chops and fish. Orange juice and a pinch of grated rind can also be added to mayonnaise for a salad dressing for cold shellfish.

MARINARA

Serve this Italian seaman's sauce over pasta. See also Five Minute Pasta Sauce (page 48).

Makes 2½ cups

1 Bermuda onion, or 2 small onions
2–3 cloves garlic, crushed or finely chopped
5 tblsp olive oil
1 lb tomatoes, skinned and chopped, or 16 oz canned
  tomatoes
1–2 tsp brown sugar
1 tblsp tomato paste
2 tblsp chopped parsley, plus extra to garnish
2 tblsp chopped fresh basil, or 1 tsp dried basil or oregano
Salt and freshly ground black pepper
¼ cup dry white vermouth or white wine
2 lb (1 quart) mussels, or 20 small clams, scrubbed

Fry the onion and garlic in the oil over low heat until soft. Add the tomatoes, chopping them with a spoon in the pan if canned, the sugar, tomato paste and herbs. Season and bring to a boil, then leave, covered, to simmer.

Pour the vermouth or wine into a wide pan and bring to a boil. Put in the mussels or clams, cover tightly and cook for 4 minutes, shaking the pan occasionally to get the top shellfish to the bottom. Discard any that persistently remain shut. Remove the shells (reserve a few on the half shell for the appearance). Boil the liquid down to 2–3 tblsp, and add the shellfish and liquid to the sauce 5 minutes before serving. Garnish with parsley.

Canned, minced clams can be used. Drain 15 oz canned clams and chop if necessary. Reduce the liquid to 6 tblsp before adding. 20 fresh clams could be used instead, with their liquid. Alternatively, substitute ½ lb cooked, peeled shrimp. If these are frozen, thaw by tossing in the vermouth until they are soft and the freezer liquid has almost evaporated.

MARSALA SAUCE

Made in the pan after frying meat, this sauce is associated with veal cutlets of all sizes in Italy. It also goes well with turkey slices and pork chops.

Makes ½ cup
Meat juices left from frying meat or poultry
½ cup Marsala wine
½ cup chicken stock (page 12) or light stock (page 15)
Salt and freshly ground black pepper
2 tblsp butter

Remove the meat or poultry from the pan and pour off the fat. Add the Marsala and half the stock and boil until reduced by half, stirring to deglaze the pan.

If possible, return the main ingredient to the pan, then pour in the remaining stock, cover and simmer for 20 minutes. (Alternatively, boil uncovered until the sauce is reduced to 6 tblsp.) Transfer the main ingredient to a serving plate. Taste the sauce and season, then whisk in the butter, in tiny pieces. Serve immediately.

MEAT GLAZE

Brown stock reduced to form a syrupy glaze, called "glace de viande" in French, this is only used in tiny quantities. It is worth keeping frozen in an ice cube tray: once made it gives an instant sauce of distinction for all meat but in particular fried chops, steak, liver and kidneys. Add the meat glaze with 1–2 tblsp wine or brandy to the pan after frying, to deglaze it.

Meat Glaze also gives the classic touch to many traditional French sauces. Add 1–2 tblsp to Béarnaise (page 24) to add more flavor, or to a savory butter to make Colbert Butter (page 91). For a quick fish sauce, make Browned Butter (page 26) adding Meat Glaze.

Makes 1½–2 cups
1 × Brown Bone Stock (page 14)

Use the stock cold, so that all fat can be removed first. Strain it into 2 saucepans and boil until reduced by half. Combine in one pan and continue boiling until thick enough to coat the back of a spoon; it will set to jelly when cold.

For a distinguished quick sauce, deglaze the pan with 1–2 tblsp (or a frozen cube) of meat glaze after frying. Add 1 tblsp lemon juice or 2 tblsp brandy or sherry too. You can also whisk in 2–3 tblsp heavy cream or 1 tblsp butter, in pieces.

Store it in small jars in the refrigerator for up to 3 weeks. If a light mold forms on top, scrape it off and reboil the glaze before use. Freeze in an ice cube tray, then bag for up to 3 months storage.

MEAT GLAZE 2

The addition of a spoonful or so of meat glaze to a sauce guarantees success, so I've also included this short cut, which knocks hours off the classic method. I keep some in empty spice jars – a ration of 2 tblsp in each – in the refrigerator (it keeps for 2–3 weeks), or frozen as cubes in the freezer. Boil up several cans of consommé simultaneously – it takes no more time than boiling one. Condensed consommé is quicker still, though not all brands are successful.

Makes 3–4 tblsp
14 oz good canned consommé

Divide the consommé between 2 pans and boil until reduced by half. Combine and boil until reduced to a syrupy liquid, about 4–6 tblsp; don't let it burn. Taste it as it starts to get low; if salt predominates, add 2–3 tblsp amontillado (medium-dry) sherry wine and reduce again. Use in the ways described for Meat Glaze.

Meat jelly from a roast or good, leftover gravy can be used (unreduced) when meat glaze is specified in a recipe, but does not have quite the same punch. If you have neither but wish to add something to finish a brown sauce, use a tiny dab of beef extract; be careful not to oversalt.

MINT BUTTER

This is an unusual variation on the well-known Béarnaise sauce, flavored with fresh mint. In France it is called "sauce Paloise," which means from Pau, the ancient capital of Béarn – a little play on words, because Béarnaise does not come from the Pyrenees region at all, but is firmly Parisian. Serve this butter sauce with roast leg of spring lamb or as a topping to young peas. Alternatives are Mint Jelly and Mint Sauce (page 93).

Makes 1 cup
2 tblsp coarsely chopped fresh mint
2 tblsp white wine vinegar
½ cup dry white wine
1 tblsp finely chopped shallots
3 medium-size egg yolks
¾ cup unsalted butter, diced small
Salt and ground white pepper

Put the chopped mint, white wine vinegar, dry white wine and chopped shallots in a small pan and boil until reduced to 2 tblsp.

Put the egg yolks and 1 tblsp cold water in the top pan of a double boiler over simmering – not boiling – water: the top pan must not touch the water. Whisk the yolks until combined, then strain in the reduced wine mixture.

Whisk in the first piece of butter until incorporated. When it has been absorbed, add the next one. Continue whisking, being careful to cover the pan's bottom and whisk around the sides regularly. Add more pieces of butter, continuing to whisk until it is all absorbed and the sauce is thick and fluffy. Check the seasonings and serve. Like other Béarnaise sauces, it can be kept warm in a wide-necked Thermos for about 30 minutes, or over simmering water – do not let it boil. It congeals when cold, so any left over can be saved and served as pats on a later dish of peas.

MOCK HOLLANDAISE

"Bastard" or "imitation" sauce – sauce bâtarde in France – this is less prone to curdling than Hollandaise because it contains flour. A quick sauce for fish, white meat and ham, it is an alternative to Velouté when you have stock. It is particularly useful, though, for serving with vegetables and is often made with vegetable cooking water.

Makes 1½ cups

6–8 tblsp butter
2 tblsp flour
1 cup boiling, salted vegetable water or salted stock
1 medium-size egg yolk
2 tblsp light cream or milk
Ground white pepper
1 tblsp lemon juice

Melt 2 tblsp of the butter in a small heavy-based pan and sprinkle in the flour. Cook, stirring, over gentle heat for 1 minute. Add the hot liquid. Whisking thoroughly to prevent lumps forming, bring to a boil and cook 1 minute.

Blend the egg yolk with the cream or milk and stir in a little hot sauce. Off the heat return to the remaining sauce and whisk. Return to a boil and whisk 5 seconds. Off the heat add pepper and lemon juice to taste. Dice the remaining butter and whisk piece by piece into the sauce. Serve at once; do not reheat.

To serve with hot ham, stir in 1 tsp mustard powder. For poached fish, 2 tblsp chopped capers and 1 tblsp chopped parsley can be added.

MOLE POBLANO

The inclusion of chocolate in this "village sauce" from Mexico always strikes outsiders as improbable, but don't be put off – chocolate is not naturally sweet, and adds a rich flavor and color to gravies. Mole means "ground" and indicates that the sauce contains chilies. A blender or food processor will make it in minutes. This is enough to cook 4 portions fried chicken or 1½ lb fried turkey or pork. Serve with rice; in Mexico cooked beans or tortillas are other likely accompaniments.

Serves 6–8

1 onion, chopped
2 cloves garlic, crushed or finely chopped
2 small hot green chilies, stalks removed, seeded and chopped, or 1 tsp chili powder
1 cup roughly chopped blanched almonds
⅓ cup raisins
½ tsp coriander seeds
¼ tsp aniseed
¼ cup sesame seeds
1 slice toasted bread, torn in pieces
16 oz canned tomatoes
2–3 sprigs of fresh coriander or parsley
½ tsp ground cloves
½ tsp ground cinnamon
1 tblsp lard or shortening
½ cup chicken stock (page 12), hot
1½ (1 oz) squares semisweet chocolate, grated
Salt and freshly ground black pepper

Combine in a bowl the onion, garlic, chilies or chili powder, almonds, raisins, coriander seeds, aniseed, 2 tblsp of the sesame seeds, the toast, tomatoes with their juice, fresh coriander or parsley and spices. Spoon into a blender or food processor a little at a time and reduce to a purée.

Heat the lard and fry the purée for 5 minutes, stirring constantly. Add the hot chicken stock, and grated chocolate and season. Stir until the chocolate has melted: the sauce should be like heavy cream. Fried chicken, turkey or pork can then be simmered in the sauce for 30 minutes; garnish the dish with the remaining sesame seeds.

MORNAY

Contrary to popular belief, mornay is not the same as "cheese sauce:" the flavoring should be so subtle that the cheese is only just recognizable. It is especially good when the Béchamel is made with half chicken stock (page 12) and half light cream. Serve with poached fish or gratins, soft-cooked or poached eggs – on a bed of spinach or pea purée – with vegetables such as poached onions, or with pasta. It is very useful for layered dishes.

Makes 1 cup

2 tblsp grated Parmesan cheese
¼ cup grated Gruyère or Emmenthal cheese

1 × Béchamel 2 (page 25), hot
Salt and ground white pepper
Tiny pinch of grated nutmeg (optional)
2 tblsp butter or heavy cream

Beat the cheeses into the hot Béchamel; taste and season. A little nutmeg can be added, if wished. Whisk in the butter, in small pieces, or the cream and use immediately: do not reheat. If the final enrichment is omitted, it makes an excellent gratin sauce.

MOUSSELINE

Many sauces have the name "mousseline" added to them to indicate they contain cream. In the classical French repertoire, however, this is the true mousseline – cream added to Hollandaise. Serve with fish or luxuries like artichoke hearts and asparagus.

Makes 1½ cups
½ cup heavy cream
1 × Hollandaise (page 52)
Few drops of lemon juice (optional)

Whip the cream before making the Hollandaise, then fold it in at the end. Taste and add a few drops of lemon juice if needed.

For **Caviar Mousseline**, fold in 3–4 tblsp caviar; the effect is pretty when served on fish and it is a practical way to extend caviar.

MUSHROOM SAUCE

I like this sauce full of meaty bits of mushroom, but if you prefer it smoother, the mushroom pieces can be puréed, or strained out: add them to the soup pot. Serve with fish or chicken; for noodles, double the amount of mushrooms to make a light supper or lunch. For a brown mushroom sauce, see Chasseur (page 31).

Makes 1½ cups
1 cup chopped button mushrooms
2 cups chicken bouillon, made with a cube
1 tblsp lemon juice

2 tblsp butter
1 tblsp flour
¼ cup heavy cream
Salt and ground white pepper

Simmer the mushrooms in the chicken bouillon and lemon juice for 20–25 minutes or until the liquid has reduced by at least half. Blend the mushrooms and bouillon to a purée, if wished.

Melt the butter and sprinkle in the flour; cook, stirring, for 1 minute. Off the heat blend in a little of the purée until smooth, then add the remainder. Bring to a boil and cook gently for 5 minutes. Add the cream and season to taste.

MUSHROOM AND WINE CREAM

Delicious with veal cutlets, this sauce also goes well with fried chicken breasts.

Makes 2 cups
¼ cup butter
½ lb mushrooms, sliced
1 cup heavy cream
½ tblsp cornstarch
2 shallots or 1 small onion, finely chopped
6 tblsp dry white port, dry white vermouth or Sercial Madeira (optional)
2 tblsp dry white wine, or ½ cup wine if not using fortified wine
2 tsp lemon juice
Salt and freshly ground white pepper

Melt half the butter in a heavy-based pan and fry the mushrooms for 5 minutes, stirring. Add three-quarters of the cream and bring to a boil. Stir the cornstarch to a paste with the remaining cream, add a little hot sauce, then return to the pan. Bring to a boil, then set aside.

Skim the pan used for frying or roasting of all fat. Fry the shallots or onion in the remaining butter in the pan until soft. Add the fortified wine, if using, and the wine and deglaze the pan, boiling until reduced to 2 tblsp. Add to the mushrooms with the lemon juice and heat through. Taste and season.

MUSTARD GLAZE

Use to paint a leg or shoulder of lamb for roasting, or as a marinade and baste for kabobs or turkey drumsticks.

Serves 6

5 oz pot Dijon-style mustard
2 tblsp soy sauce
1 clove garlic, crushed or finely chopped
½ tsp salt
¼ tsp ground ginger
1 tblsp olive oil
1 tsp powdered rosemary or dried thyme

Combine all the ingredients; use as a glaze.

MUSTARD SAUCE

Serve with ham, pork or veal meatballs, roast Cornish game hens, or chicken (adding the skimmed poultry juices to the sauce), or fish such as herring. See also Creamy Mustard Sauce (page 36).

Makes 1 cup

2 tblsp butter
1 tblsp flour
¾ cup milk, hot
1 tblsp Dijon-style mustard
⅛ tsp ground white pepper
¼ cup heavy cream
1 tsp finely chopped parsley

Melt the butter and sprinkle with the flour. Cook, stirring, for 1 minute. Off the heat stir in one-third of the milk until smooth. Add the remaining milk, mustard and pepper. Bring to a boil, stirring, and cook for 5 minutes. Whisk in the cream. Heat through, then stir in the parsley.

NANTUA

One of the great shellfish sauces, this comes from the mountains on the eastern side of France and is tradi-

tionally made with freshwater crayfish, though shrimp do just as well. The classic dish is Nantua with quenelles – oval fish dumplings – but the sauce can be served with turbot, sole or flounder or other white fish. It makes an exquisite filling for vol-au-vents for an appetizer. The lobster version is called "Cardinal Sauce," but you cannot blend the shells.

Makes 1½ cups

6 tblsp butter
½ cup finely chopped button mushrooms
2 tblsp flour
1 cup good fish stock (page 11), hot
1 tsp lemon juice
½ lb shrimp or freshwater crayfish in their shells
2 large egg yolks
5 tblsp heavy cream
Salt and ground white pepper
Pinch of cayenne (optional)
½ tsp tomato paste (optional)

Melt half the butter in a heavy-based pan and fry the mushrooms for 2–3 minutes. Sprinkle with the flour and cook for 1 minute, stirring.

Off the heat stir in one-third of the fish stock until smooth. Add the remainder, with the lemon juice, bring to a boil, stirring, and cook for 5 minutes. Simmer, covered, for 5 minutes more, then turn off the heat and leave to stand at least 10 minutes.

Peel the shellfish. Reserve a few whole for the garnish and chop the rest; set aside. To make **Shellfish Butter**, put all the debris in a small pan (smash the crayfish shells well with a hammer first). Add the remaining butter and ¼ cup water. Heat gently for 5 minutes, shaking the pan occasionally. Scrape the pan contents into a blender or food processor and add 1 tblsp boiling water if all the water has evaporated. Pulverize.

Scrape the blender contents into a sieve lined with cheesecloth. Pick up the cheesecloth and wind it down hard onto the shells, using a spoon to scrape off the shellfish butter that oozes through. (All this can be done ahead.)

Ten minutes before serving, heat the mushroom sauce and strain into the top of a double boiler, pressing the mushrooms well. Stand over simmering – not boiling – water; the top pan must not touch the water. Blend the yolks and cream and stir in a little hot liquid. Return to the pan and stir gently until thickened; the sauce must not boil.

Stir in the chopped shrimp and shellfish butter. Taste and season, adding more lemon juice if needed. For quenelles and vol-au-vents add the cayenne and tomato paste too. Garnish with the reserved shellfish.

NEWBURG SAUCE

Definitely an American invention, this creamy Madeira sauce honors an unknown individual – called Wenburg, so the story goes! Good and very easy, it is excellent for sautéed lobster, shrimp or sole, and good for heating frozen or canned shellfish destined for crêpe fillings, little pastry cases or vol-au-vents. Newburg also goes well with fried veal, pork and turkey cutlets.

Serves 4
1 tblsp butter
1 tblsp chopped shallots or white part of scallion
Pinch of cayenne
1 cup heavy cream
¼ cup dry sherry or Sercial Madeira wine
3 medium-size egg yolks
Tiny pinch of grated nutmeg
Salt and ground white pepper

In the top pan of a double boiler melt the butter and soften the shallots or scallion. Add the cayenne and three-quarters of the cream and heat through; leave over simmering water for 5 minutes to reduce slightly. Add the sherry or Madeira.

Beat the yolks with the remaining cream. Stir in a little hot sauce and return to the pan. Cook, stirring, until thickened. Season to taste with nutmeg, salt and pepper.

Up to 1 cup sliced, sautéed mushrooms can be added to bulk the sauce out if it is to be used as a filling (not traditional). Reserve a little plain sauce for dribbling over crêpes.

ORANGE CREAM

Serve with fried veal chops or poached fish such as flounder, or with mussels or scallops.

Makes 1 cup
Juice of 1 orange
Juice of ½ lemon
3 large egg yolks
¼ cup heavy cream
½ cup dry white wine
Salt and ground white pepper
Pinch of cayenne
¼ cup cold butter, diced
1 tsp finely chopped parsley

Put the orange and lemon juices, the yolks, cream and wine in the top of a double boiler. Set over simmering – not boiling – water; the top pan must not touch the water. Cook gently, stirring, until the sauce thickens to a light custard. Taste and season, adding the cayenne.

Just before serving, whisk in the butter in tiny pieces and sprinkle with parsley. Veal chops or flounder can be garnished with the segments of another orange. For mussels or scallops, add a small quantity of well-reduced shellfish liquid (see Marinara, page 56) before whisking in the butter.

ORANGE GLAZE

Useful for lamb chops and ham steaks, broiled or cooked in the microwave oven, glazes are associated with roast ham. Bake, tightly wrapped in foil, at 350°, calculating cooking time at 30 min per lb for a roast under 6 lb. Open the parcel for the last 30 minutes, remove any rind and baste with the glaze. See also Apricot Glaze (page 21), Mustard Glaze (opposite) and Redcurrant Jelly Glaze (page 65).

Glazes 4–5 lb roast
2 tblsp brown sugar
1 tblsp prepared mustard
1 tblsp frozen orange juice concentrate
Grated rind of 1 orange (optional)
1 tblsp clear honey

Skin the roast, if necessary, and prick it all over with a fork. Combine all the glaze ingredients and spread over the meat. Roast, basting 1–2 times. Alternatively, baste individual portions.

ORANGE SAUCE

Serve this fruity sauce with pork, duck or goose; use it, too, for reheating cold meat or poultry. See also Bigarade (page 26), the orange sauces on page 61 and Maltaise (page 55).

Makes about 1 cup

2 oranges
1 cup chicken stock (page 12)
1½ tblsp cornstarch
2 tblsp golden raisins
2 tblsp butter
Salt and freshly ground black pepper
Pinch of cayenne

Pare the rind from both oranges with a potato peeler. Reserve the rind from one orange and cut that from the other into thin, short julienne strips. Blanch the julienne in boiling water for 5 minutes, then refresh under cold, running water. Put the other strips in a small pan with one-third of the stock. Boil for 8 minutes or until reduced to about 2 tblsp. Squeeze the juice of 1 orange and peel and section the other.

In another pan heat the remaining stock. Make a paste with the cornstarch and 2 tblsp water. Add a little hot stock, then return to the pan. Add the reduced orange liquid, discarding the strips. Bring to a boil, stirring. Add the raisins then simmer, covered, for 5 minutes.

Tear up the orange sections, removing seeds and membrane; add, with any juice, to the sauce. Add the butter and stir until melted. Add the julienne strips and season, adding the cayenne.

Gravy can be used instead of part of the stock, making this a good, easy sauce for reheating cold pork or turkey. Add 2 tblsp port wine or 1 tblsp lemon juice, if wished.

OYSTER AND SOY SAUCE

Oyster sauce is a commercial dark-brown sauce available in Chinese supermarkets. Combined with soy sauce, it makes a quick and very good accompaniment for fried beef or chicken.

Serves 4

4 scallions, white parts only, chopped
1 in piece of fresh ginger root, grated, or ½ tsp ground ginger (optional)
1 clove garlic, crushed, with salt if necessary
3 tblsp Chinese oyster sauce
1 tblsp soy sauce
2 tblsp sherry or dry white wine
2 tblsp oil (optional)

Mix the ingredients together and marinate the food for 2 hours if possible. Add the marinade to the food after frying, as a sauce.

PAPRIKA SAUCE

This sauce, made with sour cream – "smetana" in Hungary – is also called "Hungarian sauce" or "sauce hongroise." It is traditionally served with veal, but is good for reheating cold white meat. It is also marvelous with the ribbon noodles that usually accompany chicken or veal paprikas.

A quick version can be made by adding 2 tsp paprika, plus 1 tsp tomato paste and a pinch of cayenne to any white sauce.

Makes 1 cup

2 tblsp butter
1 large onion, chopped
2 tblsp flour
2 tblsp mild paprika
1 cup sour cream
1 tblsp tomato paste
Salt and freshly ground black pepper

Melt the butter and fry the onion over low heat until soft. Stir in the flour and paprika and cook for 1 minute. Add the sour cream and tomato paste. Cook together gently without boiling, then season.

A less rich version can be made by replacing the sour cream with broth plus 2 tsp wine vinegar. Stir ¼ cup cream or sour cream in at the end; 1–2 tsp caraway seeds stirred in at the end also enhance the Hungarian ambience.

PARSLEY SAUCE

Sprightly in appearance, this simple sauce is good with fish, chicken or vegetables, but it is at its most useful with lima beans and carrots. It is sometimes called "maître d'hôtel sauce" and a quick way of making it without fresh herbs is to stir little pieces of made Maître d'Hôtel Butter (page 91), from the freezer, into a very plain Béchamel.

Makes 1 cup

2 tblsp finely chopped parsley
1 × Béchamel (page 24), Velouté (page 74) or Suprême (page 71), hot
Celery salt or salt
Ground white pepper
1 tsp lemon juice (optional)

Stir the parsley into the hot sauce and check the seasonings: try a little celery salt if the flavor is too bland. Add lemon juice if not previously included, and serve.

Chopped chives can be used in the same way for **Chive Sauce**, to serve with fish or boiled lamb or ham.

PIQUANT BROWN SAUCE

Serve with roast pork, chops and other fatty meats; it is also excellent for reheating pork and bland meat like turkey. It is good made with just the vinegar from the pickles, without the pickles themselves.

Makes 1 cup

1 shallot or ½ onion, finely chopped
1 tblsp butter
2 tblsp white wine vinegar, lemon juice or pickle liquid
1 cup canned consommé, thickened with 1 tblsp arrowroot, or 1 × Brown Sauce (page 29) or Espagnole (page 45)
1 tblsp chopped gherkins
1 tblsp chopped capers
1 tblsp chopped parsley, or mixed parsley, fresh tarragon and chervil
Salt

Fry the shallot or onion in the butter until lightly colored. Add the vinegar or lemon juice and boil to reduce to a few drops. Add to the brown sauce. Simmer 5 minutes, then add the remaining ingredients and season to taste.

POIVRADE

Peppercorn sauce is a classic for game when made with the marinade from the game or a brown sauce based on game stock. It is excellent with roast beef or steaks: use consommé or stock as the base.

Makes 1 cup

1 small onion, chopped
½ clove garlic, chopped
1 small carrot, chopped
¼ cup red wine vinegar
1 cup red wine marinade from game or beef, or ½ and ½ well-reduced game stock and a full-bodied red wine such as hearty Burgundy or Pinot Noir, or ¾ red wine and ¼ beef stock, good canned consommé or Brown Bone Stock (page 14)
1 cup canned consommé or good stock, or 1 × unstrained Brown Sauce (page 29) or Espagnole (page 45)
Meat juices from cooking game or beef
12 black peppercorns, crushed
1 bay leaf
Pinch of dried thyme
1 tblsp arrowroot (if using consommé)
Salt
4–6 tblsp heavy cream (optional)

Simmer the vegetables and garlic with the vinegar and red wine marinade or stock mixture until reduced by half. Add to the consommé or unstrained brown sauce. Simmer for 10 minutes.

Strain the sauce, pressing the vegetables well. Skim all fat from the meat juices then add with the peppercorns, bay leaf and thyme. Simmer for 10 minutes. Mix the arrowroot (if using consommé) with 2 tblsp cold water. Stir in a little hot sauce and return to the pan; cook for 1 minute. If using brown sauce, add 1 tblsp cold water to make the fat rise and skim the surface until fat free.

Strain the sauce again, taste and season. Stir in the cream, if wished, and heat through.

PORT WINE SAUCE

The red fortified wines of Portugal have been fostered and imported by Britain since the 18th century; the French much prefer white port. This long-established English sauce is traditional with venison and game; make it with a good brown sauce. The shorter version, based on canned consommé or stock, is excellent with roast beef or with chicken livers.

Makes 1 cup

*1 cup canned consommé or Brown Bone Stock
   (page 14), or 1 × Brown Sauce (page 29) or
   Espagnole (page 45), hot*
1 shallot or ½ onion, chopped
¾ cup tawny port wine
1 tblsp arrowroot (if using consommé or stock)
Grated rind and juice of 1 orange
Juice of ½ lemon
2 tblsp currant jelly
Pinch of dried thyme
Salt and freshly ground black pepper
Pinch of cayenne

Boil the shallot or onion with ½ cup of the port until reduced to 2 tblsp. Put the consommé, stock or sauce in a saucepan. If using consommé or stock, mix the arrowroot with 2 tblsp water, add a little hot liquid, then return to the pan and cook for 1 minute.

Add the reduced port, citrus rind and juices, currant jelly and thyme to the sauce and simmer for 5 minutes. Add the remaining port and season to taste, adding the cayenne.

If you like a sweeter sauce, or want something to accompany roast game such as hare, up to ⅔ cup currant jelly, or to taste, may be added.

POULETTE

This lemon-flavored sauce is so often served with poached chicken in France that it has earned the name "young chicken sauce;" "poulette" is the exact equivalent of the old English word "pullet." It is a sauce of which I am very fond – especially good when the chicken stock for it (page 12) includes a whole, unpeeled, quartered lemon; an adjustment must be made when adding lemon juice later. Serve it with poached chicken or young roast corn-fed chickens, which are notable for their yellow skin and fine flavor. Garnish with grated lemon rind or lemon quarters if wished. It also goes well with boiled veal, and vegetables such as young lima beans and carrots and new potatoes, and makes a good, simple pasta sauce before a heavy meal.

Overshadowed by the more fashionable moules marinière, and mussels with saffron or curry cream sauces, poulette is excellent with mussels. You need 2 lb or 1 quart mussels, opened, with their reduced liquor – instructions for this are given under Marinara (page 56). Serve the mussels as an appetizer or with rice as a light main course.

Makes 1 cup

2 tblsp chicken fat or butter
*6 mushroom stems or 2 button mushrooms, finely
   chopped*
2 tblsp flour
1 cup well-flavored chicken stock (page 12), hot
2 large egg yolks
4–6 tblsp heavy cream
1–2 tblsp lemon juice
Salt and ground white pepper
1 tblsp finely chopped parsley

Melt the chicken fat or butter in a heavy-based pan and fry the mushrooms, over low heat for 2 minutes. Sprinkle with the flour and cook, stirring, for 1 minute. Off the heat stir in one-third of the stock until smooth, then add the remainder. Bring to a boil, stirring, and cook for 5 minutes.

Strain the sauce into the top of a double boiler, pressing the mushrooms well. Place over simmering – not boiling – water: the top pan must not touch the water. Beat the yolks and cream together, then stir in a little hot sauce. Return to the pan and stir gently until thickened. Add the lemon juice to taste and season, then stir in the parsley.

PRUNE SAUCE

Serve with roast pork or goose.

Makes 1 cup

½ lb unpitted prunes, or 6 oz (about 1 cup) pitted prunes
Grated rind and juice of 1 lemon
6 cloves
4 allspice berries
Pinch of grated nutmeg
½ cup sugar
¼ cup cider vinegar or sherry vinegar

Put the prunes in a small pan and cover with water. Add the lemon rind and juice, and all the spices. Cook very gently until soft and the liquid is well reduced. Rub through a sieve, and discard the pits and spices.

Return the purée to the pan and add the sugar and vinegar. Reheat gently, stirring, until the sugar is dissolved. Taste and check the seasonings.

RAISIN SAUCE

Serve this American sauce with hot ham; it is equally good with English crackling roast pork.

Makes 1 cup

1¼ cups grape juice or hard cider
½ cup raisins
Strip of thinly pared lemon rind
1 tblsp cornstarch
½ tsp prepared English mustard
Pinch of ground mace, or tiny pinch of grated nutmeg
1 tblsp butter

Simmer the grape juice or cider with the raisins and lemon rind for 10 minutes, until the fruit has plumped and the liquid reduced. Discard the lemon strip.

Mix the cornstarch and mustard with 2 tblsp cold water, stir in a little hot sauce and return to the pan. Cook, stirring, for 1 minute. Add the mace or nutmeg. Just before serving, whisk in the butter, in tiny pieces.

RASPBERRY PUREE

The nouvelle cuisine style is to spread a thin layer of rich berry sauce over a hot plate and on it arrange delicate slices of broiled calf's liver or lightly roasted duck breast.

Serves 4

6 tblsp currant jelly
1 tblsp lemon juice
¾ lb (3 cups) fresh or frozen raspberries
Freshly ground black pepper

Heat the currant jelly and lemon juice together until melted. Meanwhile, purée the raspberries in a blender or food processor and sieve to remove the seeds. Add the purée to the pan, heat through, taste and season with black pepper. Garnish the dish in style with flat-leafed parsley and pairs of raspberries.

REDCURRANT JELLY GLAZE

Use the glaze for basting chops, or for painting over a roast of any meat, or a small turkey. See also Apricot Glaze (page 21) and Orange Glaze (page 61).

Makes ½ cup

⅔ cup currant jelly
2 tsp butter
1 tblsp malt or red wine vinegar
¼ tsp mustard powder
Salt
Cayenne

Melt the currant jelly gently in a small heavy-based saucepan and stir in the butter, vinegar and mustard. Taste and season with salt and cayenne.

RED WINE SAUCE

This butter sauce is quickly made in the skillet after cooking chops or steaks, or in the corner of a small roasting pan while the beef rests before carving. See also Bourguignonne (page 28). Curiously, red wine sauce is in origin a fish sauce.

Makes ½ cup

¼ cup cold butter, in small pieces
2 shallots or 1 small onion, finely chopped
½ cup red wine
1 clove garlic, crushed or finely chopped
1 sprig of fresh thyme, or pinch of dried thyme
Salt and freshly ground black pepper

Remove the meat from the pan and keep warm. Skim off all fat from the pan, keeping any meat juices. Add 1 tblsp of the butter and fry the shallots or onion over high heat for 2 minutes. Add the wine, garlic and thyme and boil until reduced to 3–4 tblsp. Whisk in the remaining butter in small pieces. Season and serve without reheating.

For **Red Wine Foam**, which is much fluffier, use 1 cup red wine and ½ cup butter – but the chances of the sauce separating are higher, so whisk as little as possible and off the heat: never stir with the flat of the spoon. Enrich the sauce with ¼ cup meat jelly from a roast, or Meat Glaze (page 57).

For **Red Wine Fish Sauce**, add 1 tblsp fish glaze (page 12) from cooking, ¼ tsp anchovy paste, plus cayenne. Though I am not overfond of red wine sauces with fish, it makes a talking point when served with salmon steaks and masks the dull color of mackerel or carp.

RICH GRAVY

Make this sauce in the roasting pan after roasting beef, game birds, Cornish game hens or just plain chicken. It also goes well with chops and steaks.

Makes 1 cup

½ cup red wine
Fat and meat drippings in the pan

2 unpeeled garlic cloves, crushed with the flat of a knife
Pinch of dried thyme
¾ cup chicken stock (page 12), light stock (page 15) or canned consommé
¼ chicken or beef bouillon cube (if necessary)
1 tblsp currant jelly
Beurre manié made by mashing together 1 tblsp butter and 1 tblsp flour
2 tblsp brandy
Salt and freshly ground black pepper

Pour the red wine over the roast and baste during the last 5 minutes of cooking. Remove the roast and keep it warm. Skim off all possible fat from the roasting pan. Add the garlic cloves and thyme and stir to deglaze the pan. Boil to reduce the liquid by half.

Add the stock and bring back to a boil. Taste and add the piece of bouillon cube if needed. Stir in the currant jelly and then tiny pieces of beurre manié. Cook for 1 minute, then remove the garlic cloves and add the brandy. Cook 2 minutes, taste again and season. If wished, 2 tblsp heavy cream can be added, too.

ROBERT

The identity of Robert, immortalized in this classic brown sauce, is unknown. It is especially good with pork – from roast to chops – and for this reason is sometimes known as "sauce charcutière," or "pork butcher's sauce." Make the piquant additions to Espagnole (page 45) or to Demi Glace (page 40) and you have a sauce for a dinner party. The following version is rather quicker.

Makes 1 cup

2 shallots or 1 onion, finely chopped
1 tblsp butter
2 tblsp white wine vinegar, lemon juice or pickle liquid
1 cup canned consommé, thickened with 1 tblsp arrowroot, or 1 × Brown Sauce (page 29) or Espagnole (page 45)
1 tsp Dijon-style mustard
Pinch of sugar
1 tblsp chopped gherkins
1 tblsp chopped capers
Salt and freshly ground black pepper

Fry the shallots or onion in the butter until lightly colored. Add the vinegar or lemon juice and boil to reduce to a few drops. Add to the consommé with the mustard and sugar and simmer for 5 minutes.

Stir in the remaining ingredients. If wished the amount of cooked onion can be halved and 1 tblsp finely chopped raw shallot or onion can be stirred in at the end: this gives a crisper texture.

SAFFRON CREAM

A lovely sauce for fine-flavored shellfish like scallops, clams and mussels, and also for fish. Instructions for opening mussels and clams are given under Marinara (page 56).

Makes 1 cup
2 tblsp butter
1 onion, finely chopped
1 clove garlic, crushed or finely chopped
½ cup dry white wine
Up to 1 cup liquid from cooking shellfish or fish
½ cup heavy cream
½ tsp saffron powder, or pinch of saffron threads soaked in 2 tblsp hot water for 15 minutes
2 large egg yolks
Salt and ground white pepper
Pinch of cayenne

Melt the butter in a heavy-based pan and fry the onion and garlic gently until soft. Add the wine and the fish liquid. Boil until reduced to ½ cup. Add three-quarters of the cream and the saffron powder or liquid and bring gently to a boil.

Mix the yolks and remaining cream and stir in a little hot liquid. Stir back into the pan and bring just to a boil over low heat, stirring. Add the shellfish or fish and heat through gently. Season to taste, adding the cayenne.

Curry Cream can be made the same way; add 1 tsp curry powder to the frying onion. Omit the saffron and cayenne and flavor with 1 tsp Dijon-style mustard and 1 tblsp lemon juice.

SAGE AND ONION SAUCE

This medieval sauce, thickened with bread crumbs, is traditionally served with roast duck in England. It is also good with roast pork.

Makes 1 cup
2 tblsp butter
2 small onions, finely chopped
1 cup well-flavored stock
1 tsp chopped fresh sage leaves, or ½ tsp dried sage
2 tblsp soft white bread crumbs
Salt and freshly ground black pepper

Melt the butter in a saucepan and fry the onions until soft and lightly browned. Add the stock and bring to a boil, then stir in the sage and bread crumbs; season to taste.

SESAME SAUCE

Use this hot Chinese sauce as a marinade for chicken or cod, then add it to the pan after frying. It can also be served as a dip. The amount of chili can be reduced.

Serves up to 6
2 tblsp sesame seed paste or tahini
2 tblsp sesame oil
1 tblsp hot pepper oil, ¼ tsp hot pepper sauce, or 1 tsp Chinese chili sauce
2 tblsp dry sherry wine, or 2 tsp red wine vinegar
¼ cup soy sauce
3 scallions, chopped
½ tsp ground Szechuan peppercorns (anise pepper) or freshly ground black pepper
½ tsp salt

Mix all the ingredients and use as a marinade or dip: you may like an additional 1 tsp sugar.

A milder Japanese sesame dip can be prepared from sesame seeds. Toast 2 tblsp in a pan (without liquid or oil), then blend to a purée with 2 tblsp chicken broth, 1 tblsp dark soy sauce, 1 tsp lemon juice and a pinch each of salt and sugar.

SHRIMP SAUCE

This is a party sauce when made with fish stock and/or cream, but plain Béchamel will serve – I have even made it successfully with half milk and half fish stock from a cube. With frozen cooked shrimp it is a good standby for fish fillets from the freezer. Add extra shrimp to make a pasta sauce or turn new potatoes into a light lunch dish. This will also make a filling for tiny bouchées to eat with cocktails and makes a crêpe filling, for an appetizer. Nantua (page 60) is a more elaborate shrimp sauce, for which the shells are needed.

Makes 1 cup

½ cup finely chopped peeled cooked shrimp, fresh or frozen
1 scallion, white and green chopped separately (optional)
2 tblsp dry white vermouth
1 × Allemande (page 20) or Velouté (page 74), made with fish stock (page 11), or Béchamel 2 (page 25), made with ½ fish stock and ½ heavy or light cream, or plain Béchamel, hot
Salt and ground white pepper
Pinch of ground mace (optional)
Pinch of cayenne (optional)

Toss the shrimp in a small pan with the white of the scallion, if using, and the vermouth until the liquid has almost evaporated. Stir into the white sauce. Taste and season, adding mace if not using onion, and the cayenne if needed. Garnish with the green of the scallion (optional).

If the original sauce was a bland Béchamel, the fishy taste can be pointed up by adding ¼ tsp anchovy paste, while 1 tsp tomato paste will give it a shrimpy color. This is a good idea for fillings for bouchées or crêpes.

If you use Allemande as the base, and purée the shrimps, it becomes **Sauce Marguéry**.

SOUBISE

This superior onion sauce which goes back over 250 years is one of many French sauces a talented chef named after his master – other examples are Béchamel and duxelles. It is my choice for Easter day, to accompany a leg of spring lamb, fast roasted and rare in the French manner. It also goes well with lamb chops, poached or hard-cooked eggs and braised rabbit. The sauce is good cold; strip all the skin from a cold, roast leg of lamb and coat thickly with cold Soubise (instead of Chaudfroid), smoothing with a palette knife. Presented on a bed of fresh mint leaves it looks beautiful and tastes as delicious as it looks.

Makes 1 cup

2 cups chopped onions
¼ cup butter
Salt
1 tblsp flour
1 cup milk
Tiny pinch of grated nutmeg
Ground white pepper
¼ cup heavy cream

Put the onions and butter in a heavy-based pan with a pinch of salt and cook, covered, over gentle heat for about 30 minutes or until the onions are disintegrating; do not let them color or burn. Sprinkle with the flour and cook, stirring, for 1 minute.

Off the heat stir in one-third of the milk until smooth. Add the remainder and season lightly, adding the nutmeg. Bring to a boil, stirring. Cover and simmer gently for about 20 minutes until reduced to about two-thirds the volume; it should look like a thick, cheesy paste – do not let the sauce burn.

Stir in the cream, check the seasonings, warm through and serve.

SOUFFLE CHEESE SAUCE

A cheese sauce with a different texture; beaten egg whites give it its special lightness. It is good with leeks, broccoli or asparagus; use it, too, as a gratin sauce for vegetables or fish.

Makes 2 cups
¼ cup butter
2 tblsp flour
1 cup milk, hot
½ cup grated Cheddar cheese plus ¼ cup grated Parmesan cheese, or ¾ cup grated Gruyère, Emmenthal or Swiss cheese
Salt and freshly ground black pepper
1 medium-size egg yolk
Pinch of cayenne
3 medium-size egg whites

Melt the butter and sprinkle in the flour. Cook for 1 minute, stirring. Off the heat stir in one-third of the milk until smooth. Add the remainder and bring to a boil; cook 1 minute, stirring. Stir in the cheese and season; heat through. Stir in the egg yolk and cayenne off the heat.

Beat the whites until stiff and fold in; taste for seasoning and serve at once.

SOUR CREAM GRAVY

This rich, classic game sauce for roast saddle of hare and game birds such as pheasant and wild duck (all of which can be a little dry), can be white or brown, according to the fat and stock used. Make it in the roasting pan after roasting beef or chicken for a pleasant change. It is also good with boiled beef. Made with sour cream – "smetana" in Eastern Europe – the sauce is called "smitane" in the U.S. and France. See Paprika Sauce (page 62) for a sour cream sauce that does not contain beef stock.

Makes 1 cup
3 tblsp butter, meat drippings or chicken fat
2 small onions, chopped
1 cup consommé or Brown Bone Stock (page 14) or other beef stock
½ cup dry white wine
Meat juices from game, meat or poultry, skimmed of all fat
¾ cup sour cream
Salt and ground black or white pepper
1 tsp lemon juice

Melt the butter or drippings and fry the onions gently until soft. Add the stock and wine and boil until reduced by half – about 15 minutes. Add any meat juices and stir in the sour cream. Bring to a boil and cook for 5 minutes or until reduced to 1 cup. Strain for a smooth sauce. Season to taste and add lemon juice; do not reboil but serve immediately.

SOY GLAZE

This can be used to baste steaks, fillet of beef and pork, but the meat tastes even better if it is marinated in the sauce for 4 hours before cooking. See also Soy and Ginger Dipping Sauce (page 104), Oyster and Soy Sauce (page 62) and Teriyaki Sauce (page 72).

Makes ¾ cup
2 garlic cloves, crushed, with salt if necessary
6 tblsp soy sauce
3 tblsp olive oil
3 tblsp dry sherry wine

Put all the ingredients in a bowl. Baste the meat with the sauce during broiling or roasting.

SPRINGTIME GREEN SAUCE

This spring-tasting Velouté goes well with lamb or chicken. It can also be poured over noodles as an appetizer, or used to fill little tart cases for a light hors d'oeuvre.

Makes 1 cup

2 tblsp butter
1 clove garlic, finely chopped
2 tblsp flour
2 cups well-flavored chicken stock (page 12), hot
2 tblsp finely chopped parsley
½ cup asparagus tips, fresh or frozen
½ cup green peas, fresh or frozen
¼ cup heavy cream

Melt the butter in a small heavy-based pan and fry the garlic briefly. Sprinkle with the flour and cook over low heat, stirring, for 1 minute.

Off the heat, stir in one-third of the stock until smooth. Add the remainder and the parsley and bring to a boil, stirring. Leave the sauce to simmer for 30 minutes or until reduced by half.

During this time add the vegetables: fresh asparagus tips after 15 minutes, fresh peas after 20 minutes; frozen asparagus tips after 20 minutes and frozen peas after 25 minutes. Stir in the cream, taste and season, then serve.

If wished, for noodles or a pastry case filling, ¼ cup chopped cooked ham and the same quantity of frozen green beans can also be included.

STIR-FRY CHINESE SAUCE

A quick Chinese sauce to make in the pan when stir-frying vegetables; bean sprouts, green pepper strips and snow peas are popular, as are thin slices of carrot or tiny florets of cauliflower and broccoli.

Serves 4

2 tsp cornstarch
2 tblsp soy sauce
1 tblsp dry sherry
Salt and freshly ground black pepper
2 tblsp white wine vinegar (optional)
1 tblsp sugar (optional)

Mix the cornstarch with 3 tblsp water. Sprinkle the soy sauce and sherry over the vegetables (in China they are often poured around the rim of the wok and allowed to run down and half evaporate, making a fragrant sauce with the vegetable juices). A spoonful or so more water may be required if the vegetables themselves have given no juice. Pour the cornstarch mixture over the vegetables and stir-fry for 1 minute. Taste and season.

For a sweet and sour taste, include the vinegar and sugar as well.

SUGO

Real Italian spaghetti sauce! In Naples it is known as "sugo di carne" – meat sauce – to distinguish it from "sugo di pomodore" – plain tomato sauce.

Serves 6

½ lb beef top round, diced very small
3 tblsp olive oil
2 cloves garlic, finely chopped
4 shallots or 1 onion, chopped
2 tblsp chopped parsley
2 tblsp chopped celery leaves
1 tblsp chopped fresh basil
1 tsp each chopped fresh sage, rosemary and thyme or ½ tsp each dried herbs
1 oz dried mushrooms, soaked in water for 30 minutes, drained and liquor reserved, hard stems trimmed off, and chopped
Salt and freshly ground black pepper
Pinch of ground allspice
Tiny pinch of grated nutmeg
¼ cup dry white vermouth or white wine
1½ lb tomatoes, skinned, seeded and chopped
½ cup chicken stock (page 12) or light stock (page 15)
2 strips of lemon rind, very finely chopped

Fry the meat in the olive oil over high heat, tossing until brown. Add the garlic and shallots or onion. Cook over the lowest heat for 5–10 minutes until the onion softens. Add each herb as it is chopped. Add the soaked mushrooms and all the seasonings. Add the vermouth or wine and the mushroom liquor and simmer gently while you prepare the tomatoes.

Add the tomato flesh with the stock. Simmer, covered, for about 1½ hours, checking occasionally that the sauce is not burning: it should reduce to a rich, thick dark brown. Just before serving, stir in the lemon rind.

SUPREME

A rich dinner party sauce. The flavor of the stock is all-important: it must be well reduced, and not salty – check before you start. The sauce gets its name from its partnership with suprêmes – skinned and boned chicken breasts with the first wing joint still attached; fry them in butter. It is also excellent with poached or roast chicken, with fish and with hot ham.

Makes 1 cup

2 tblsp butter
½ cup finely chopped button mushrooms
2 tblsp flour
1 cup reduced, well-flavored chicken stock (page 12) or fish stock (page 11), hot
½ cup heavy cream
Salt and ground white pepper

Melt the butter in a heavy-based saucepan over low heat and fry the mushrooms for 2 minutes. Sprinkle with the flour and cook gently, stirring, for 1 minute. Off the heat stir in one-third of the hot stock until smooth, then add the remainder. Cook, stirring, for 1 minute, then simmer, covered, for 20 minutes or until reduced by one-quarter. This can be done ahead.

Strain out the mushrooms, pressing them well, and return the sauce to the pan. Stir in the cream and bring the sauce back to a boil. Taste and season.

SWEET AND SOUR CHINESE STYLE

Well known from Chinese restaurants, this is the sauce poured over deep-fried pork balls. It can also be used to reheat strips of pork or turkey.

Makes 1 cup

1 clove garlic, crushed or finely chopped
1 onion, finely chopped
1 tblsp oil
6 tblsp chicken stock (page 12)
1½ tblsp wine vinegar
1½ tblsp sugar
1½ tblsp soy sauce
2 tsp tomato paste or ketchup
2 tblsp sherry wine
1½ tblsp cornstarch
Salt and freshly ground black pepper
1 tsp Chinese chili sauce (optional)

Fry the garlic and onion in the oil until soft but not colored. Add the stock and the next 5 ingredients. Blend the cornstarch to a paste with ¼ cup water and stir in. Cook for 1 minute. Taste and season, adding the chili sauce if wished.

SWEET AND SOUR ITALIAN STYLE

Zucchini, carrots and cauliflower are delicious this way. See also Agrodolce (page 20).

Serves 4

1 lb vegetables, par-boiled or half-sautéed
2 tblsp olive oil (optional)
Salt and freshly ground black pepper
Pinch of ground cinnamon
¼ cup wine vinegar
2 tblsp sugar

If the vegetables are sautéed, you do not need the extra oil. If they are par-boiled, heat the oil in a pan large enough to hold them in a single layer. Toss the vegetables in the oil until almost cooked, then season and sprinkle with the cinnamon. Add the wine vinegar and sugar; cook until evaporated.

Pearl onions and parsnips can take a more robust sauce. Use the vegetables raw and fry until browned on all sides. Add 6 tblsp port wine and 6 tblsp red wine vinegar with 2 tblsp raisins and 2 tblsp brown sugar. Cover and simmer, shaking the pan regularly to prevent sticking, until the sauce is reduced to a few rich spoonfuls. Check the seasonings, adding a little cayenne.

TARRAGON SAUCE

Tarragon has a natural affinity with chicken, but can also be served with poached eggs or fish, and hot vegetables like new potatoes. A quick method is to add the chopped herbs to a Béchamel (page 24); a purée, used here, is more sophisticated, so it is worth using one of the better white sauces as a base.

Makes 1 cup

¼ cup fresh tarragon leaves, stalks removed
1 × Allemande (page 20), or Suprême (page 71) or
  Cream Sauce (page 36), hot
Salt
Cayenne

Reserve some tarragon leaves for a garnish and put the remainder in a small saucepan. Cover with a little water and boil for 5 minutes until almost evaporated. Purée the leaves with their liquid in a blender.

Stir the purée into the hot sauce. Season to taste, adding cayenne, and serve with poached or roast chicken, garnished with more tarragon leaves.

TERIYAKI SAUCE

"Teri" means glossy and "yaki" means grilled, but this Japanese marinade and baste can also be used to deglaze a pan after frying. Serve with strips of fillet or sirloin steak, chicken drumsticks or kabobs of firm fish or pork. It makes an excellent dip.

Serves 4

1 in piece fresh ginger root, grated
2 cloves garlic, crushed, with salt if necessary
4 scallions, finely chopped, or ½ onion, grated
6 tblsp light soy sauce or Japanese shoyu
6 tblsp sake (rice wine) or dry sherry
3 tblsp brown sugar

Mix all the ingredients and marinate the food for 2 hours; then use as a basting sauce.

If wished, the first 3 ingredients can be omitted and ¼ cup light broth (page 15), and/or 2 tblsp sesame or peanut oil can be included. The grated rind of 1 orange is a good addition for pork.

TOMATO AMATRICIANA

Made from canned tomatoes, this is a useful pizza topping and all-purpose tomato sauce, from Amatrice, a small town near Rome. Serve it with pasta and vegetables such as peppers, eggplant, zucchini and onions.

Makes 1 cup

¼ lb slab bacon or fat salt pork, chopped
2 tblsp olive oil
2 onions, chopped
2 cloves garlic, crushed or finely chopped
2 lb canned tomatoes
2 tblsp tomato paste
½ tsp sugar
1 small sweet red pepper, seeded and chopped, or pinch of
  paprika
Salt and freshly ground black pepper

Fry the bacon or salt pork in the oil until the fat runs and the morsels are crisp. Add the onions and garlic and cook gently until soft.

Add the tomatoes with their juice, chopping them with a spoon, the tomato paste, sugar and red pepper or paprika. Simmer gently for about 30 minutes, stirring regularly. Season to taste.

For a **Pizza Sauce**, blend to a purée; return to the pan and cook until thick, then stir in 1 tblsp olive oil.

TOMATO AND CORIANDER BOUILLON

Poach vegetables that are to be served cold as a salad in this tomato-flavored bouillon, then cool them in the liquid, which will form part of the salad dressing. The French call vegetables in this style "à la greque," though there is no connection with Greek cooking.

Serves 4

5 tblsp tomato paste
5 tblsp olive oil

5 tblsp dry white wine or vermouth
1 onion or ½ Bermuda onion, finely chopped
1 clove garlic, finely chopped
12 coriander seeds, crushed
1 tblsp olive oil
1 tblsp lemon juice
Salt and freshly ground black pepper
Pinch of cayenne
2 tblsp finely chopped parsley

Combine the first 6 ingredients in a saucepan large enough to hold about 1 lb vegetables. Add 2 cups water and simmer for 20 minutes.

Cook only one vegetable at a time, choosing from carrots, celery, leeks, fennel, pearl onions or button mushrooms; they should be cut into even-sized strips or broken into florets. Cook until only just tender, then cool in the sauce and chill.

If there is more sauce than just coats the vegetables, pour off the extra. Combine the olive oil and lemon juice, pour over the vegetables and check the seasonings. Sprinkle with the parsley.

TOMATO SAUCE

Really ripe tomatoes are essential for this sauce – a "couli de tomates" in French – otherwise use canned tomatoes; see Winter Tomato Sauce (page 76) and Emergency Tomato Sauces (page 44). Serve with red snapper, shrimp, lobster or homemade pasta. It is also good with vegetables like eggplant and zucchini. The sauce stores well, so make double.

Makes 2 cups
2 medium-size onions, chopped
1 clove garlic, crushed or finely chopped
¼ cup butter
2 lb ripe tomatoes, coarsely chopped
1 tsp sugar
Fresh bouquet garni, made of 1 sprig each of fresh thyme, parsley and celery leaves, 1 bay leaf and strip of lemon rind, tied together
Salt and freshly ground black pepper
1 tblsp tomato paste (optional)

Fry the onions and garlic in the butter until soft. Add the chopped tomatoes, sugar and bouquet garni and season to taste. Simmer, covered, for

30–45 minutes, stirring occasionally, until soft. Add the tomato paste if needed for color.

Remove the bouquet garni and paste the sauce, then press through a sieve to remove skin and seeds. Taste and season.

For a **Mediterranean Tomato Sauce**, double (or treble) the garlic and use ¼ cup olive oil instead of butter. Add 2 tblsp chopped fresh basil (or 1 tblsp dried basil); a good pinch of dried oregano or thyme could be substituted.

In Spain a **Spicy Tomato Sauce** is made with ½ tsp crushed cumin seeds (or a pinch of ground cumin) with 2–3 tblsp red wine.

All these sauces will keep, covered, in the refrigerator for 5 days and can be frozen. Delicate herb sauces lose something after about 1 month in the freezer, while cumin will become stronger after this time frozen.

TRUFFLE SAUCE

Looking like small, dirty potatoes, black truffles are in season around Christmas, but are almost unobtainable fresh. Even canned ones are desperately expensive, so there is no point in making anything less than the best brown sauce. Truffle sauce is often called sauce Péri-gueux, after the district in South-West France where the best black truffles grow. A 1 oz can will make twice this quantity: freeze ½ the truffles in ½ the liquor, or double the sauce. It is traditionally served with fillet of beef, fresh foies gras and very classy timbales and vol-au-vents: it is very rich.

Makes 1 cup
½ cup Madeira wine
1 cup Demi Glace (page 40)
1 tblsp truffle liquor, from the can
½ oz truffles, chopped
Salt

If you have been frying meat, pour off the fat from the pan, then add the Madeira and stir to deglaze the pan; boil to reduce by half. Alternatively, boil the Madeira in a small pan to reduce by half.

Meanwhile boil the demi glace until reduced by one-quarter, then stir in the Madeira, truffle liquid and chopped truffles; season to taste.

TURKEY GRAVY

Very fatty meats like shoulder of lamb and roasts like turkey or beef cooked with potatoes roasting around them in fat need special attention. This gravy is largely fat-free. For others suitable for the festive turkey, see Beef Broth Gravy (page 25), Brown Sauce (page 29) and Herby Onion Gravy (page 51). Espagnole (page 45) and sauces based on it, like Madeira Sauce (page 55), can also be used; make these ahead and add the turkey juices (without any fat), in the manner described below, on reheating. Use any left over sauce for reheating sliced meat and chestnut stuffing.

Makes 1¼ cups
Fat and meat drippings in the pan
2 tblsp flour
1 cup giblet (page 12) or other light stock (page 12)
Salt and freshly ground black pepper

Remove the meat (and roast vegetables) to a warm place and pour all the fat and juices from the pan into a tall heatproof pitcher. Pop in an ice cube so the fat rises (then remove). Return 3 tblsp fat to the pan, sprinkle in the flour and cook, stirring, for 1 minute. Remove from the heat.

Either use a bulb baster to extract the juices from the bottom of the pitcher (leaving the fat) or pour off the fat from the pitcher, then skim the surface with a spoon. Stir the juices into the pan, and add the broth. Stir until boiling, then simmer for 5 minutes. Check the seasonings and strain into a sauceboat.

I avoid flour-thickened sauces at the traditional turkey-eating festivals, which often end up as orgies of eating, and serve **Turkey Vegetable Gravy**. After straining the giblet stock, I purée the vegetables used to make it in a blender or food processor (or, if I am really trying, cook 1 carrot, 1 celery stalk and 1 small onion, all chopped, in the strained stock, and purée these). Empty all the drippings from the roasting pan into a pitcher as before, then return only the poultry juices to the pan. Add ½ cup white wine and boil for 5 minutes until slightly reduced. Then add the vegetable purée; boil again, if necessary, until you have the right consistency. Taste and season.

VELOUTE

"Velvet" sauce is probably the most useful ever invented; a flavored stock thickened with butter and flour, it can be adapted to any liquid on hand, including one that comes out of a bottle. Serve with chicken, veal, vegetables, eggs and lamb. Made with fish stock, it is a popular fish sauce.

Makes 1 cup
1 cup well-flavored white stock (see introduction to this section) or a combination of stock and white wine, hot
2 tblsp butter
6 mushroom stems or 2 button mushrooms, finely chopped (optional)
2 tblsp flour
Salt and ground white pepper

Melt the butter in a heavy-based saucepan over low heat and fry the mushrooms, if using, for 2 minutes. Sprinkle in the flour and cook gently, stirring, for 1 minute.

Off the heat, stir in one-third of the hot stock until smooth, then add the remainder. Return to the heat and cook for 5 minutes; the sauce can wait at this point if necessary. Strain out the mushrooms, if using, taste and season. This sauce is coating consistency and can be thinned with a little white wine or dry white vermouth, if wished. You can also add a little duxelles (page 17) to the finished sauce.

For **Mustard Velvet Sauce** for fish, add 1 tsp mustard powder, mixed to a paste with a little cold water; 1–2 tsp lemon juice and a little cayenne will make this quite fiery and suitable for herrings. A milder sauce is made by adding 2 tsp Dijon-style mustard – suitable for soft roes.

VINDALOO CURRY SAUCE

"Vindaloo" means pork marinated overnight in vinegar and spices: this type of curry can be quite mild. In Goa chilies are added and this gives the fiery combination

served as vindaloo in Western restaurants. This quantity is enough for up to 1½ lb pork – fry the meat before adding it to the sauce.

Serves 6

2 tblsp coriander seeds
1 tblsp cumin seeds
½ tsp each cardamom seeds (husks discarded) and black
    peppercorns
½ tsp each ground cinnamon and ground cloves
1 tblsp turmeric
2 in piece fresh ginger root, finely chopped, or 1 tsp
    ground ginger
1 tsp onion salt
½ tsp cayenne
1 cup malt vinegar
4 cloves garlic
2 tblsp clarified butter (page 18)
2 bay leaves
2 tsp ground mustard seeds
Salt

Dry-fry the coriander seeds in a pan with a lid. Add the cumin seeds and toast. Grind, blend or crush in a mortar with the cardamom, peppercorns, cinnamon, cloves, turmeric, ginger, onion salt, ¼ tsp cayenne and a little of the vinegar. Fry the garlic in 1 tblsp of the butter until gold, then mash. Combine with the aromatic paste and add the remaining vinegar and bay leaves. If possible marinate the meat in this for 24 hours.

Fry the mustard seeds in the remaining butter and add the vinegar liquid. Fried pork should be simmered in the sauce until tender. Taste and season with salt and the remaining cayenne if wished.

WATERCRESS SAUCE

For broiled mackerel or hot sea trout.

Makes 1 cup

2 bunches watercress, washed and coarse stems
    chopped off
5 tblsp butter
2 canned anchovies, drained, or ¼ tsp anchovy paste
Freshly ground black pepper
Pinch of cayenne

3 in piece cucumber, seeded and diced very small
2 tsp flour
1 cup well-reduced fish poaching liquid (page 11)
Salt
1 tsp lemon juice

Blanch the watercress in boiling water for 5 minutes. Drain and refresh in a sieve under cold running water, then drain and blot with paper towels. Purée the herb in a blender. Add ¼ cup of the butter, the anchovies or anchovy paste, pepper and cayenne and blend. Blanch the cucumber in boiling water for 2 minutes, then refresh, drain and reserve. This can all be done ahead.

In a small heavy-based pan melt the remaining butter and sprinkle in the flour. Cook, stirring, for a few seconds. Off the heat stir in one-third of the fish liquid until smooth. Add the remainder, stirring, and cook for 5 minutes. Add the cucumber.

Off the heat whisk in the watercress purée, in little pieces. Taste and season, adding lemon juice. Do not reheat; serve immediately.

WHISKEY CREAM

Serve with butter-fried chicken or sole.

Makes 1½ cups

4 button mushrooms, sliced
2 tblsp butter
6 tblsp bourbon or other whiskey
1 cup heavy cream
2 tsp beurre manié, made by mashing together 1 tsp each
    butter and flour
Salt and ground white pepper

Fry the mushrooms in the butter for 2 minutes. Add the whiskey and bubble gently for 2 minutes. Add the cream and bring to a boil. Drop in little pieces of beurre manié, and cook, stirring, for 1–2 minutes. Season to taste and serve.

WHITE WINE SAUCE

A straightforward sauce vin blanc of coating consistency, for white meat including boiled lamb, sweetbreads and brains. Mushroom and Wine Cream (page 59) is an alternative. If you are serving fish, use fish stock or substitute the more elaborate Bercy (page 25). Two nouvelle cuisine butter sauces based on white wine are Foaming Wine Sauce (page 48) and Orange Cream (page 61).

Makes 1 cup
1 shallot or ½ onion, chopped
3 tblsp butter
2 tblsp flour
½ cup well-flavored chicken stock (page 12), hot
½ cup dry white wine
Salt and ground white pepper
2 tblsp heavy cream (optional)
1 tblsp chopped parsley or chives

Fry the shallot or onion in the butter over low heat until soft and golden. Sprinkle with the flour and cook for 1 minute, stirring. Off the heat, stir in the stock until smooth.

Return to the heat and add the wine. Cook, stirring, for 5 minutes, then check the seasonings. Finish with the cream, if wished, and stir in the chopped herbs.

For oily fish such as mackerel make **Fennel Wine Sauce**; add 1 tblsp chopped, blanched fennel with a pinch of parsley (do not cook further as fennel is rather pervasive).

If you have flavored butters made – perhaps stored in the freezer – these make wonderful additions to a plain white wine sauce. Add a little Maître d'Hôtel Butter (page 91), Anchovy Butter (page 80) or Watercress Butter (page 106) in tiny pieces, whisking it in just before serving; omit the cream and herbs.

WINTER TOMATO SAUCE

A good basic sauce using canned tomatoes, this is suitable for vegetables, pasta and pizza toppings. See also Emergency Tomato Sauces (page 44).

Makes 2½ cups
1 large onion, chopped
1 clove garlic, crushed or finely chopped
2 tblsp oil, butter or margarine
1 small carrot, chopped
1 celery stalk, chopped
½ cup chopped mushrooms (optional)
2 lb canned tomatoes
2 tblsp tomato paste
Large pinch of dried mixed herbs
¼ cup red wine, or 2 tblsp red wine vinegar
Salt and freshly ground black pepper

Fry the onion and garlic in the oil or fat until soft. Add the carrot, celery and mushrooms, if using, and cook, stirring occasionally, for 3 more minutes.

Add the tomatoes and their juice, breaking them up with the spoon. Stir in the tomato paste, herbs and wine or vinegar and season. Cover and leave to simmer for 30–45 minutes, or until well reduced. Blend to a paste if wished, then press through a sieve to remove seeds.

The sauce will keep, covered, in the refrigerator for 5 days. Freeze in 1 cup packs (leaving ½ in headspace) for up to 6 months, though the flavor of the herbs and garlic grows coarser if kept so long.

Cold Savory Sauces

Dips and relishes from the Orient and Middle East give new interest to barbecues, kabobs and satés or fondue bourguignonne. Nut sauces add sophistication to hand-made pasta and are a novelty with poached chicken. Or try a fresh herb sauce from Scandinavia with cold fish. Here, too, are the traditional English garnishes for lamb chops, duck and fried sole, and the classic savory butters. There are suggestions for familiar dishes like shrimp cocktail and cold chicken from the New World and from Europe, plus ideas for summer buffets and picnics. There are also instructions for making mayonnaise the classic way, plus ideas for cheering up the store-bought version.

MAYONNAISE AND OTHER COLD SAUCES

Mayonnaise – where did it come from? The great French chef Carême, at the beginning of the 19th century, said it came from *manier*, French for "to wield." Others claim it was brought back from the port of Mahon in the Balearic Isles 50 years earlier by a victorious French army. Yet other versions are that it comes from *moyeu*, an "egg yolk," or that it is really *bayonnaise* – from Bayonne over the French border from Catalonia, which claims to have originated Aïoli or garlic mayonnaise. Two versions give Spain as the country of origin and in any event it is a southern sauce – easy to make in warm weather and sometimes obstinate in cold.

Whatever its origin, **Mayonnaise** (page 92) is the most famous of the emulsion sauces: egg yolks are whisked to suspend the particles in oil. Do not use eggs straight from the refrigerator: the emulsion forms most easily if all the ingredients are at room temperature. If you are in a hurry warm the yolks slightly by whisking them initially, then leave them to stand for 5 minutes at room temperature. I sometimes take the chill off the oil by warming it gently: it should still feel cold to your finger. If you do this, infuse a crushed or halved garlic clove in the oil at the same time. You can also warm the bowl in hot water before starting; dry it scrupulously.

Separate the eggs properly, removing the thread of white which attaches the yolk to the shell (if left in, this looks unattractive later). Mayonnaise is most difficult to make in small quantities. Use at least 2 yolks and not too large a bowl, so that the whisk can scoop the yolks. A ready-made emulsion of yolks and a little mustard to start makes it easier still. Add lemon juice or vinegar and salt to the yolks. Acid is essential for making the emulsion work and lack of it can cause curdling later on. Whisk them together until lemon-colored and fluffy.

Different types of oil (page 108) will make a considerable difference to the final mayonnaise; olive oil is the original and classic oil, giving most character to the sauce. Measure the oil into a lightweight cup and pour with one hand, whisking with the other. A hand electric beater is ideal for mayonnaise. Add the first few drops of oil – this is the crucial stage – and whisk until incorporated. Add the next few drops, ½ tsp only, and make sure this is absorbed with no little lines of oil trailing behind the beater, before adding more. Once the emulsion has started to form, you can add the oil faster or take a break.

The most frequent cause of **curdling** is adding the oil too fast, followed by cold or lack of acidity plus, it must be confessed, hurrying, not paying attention – and bad luck. If the mayonnaise curdles, try whisking in 1 tblsp very hot water. If this is no good, break another yolk into a small bowl and start again. Get the emulsion going by adding lemon juice, slowly at the beginning. Once you have made a light cream with the first few drops of oil, you can whisk in the curdled egg and oil alternately. Remember that as you have increased the number of yolks you must proportionately increase the quantity of oil.

Indispensable as a summer coating sauce, mayonnaise can take a myriad additions (see recipes page 92), though the quicker version (page 93) is less opaque than the classic one. If the oil used is bland and seasoning is minimal, mayonnaise can be served with a fruit dessert – its creamy texture is attractive. It can also be cooked – if it is layered into dishes, it won't separate.

By far the oldest versions of mayonnaise, stretching back into antiquity, are made from the mashed yolks of hard-cooked eggs, beaten with oil to make an emulsion. One that has survived into modern times is Sauce Tartare (page 105), for which I have given the European, not the American, version.

Garlic and bread **purées,** such as Skordalia (page 101) and nut purées like Pesto (page 95) and Tarator (page 105) come from the same period; they are common in the Mediterranean with pasta, fish and chicken. Puréed vegetables and legumes with oil including Hummus (page 90) and Poor Man's Caviar (page 96) can be treated as dips, side salads or sauces for fried meat and poultry.

Finally a word on **flavored butters** which are part of the French classic cuisine. Quite simply these are butters with seasoning, lemon juice, herbs and spices beaten in to give them character. They are best served cold on very hot food, where they will melt and lubricate it. They can be made ahead and stored in rolls in the freezer, ready for cutting. The most famous is Maître d'Hôtel Butter (page 91).

ASPIC

True aspic is made by boiling bones with flavoring ingredients to produce stock, then clarifying the stock to remove floating particles. This is done by boiling it with egg shells and raw whites then straining through cheesecloth. Though I often include a pig's foot in stock to make a sauce set to a firm jelly, I have managed to dodge the cumbersome process of making aspic all my life. The trick is to start with the type of jelly needed for the final dish and then work backwards.

A dark brown jelly is occasionally needed to coat a cold roast or poultry (duck or pheasant) served whole and eaten cold. The aspic layer is thin and **jellied consommé** does the job well. This sets in the can when refrigerated but is unstable at room temperature, so add 2 tsp unflavored gelatin to each 2 cups consommé, dissolved as described opposite.

The taste of the aspic is more important when it is to be used for glazing sliced, cold meat, as in boeuf à la mode. Reduce the consommé by one-quarter by fast boiling and make up the difference with sherry or white wine. Dissolve 1 tblsp unflavored gelatin (see right) in the liquid.

For a quantity of cold, sliced meat, cold tongue or sliced duck or game, use **jellied chicken stock**. This relies on the bones of the bird for part of the set and is made with the carcass, or better still the whole bird (page 12). Let the strained stock stand overnight in a tall pitcher, then remove all traces of fat. Leave the sediment in the bottom of the pitcher and strain the stock above it through a cheesecloth-lined sieve to make sure it is clear.

When reduced to 2 cups, the stock of 1 bird will set to a light jelly. For a coating and some other purposes this will need strengthening; dissolve ½ tblsp unflavored gelatin (see right) and blend it into the liquid.

I also use jellied chicken stock if a lot of aspic is needed and its flavor is important to the dish, for example to fill the empty spaces in a cold meat pie or for suspending vegetables, ham or bits of cold poultry in a mold. It is also good for glazing chops, poultry and white meat and for topping canapés and cold timbales or small molds for hors d'oeuvre.

It is important to test the set of aspic before using. Pour 2 tblsp into a saucer and put it in the freezer while you count to 10; it should set firm. If it does not, fortify it with more unflavored gelatin.

Aspic powder is a ready-flavored gelatin: dissolve it like gelatin (below). **Quick aspic** is made from a clear bouillon based on a cube. Dissolve a chicken (or fish) bouillon cube, according to the dish and the manufacturer's instructions, in 2 cups water. Add 3 tblsp chopped celery, 2 parsley stalks, snapped in 3–4 places, ½ crumbled bay leaf and a sprig of fresh thyme (or tiny pinch of dried thyme). Simmer for 20–30 minutes, until reduced by one-third. Strain through a cheesecloth-lined sieve, then add ½ tblsp dissolved unflavored gelatin.

To dissolve gelatin, put 2 tblsp hot white wine or sherry in a cup and sprinkle with the gelatin. Stand the cup in a little simmering water and stir gently until dissolved. Stir the gelatin into the warm liquid and leave until half set; 1 tblsp or 1 envelope sets 2 cups.

Aspic should not be frozen. If you are running late, 1–2 hours in the freezer may chill and set it, but after about 12 hours the gelatin will lose its setting strength. Never freeze a savory mousse that you intend to unmold for serving.

Use the aspic when syrupy – the consistency of unbeaten egg whites. It will then cling as it flows over the food. **To coat meat or poultry** with aspic, stand it on a wire rack over a plate. **Coat fish** on the serving plate – it might break up. Pour the aspic in one movement to avoid a patchy surface. Recover the drips, melt them gently and use them again. After coating fish, mop up the plate with paper towels.

For **herby aspic,** add chopped fresh herbs – parsley, tarragon, basil or chives – before coating. See also Tomato Aspic (page 105).

Other **jellied sauces** may be used for coating: Jellied Mayonnaise (page 90), *mayonnaise collée* in French, has sufficient gelatin to be piped and is very decorative on canapés, summer salads and salmon. Chaudfroid (page 82) is simply a hot sauce with added gelatin. Any sauce, Espagnole for example, which is brown, can be jellied. However, a white one, made with jellied Béchamel or Velouté, is most useful. Coat as for aspic. Decorations can be arranged on top of the chaudfroid; coat it again, this time with aspic, to give an extra sheen.

AIOLI

This garlic-scented mayonnaise from the South of France is sometimes called a butter – "beurre de Provence." The Spanish claim that aioli is a version of the Catalan "all-i-oli" (a purée of garlic and olive oil), which is often served on barbecued meat. Serve with cold fish – it is most famous with cooked salt cod – cold potatoes, hard-cooked eggs and coarsely chopped salads. It is also good with hot new potatoes and chick-peas.

Makes 1¼ cups

2 medium-size egg yolks, at room temperature
1 tsp lemon juice
4 cloves garlic, crushed, with salt if necessary
Salt and freshly ground black pepper
1 cup olive oil

Put the yolks and lemon juice in a bowl and whisk in the garlic and salt until light and fluffy.

Pouring with one hand and whisking with the other, add ½ tsp oil, then another. Proceed slowly with the first 2–3 tblsp oil, adding a few drops at a time, and making sure each addition is absorbed before adding the next. When the oil is incorporated, season to taste, adding extra lemon juice if needed.

ANCHOVY BUTTER

Stir into hot pasta, or chill and serve with poached or broiled fish. It can also be spread on small crackers to serve with cocktails before dinner.

Makes ¼ cup

¼ cup butter, at room temperature
4 canned anchovy fillets, drained and finely chopped
2 tsp lemon juice
2 tsp finely chopped parsley

Cream the butter until it is soft. Mash the anchovies on a plate with a fork, then beat into the butter until smooth. Beat in the lemon juice and parsley.

To make **Sardine Butter**, blend 1 canned sardine with the butter and add ⅛–¼ tsp anchovy paste. Taste and add 1 tsp lemon juice, if needed, and black pepper. Use it to enrich a fish sauce or spread it on crackers. The butter can be made more piquant by using Worcestershire sauce instead of lemon juice.

For **Smoked Salmon Butter**, blend ¼ cup smoked salmon trimmings with the butter. It makes a luxury canapé and is a good enrichment for a white fish Velouté for flounder.

ANCHOVY SAUCES

Cold anchovy sauces are too numerous to list, so consult the index. Prominent among them are Anchoïade (page 109), Montpellier Butter (page 94), Rémoulade (page 97) and Tapenade (page 104).

APPLE MAYONNAISE

This cold fruity sauce, also called "sauce suédoise," was probably invented for cold goose, but goes well with lamb chops and hot or cold roast pork; this quantity will serve 6–8 people. It also makes an unusual coleslaw dressing.

Makes 1½ cups

2 medium-size apples, peeled and chopped
¼ cup white wine
1 cup Mayonnaise, homemade if possible (page 92)
1 tblsp grated horseradish
Salt and ground white pepper

Cook the apples gently with the white wine in a covered pan until soft and pulpy. Press them through a food mill, then return the purée to the pan. Cook over low heat, stirring all the time, until all excess liquid evaporates; leave until completely cold.

Beat the apple purée into the mayonnaise with the horseradish and check the seasonings. A similar sauce can be made by using thick, whipped cream instead of mayonnaise; sharpen the sauce with 1 tblsp lemon juice. For lamb, a sprig of mint can be included.

For **Apple Horseradish**, popular in Eastern Europe with hot cooked beef and smoked tongue, add 2–3 tblsp grated or prepared horseradish to 1 cup cold, cooked apple purée (page 130).

ASPIC

Aspic (page 79), with or without herbs, makes an excellent cold dressing. See also Tomato Aspic (page 105).

BANANA RAITA

An excellent side sauce to any curry, this also makes a pleasant relish for cold meat and cold turkey. Make it more spicy for a relish, or serve it cool, without the chilies, if it is to accompany fiery food. See also Raita (page 96).

Makes 1½ cups

½ tsp garam masala or ground cumin
¼ tsp ground coriander
1 cup plain Yogurt, homemade if possible (page 106)
2 bananas, chopped roughly
½ green chili, stalk removed, seeded and finely chopped, or pinch of cayenne (optional)
Salt
2 tsp finely chopped fresh coriander leaves (optional)

Stir the garam masala or cumin and ground coriander into the yogurt and add the bananas. Include the chili or cayenne if you like a hotter flavor. Taste and season. Chill. Scatter chopped coriander leaves over the surface, if wished.

BASIL SAUCE

The most famous cold Basil Sauce is the Genoese Pesto (page 95).

BUTTERS

The principal cold, savory butters are given under Maître d'Hôtel Butter (page 91), while there are separate entries for Anchovy Butter (see left), Green Butter (page 87), Shellfish Butter (page 100) and Snail Butter (page 101).

CAMBRIDGE SAUCE

A 19th century sauce from a university where the professors are known to be fond of dining, this goes well with cold meat, especially bland turkey, ham and cold pork. It belongs to the same famous family as Montpellier Butter which, in the 20th century, inspired Green Goddess dressing in the U.S.

Serves 6–8

4 medium-size hard-cooked egg yolks
4 canned anchovy fillets, drained
1 tblsp capers
2 tsp Dijon-style mustard
1 tsp prepared English mustard
1 tblsp tarragon or white wine vinegar
1 tblsp finely chopped parsley
1 tblsp finely chopped fresh chervil or chives
1 tblsp finely chopped fresh tarragon
½ tsp cayenne
6 tblsp olive oil
Salt and freshly ground black pepper

Put the first 6 ingredients in a blender and purée. Add the herbs and cayenne and purée again. With the blender running, add the oil slowly through the hole in the lid, making sure each addition is absorbed before adding the next. Season to taste. Chill until needed.

CAPER SAUCE

See Tapenade (page 104), Cambridge Sauce (above), Tartare (page 105), Rémoulade (page 97) and Montpellier Butter (page 94).

CASHEW CREAM

Use this thick purée of nuts instead of mayonnaise; it goes well with cold chicken, and makes an inspired dressing for cheese, carrot and apple salads.

Makes 1 cup

½ cup cashew nuts
½ clove garlic, crushed, with salt if necessary
3 tblsp lemon juice
½ cup oil
Salt and ground white pepper
Pinch of paprika

Put the nuts and garlic in a blender with the lemon juice and ½ cup water and purée. Add the oil gradually through the hole in the lid. Taste and season, adding paprika.

CHANTILLY MINT SAUCE

Excellent with cold lamb, this sauce also makes a good salad dressing to turn boring old frozen peas into something special, or new peas into something very special! Decorate a pea salad with fresh mint leaves or strips of pimiento. See also Mustard Chantilly (page 94).

Makes 1¼ cups

½ cup sour cream or whipping cream
½ cup Mayonnaise, homemade if possible (page 92)
¼ tsp Dijon-style mustard
2 tsp lemon juice (for whipping cream only)
1 cup roughly chopped fresh mint
Salt and freshly ground black pepper

Whip the cream until very creamy, then stir all the ingredients together. Chill.

CHAUDFROID

The name "hot-cold" in French describes any sauce that is made hot, but eaten cold and jellied. This elegant coating sauce is ideal for summer parties because it keeps food moist for 24 hours or more. Whole chickens, galantines of meat and whole fish can be coated, but so can cold lamb chops, fish steaks, chicken pieces – and even rolls of stuffed ham. This white chaudfroid is best known, but any smooth sauce can be set with unflavored gelatin to make chaudfroid.

Coats 1 chicken or 8 portions

2½ cups chicken stock (page 12) or fish stock (page 11), hot
2 tblsp butter
2 tblsp flour
2 tblsp dry white wine
½ cup whipping cream
Salt and ground white pepper
1–3 tsp lemon juice
1½ envelopes unflavored gelatin

Melt the butter, sprinkle in the flour and cook 1 minute, stirring. Off the heat stir in one-third of the hot stock until smooth. Add the remainder with the wine. Bring to a boil, stirring, then simmer 10 minutes or until slightly reduced. Stand for 10 minutes, then stir in the cream and season, adding lemon juice to taste.

Sprinkle the gelatin over 2 tblsp water, then stir over hot water until dissolved. Stir into the warm sauce. Cool until syrupy (it can be gently reheated if you forget it). Use when it is the consistency of unbeaten egg whites. Whole fish and fish steaks should be coated on the serving plate as there is the risk of them breaking up. Spoon the sauce over them and mop up with paper towels. Stand portions, whole birds and roasts on a wire rack over a plate then pour the sauce from the pan, in one movement, over them. Retrieve spare sauce from the plate and repeat as necessary.

Chaudfroid sauce can be used to serve cold chicken "**en demi-deuil**," which is French for "half-mourning" and is therefore black-and-white. The white chicken is decorated with thin strips of black truffle or – more practically – black olive strips, which gives the appearance but not, alas, the taste. Strictly speaking the dish should be hot with Suprême Sauce and truffles, but decorating is easier with a cold dish. Glaze the finished pattern with a layer of aspic.

CHILI DIP

This is a homemade substitute for "harissa," the North African hot red pepper sauce. It can be served with couscous, but is more useful for vegetable kabobs and as a barbecue dip for sausages and grilled meat. It also livens up hamburgers.

Makes 5 tblsp

½ tsp seeded, chopped fresh chili or chili powder
1 tsp ground cumin
1 tsp ground coriander
½ tsp celery salt
2 tblsp tomato paste or tomato ketchup
2 tblsp stock, hot

Pound the chili to a paste in a mortar, keeping it as far from your face as possible. Add the next 4 ingredients, and stir in the stock.

COCKTAIL SAUCE

For shrimp cocktails! It is also called "sauce Caribbee." See also Hot Tomato Sauce (page 89) and Creamy Tomato Sauce (page 84).

Makes 1 cup

1 unpeeled garlic clove, halved lengthwise
¾ cup Mayonnaise, homemade if possible (page 92)
¼ cup sour or heavy cream
1–2 tsp lemon or lime juice
⅛ tsp anchovy paste
3 tblsp finely chopped parsley
Pinch of cayenne
Salt and freshly ground black pepper

Wipe the cut sides of both garlic halves around a bowl, crushing the garlic well, then discard. Add the remaining ingredients, using less citrus juice with sour cream, and seasoning to taste.

COCONUT SAMBAL

Sambals are small side dishes served at an Indonesian or Sri Lankan meal, often with curry; some are mild, some chili-flavored, but all are different from the chutney tray that accompanies Indian curries. This makes a good dip.

Makes ¾ cup

1⅓ cups shredded coconut
2 tblsp warm milk
1 onion, finely chopped
1 tsp paprika
1 tsp balachan (Indonesian dried shrimp powder or paste), or Indian-style bottled shrimp balichow, or shrimp paste, or anchovy paste, or ½ canned anchovy fillet, drained and mashed
1 tsp chili powder (less for balichow)
About 1 tblsp lemon juice

Mix together the first 5 ingredients, then add chili powder and lemon juice to taste. It keeps for 4–5 days, covered, in the refrigerator.

CORONATION SAUCE

Curried mayonnaise was served at the banquet for British King George V's Jubilee celebrations and again after Elizabeth II's Coronation – with cold chicken. This delicate version would also suit shellfish. It will serve 8. For big buffets, I sometimes use it to dress potato salad.

Makes 2½ cups

1 small onion, finely chopped
1 tblsp oil
2 tsp curry powder
¾ cup red wine
1 tsp tomato paste
1 bay leaf
Pinch of sugar
1–2 tblsp apricot purée or apricot jam
1–2 tsp lemon juice
Salt and freshly ground black pepper
2 cups Mayonnaise, homemade if possible (page 92)
¼ cup heavy cream, whipped

Fry the onion in the oil for 5 minutes or until soft. Sprinkle with the curry powder and cook for 1 minute. Stir in the wine, tomato paste and ½ cup water. Add the bay leaf, sugar, apricot purée or jam and 1 tsp lemon juice. Simmer, uncovered, for 10 minutes or until reduced to a soft paste. Taste and season, adding more lemon juice if needed. Sieve and leave until cold.

Stir the cold sauce into the mayonnaise, tasting as you go. Fold in the whipped cream, taste and season if necessary.

For a smaller quantity of a quicker **Curry Mayonnaise**, stir the following ingredients into ¾ cup mayonnaise: 1 tblsp lemon juice, 1½ tblsp curry powder, 1½ tblsp mango chutney, 1½ tblsp grated onion and 6 tblsp heavy cream, lightly whipped. Garnish with 2 tsp chopped parsley.

CRANBERRY RELISH

This raw relish goes back to early 19th century America. Make it 48 hours before eating, otherwise the berries remain tart, rather than absorbing the syrup.

Makes 2½ cups
½ lb cranberries
1 orange, peeled, sectioned and seeded
½ cup golden raisins
6 tblsp sugar
¼ cup clear honey (warm it to help measuring)
½ tsp powdered ginger
½ cup chopped walnuts

Put the cranberries and orange in a food processor and chop roughly, or chop then combine. Add the remaining ingredients and chill for 48 hours, turning occasionally.

CRANBERRY SPICY JELLY

Serve with festive turkey, poultry and game birds. It also makes an excellent dessert sauce; spread it on waffles or biscuits.

Makes 3 cups
1 lb cranberries
1 cup sugar
⅔ cup coarse-cut marmalade
¼ tsp ground allspice, or ½ tsp crushed allspice berries
Pinch of ground ginger

Bring the cranberries, sugar and ½ cup water to a boil and cook for 5 minutes. Add the marmalade and spices and stir over low heat until dissolved. Leave until cold.

CRANBERRY WHOLE BERRY SAUCE

Translucent, red cranberries are a necessary part of a traditional Christmas dinner. This sauce has none of the bitterness associated with the raw berry. I like it both hot and cold. This quantity is enough for the hot bird and for the cold roast on the following day.

Makes 3 cups
2 cups sugar
1 orange
1 lb cranberries

Put the sugar with 1½ cups water in a heavy-based pan and heat slowly, stirring until the sugar dissolves. Pare the rind from the orange with a potato peeler and add to the syrup. Boil for 5 minutes.

Add the berries and simmer for 5 minutes. Remove the rind before serving hot or cold.

For **Cranberry and Orange Sauce**, section 2 oranges, removing all membrane, and tear each section in 2 or 3. Drain off a little syrup from the cranberry sauce and mix the orange into the cranberries. When cold this will set to a light jelly.

CREAMY TOMATO SAUCE

Serve this fresh vegetable sauce instead of mayonnaise with shellfish, mixed chicken or fish salads, a variety of vegetables and even potato salad. See also Raw Tomato Sauce (page 96).

Makes 1 cup
½ lb very ripe tomatoes, skinned, seeded and coarsely chopped
Salt
¼ cup heavy plain cream, or Yogurt, homemade if possible (page 106)
2 tblsp white wine vinegar
1 tsp Dijon-style mustard
1 tsp finely chopped fresh tarragon leaves
1 tblsp finely chopped parsley
1 tsp finely chopped fresh chervil or chives
Ground white pepper
Pinch of cayenne (optional)

Put the tomato flesh in a sieve and salt lightly; leave for 30 minutes to drain. Whip the cream until thick, if using. Reserve one-third tomato for a garnish, then purée the remainder into the cream or yogurt. Stir in the vinegar, mustard and herbs.

Stir in the reserved tomato, taste and season with pepper and cayenne if needed.

For **Tomato Sour Cream Sauce**, omit the vinegar; use up to ½ cup sour cream and a single herb – fresh basil if you can get it.

CREME DES FOIES

This smooth sauce is made from puréed chicken livers. Make it with cream and green peppercorns to dress pasta – it makes a delicious dinner party appetizer. The olive oil version goes well with a mixed watercress and raw mushroom salad, and would make an excellent beginning for a nouvelle cuisine meal.

Makes ¾ cup

4 chicken livers, trimmed of membrane and green patches
2 tblsp butter
Salt and freshly ground black pepper
3 tblsp dry white vermouth, preferably French
1 clove garlic, finely chopped
2 large hard-cooked egg yolks
1 tblsp lemon juice
1 tsp coarse-grained mustard, such as Meaux
¼ cup heavy cream or olive oil
8 green peppercorns, crushed, or 3 tblsp chopped watercress leaves
1 tblsp finely chopped parsley (optional)

Fry the chicken livers in the butter until lightly browned on all sides, but still pink in the middle. Season them and place in a blender or food processor. Deglaze the pan with the vermouth, then add the liquid to the blender; purée. Add the garlic, yolks, lemon juice, mustard and cream or oil and blend to a purée. Stir in the green peppercorns or watercress leaves and serve at room temperature. Garnish a noodle dish with parsley.

CREME FRAPPE

Serve this iced horseradish sauce with cold cod, or with party fish such as salmon, turbot or smoked trout. Chilling reduces the effect of all seasoning, so it should be both tart and piquant to the taste before freezing.

Makes 1 cup

2 large egg yolks
1 tblsp tarragon or white wine vinegar
¼ cup corn oil
2 tblsp grated or prepared horseradish
1 tsp white wine vinegar
1 tsp Worcestershire sauce
¼ tsp anchovy paste, or ½ canned anchovy fillet, mashed
¼ cup heavy cream, whipped

Whisk the yolks in a small bowl with the vinegar, then add a few drops of corn oil and whisk. Continue adding oil, making a mayonnaise. Stir in the next 4 ingredients, then fold in the cream. Either freeze for 30 minutes, until barely firm, or freeze until firm, then remove to the refrigerator 15 minutes before serving to allow it to soften – it should be soft to the spoon.

CUCUMBER CREAM

Serve this with egg or tomato salads or cold salmon. It can also be heated gently to accompany hot poached fish such as salmon. The sour cream version is good with cold meat.

Makes 1 cup

½ cup cottage cheese
½ cup buttermilk or milk
½ cucumber, unpeeled, grated
2 tsp lemon juice or white wine vinegar
Salt and freshly ground black pepper
1 tsp finely chopped parsley or fresh dill (optional)

Blend the cheese and milk until smooth. Press the cucumber in several sheets of paper towel to remove much of its moisture. Stir into the cheese mixture and add lemon juice or vinegar and seasoning to taste. Add chopped herbs, if wished.

Sour cream – use 1 cup with 1 tsp lemon juice or vinegar – can be used instead of cottage cheese. Or use heavy cream with 1 tblsp white wine vinegar. If serving cold with cold meat, add a pinch of cayenne or chili powder.

CUCUMBER RELISH

Serve as a side relish to satés – bite-sized pieces of pork, chicken or beef cooked on wooden skewers – or with cold beef or other cold meat.

Makes ¾ cup
½ cucumber, peeled and very thinly sliced
Salt
¼ cup lemon juice or white wine vinegar
2 tblsp sugar
2 tblsp chopped scallion (optional)
½ red or green chili, stalk removed and thinly sliced in
  rings (optional)
Few drops of olive or sesame oil (optional)

Spread out the cucumber slices in a colander, sprinkle with salt and leave 30 minutes to drain. Put the lemon juice or vinegar, sugar and 2 tblsp water in a small pan and bring to a boil; leave until cold.

Rinse the cucumber under cold running water, then drain and blot dry with paper towels. Pour the cold liquid over the cucumber in a bowl. Add the scallion, and chili and oil, as wished.

CUCUMBER AND YOGURT DIP

This Turkish salad called "caicik" (pronounced gee-ah-jēēk) is extremely popular throughout the Middle East where it is eaten with other salads. Dried mint is often used. It makes an excellent dip, as well as an accompaniment to cold pork and cold lamb. See also Raita (page 96), the spicy Indian version.

Makes 1½ cups
½ cucumber, peeled and diced
Salt and freshly ground black pepper
2 cloves garlic, crushed, with salt if necessary
1 cup plain Yogurt, homemade if possible (page 106)
2 tblsp finely chopped fresh mint, or 2 tsp dried mint

Spread out the diced cucumber in a colander and sprinkle with salt; leave 30 minutes to drain. Rinse under running cold water and drain well. Stir the garlic and cucumber into the yogurt. Add the mint, taste and season with pepper.

CUMBERLAND SAUCE

This sauce commemorates the Duke of Cumberland, the general who won the last battle on English soil – against the Scots in 1745. He was known as "Sweet William" or "Butcher Cumberland" according to which side you were on. The sauce can be served hot, but is usually served cold with cold venison. It can also be used to baste ham steaks or a baked ham during the last 30 minutes of cooking.

Serves 4
½ cup tawny port wine
½ small shallot, finely chopped
⅓ cup currant jelly
1 orange
1 lemon
¼ tsp ground ginger
1 tsp mustard powder
Pinch of cayenne

Put the port, shallot and jelly in a small saucepan and heat until the jelly melts, stirring occasionally.

Grate the rind from the orange and lemon and add to the pan. Squeeze and add the juice of the orange and half the lemon. Stir in the ginger, mustard powder and cayenne. Bring to a boil.

Combined with Brown Sauce (page 29), this makes an excellent sauce for reheating cold pork or ham. For more texture, pare off the rind of the orange and cut into very fine julienne strips. Boil these for 5 minutes, drain and refresh under cold running water, then add to the sauce.

CURRY MAYONNAISE
Two simple recipes are given on page 92 and page 83, as well as the more ambitious Coronation Sauce (page 83).

DAMSON CHEESE

Fruit "cheeses" were popular medieval accompaniments to cold meat. Slightly tart fruit is best, though most types of plums could be used in this recipe. The "cheese" can also be served as a dessert sauce with molded creams, baked custard or creamy grain puddings – add more sugar to taste.

Makes 2–3 × 1 lb jars
6 lb damsons or other purple plums
About 5 cups sugar
2 tsp ground allspice (optional)

Put the fruit in a preserving kettle and pour in 1¼ cups water. Simmer, covered, until the fruit is tender. Purée the fruit, removing the pits – a rather tedious process.

Measure the purée; for each 1 cup purée you need 1 cup sugar. Return the purée to the pan and add the sugar, and spice if using. Stir gently over low heat until the sugar is dissolved. Continue stirring until the purée is very thick, then pack into jars and cover. The cheese can be eaten immediately, but will keep for up to 1 year. (For long storage, first process in a boiling-water bath.)

DILL AND SOUR CREAM SAUCE

This Scandinavian-style sauce is served with cold fish and shellfish such as cold crab. See also Dill and Mustard Cream (page 112).

Makes 1 cup
1 cup sour cream
1 tblsp lemon juice or cider vinegar
Pinch of sugar
2 tblsp chopped fresh dill, or 1 tsp dried dill
Pinch of celery seeds (optional)
Ground white pepper

Stir the ingredients together, seasoning to taste. **Fennel Sour Cream Sauce** can be made the same way (omitting the celery seeds). Add 1 tblsp Dijon-style mustard to either version if wished.

FRUIT SAUCES

Cold sauces for serving with hot or cold meat or fish include Apple Mayonnaise (page 80), Apple Sauce (page 130), Banana Raita (page 81), Damson Cheese (left), which can also be made with plums, Gooseberry and Rhubarb Sauces (page 49) and Orange Pickle (page 94).

GARLIC SAUCES

Cold sauces containing garlic are too numerous to list so consult the index. Notable ones are Aïoli (page 80), Herby Garlic Mayonnaise (page 92), Snail Butter and Garlic Butter (page 101), Pesto (page 95), Rusty Sauce (page 97) and Skordalia (page 101).

GREEN BUTTER

This colorful butter cheers up poached white fish; it can also be whisked, in tiny pieces, into a Béchamel or Velouté just before serving to give them a lift. Serve pats on hot vegetables such as green beans or cauliflower or use as a soup garnish. See also Snail Butter (page 101) and Montpellier Butter (page 94).

Makes ¼ cup
6–8 spinach leaves, stalks trimmed
Salt
1 tsp chopped fresh tarragon
1 tsp chopped fresh chervil or chives
1 tsp chopped parsley
1 tsp chopped watercress (optional)
2 shallots or ½ small onion, chopped
¼ cup butter

In a small pan of boiling salted water, blanch the spinach leaves for 3 minutes. Add the herbs and boil for ½ minute more. Drain in a sieve, then refresh under cold running water. Squeeze lightly in paper towels. Purée in a blender or food processor, adding the raw shallot or onion, then add the butter in pieces. For more texture the shallot or onion can be beaten in, finely chopped, at the end. Taste and add salt if needed.

GREEN PEPPERCORN BUTTER

Made fashionable by nouvelle cuisine, this butter is on page 91.

GREMOLATA

This savory Italian mixture is sprinkled over soups and dishes of braised meat before serving; it is best known on the Milanese dish osso buco.

Makes 6 tblsp

1 large clove garlic, crushed, with salt if necessary
Finely grated rind of 1 lemon
5 tblsp chopped parsley

Mix all the ingredients together and sprinkle over the cooked dish.

GUACAMOLE

This avocado purée from Mexico is well known as a dip, served with sticks of fresh, raw vegetables and taco chips, and as a salad dressing; surprisingly, it also makes an excellent sauce for hot fried chicken. In Mexico, guacamole is rolled inside hot tortillas.

Makes ¾ cup

2 avocados
2 tblsp lemon or lime juice
¼ tsp coriander seeds, or pinch of ground coriander
1 clove garlic, crushed, with salt if necessary
1 tsp grated onion (optional)
1 tomato, skinned, seeded and chopped
Few drops of hot pepper sauce, or pinch of cayenne
Salt and freshly ground black pepper

Halve the avocados, remove the seeds and scoop the flesh into a bowl. Immediately mash it with the citrus juice, or it will discolor.

Crush the coriander seeds in a mortar with a pestle. Add to the avocado with the garlic and onion, if using. Add the tomato flesh. Stir well, then add pepper sauce or cayenne and season to taste. More lemon or lime juice can be added.

If the guacamole is to be a salad dressing, stir in up to ¼ cup olive oil. In Mexico seeded, chopped serrano chilies are often included. Seed and chop 1 fresh hot green chili and add if wished (see also Green-Green Dressing, page 116).

For economy or a less rich purée, 1 avocado can be replaced by up to ¾ cup cottage cheese. Other vegetables may also be included, such as 1–2 tblsp crisp chopped celery, and the amount of tomato can be doubled. Sometimes small ham dice are included while 1 tblsp parsley is often added to garnish.

HAZELNUT AND ALMOND SAUCE

Also called "salsa romesco," this is a specialty of Catalonia in Spain, where it is made with red Romesco peppers, which are smaller and hotter than ordinary green or red peppers. One chili is the equivalent of 8 of them. Serve with hot fish, such as red snapper, or shellfish, or broiled chops and spicy sausages. Spoonfuls can be added to a fish or chicken stew while it is cooking, in the same way that the French rouille (Rusty Sauce, page 97) is used. See also Tarator (page 105).

Makes 1½ cups

½ lb tomatoes
3–6 large cloves garlic, or even more
½ cup hazelnuts
½ cup blanched almonds
1 dried hot chili, stalk removed, seeded and crumbled, or 1–2 tsp cayenne
Salt
2 tblsp wine vinegar
½ cup olive oil
¼ cup sherry wine
1 tblsp finely chopped parsley

Heat the oven to 425–450°. Bake the tomatoes and unpeeled garlic cloves (up to 12 fat cloves can be used: they lose their pungency when cooked) for 15 minutes. Add the nuts and bake for a further 5 minutes.

Rub off the hazelnut skins. Put all the nuts in a blender with the dried chili, if using, and purée. Peel the garlic cloves, roughly chopping them and add to the blender with the cayenne, if using.

When the tomatoes are cool enough to handle, remove their skins and add them too. Purée to a paste, and add the salt and vinegar.

With the blender running, add the oil through the hole in the lid, a little at a time, making sure each addition is absorbed before adding more. Beat in the sherry and mix in the parsley. Chill for several hours to allow the flavors to blend.

HERB SAUCES

For creamy herb sauces see Dill and Sour Cream Sauce (page 87), Dill and Mustard Cream (page 112) and Watercress Cream (page 106). For mayonnaise-based sauces see Herby Garlic Mayonnaise and Tarragon Mayonnaise (page 92), Chantilly Mint Sauce (page 82) and Sauce Verte (page 100). See also Pesto (page 95).

When you have a selection of herbs available, sophisticated sauces containing several herbs are Cambridge Sauce (page 81), Montpellier Butter (page 94), Ravigote (page 122) and Rémoulade (page 97).

Mint Jelly and Mint Sauce are on page 93, where you will also find Parsley Jelly and Rosemary Jelly.

HOISIN SAUCE

Hoisin, a sweetish commercial bottled Chinese sauce, is often an ingredient in Chinese recipes. It is also called "Chinese plum sauce" and this is a fair substitute which can be made at home. It is a popular dip with roast meats and is also served with Peking duck, rolled up in pancakes.

Makes ½ cup

3 cloves garlic, crushed, with salt if necessary
1 scallion, finely chopped
¼ cup dark, thick soy paste
5 tsp plum chutney or plum jam
2 tblsp tomato paste
1 tblsp corn oil
1 tsp Chinese chili sauce

Stir all the ingredients together. Keep, covered, in the refrigerator for up to 1 week.

HORSERADISH CREAM

Still one of the best sauces for roast or boiled beef, this can also be served with smoked fish, such as trout or mackerel, and with roast chicken. For a chilled horseradish sauce, see Crème Frappé (page 85) and also Apple Horseradish (page 80).

Makes 1 cup

¾ cup heavy cream
2 tblsp freshly grated or prepared horseradish
1 tsp Dijon-style mustard
2 tsp tarragon or white wine vinegar
Salt and ground white pepper
Pinch of cayenne

Whip the cream until stiff peaks form, then stir in the other ingredients, seasoning to taste and including the cayenne. Chill before serving. Horseradish cream can also be made with sour cream; omit the vinegar.

HOT TOMATO SAUCE

For seafood cocktails, or as a barbecue side sauce for dipping sausages or kabobs.

Makes 1¼ cups

¾ cup Blender Tomato Sauce (page 96) or tomato ketchup
1 tblsp grated or prepared horseradish
1 tblsp Worcestershire sauce
2 tblsp olive oil
2 tblsp lemon or lime juice
Salt and freshly ground black pepper
1 tblsp hot pepper sauce

Stir or blend together the first 5 ingredients. Season to taste, adding the pepper sauce 1 tsp at a time.

HUMMUS

This chick-pea dip is well known outside the Middle East; serve it with cocktails before dinner with strips of hot pocket bread or raw vegetables. It can also be used as a sauce for fried meat. Make it quickly with canned chick-peas – already cooked – often sold under their Spanish name "garbanzos" or their Italian name "cecis."

Makes 1½ cups

⅔ cup dried chick-peas
¼ cup lemon juice
2 cloves garlic, crushed, with salt if necessary
½ cup tahini paste
Salt

Cover the chick-peas generously with cold water and soak for 24 hours; alternatively, cover with boiling water and soak for 1 hour. Drain and cover again with water. Bring to a boil and cook for 1 hour or until tender – the time depends on the age of the beans – or for 20 minutes in a pressure cooker on high.

Drain the chick-peas, reserving the liquid. Purée in a blender with the lemon juice, adding a few spoonfuls of cooking liquid to make a smooth paste.

Add the garlic to the blender with the tahini and purée. Add a little more cooking liquid, drizzling it through the hole in the lid, until you have a thick cream. Season with salt. Hummus will keep, covered with plastic wrap, in the refrigerator for up to 5 days. To serve as a traditional dip pour 1 tblsp olive oil on top, then tilt the bowl to film the surface. Sprinkle a little parsley in the center or make a pattern with paprika.

JELLIED MAYONNAISE

Mayonnaise collée, "clinging mayonnaise" in French, can be piped on canapés or around a salmon when freshly made, but then sets firmly. It can be used to suspend vegetables or seafood for a salad or to make a jellied appetizer salad. Use homemade Mayonnaise.

Makes 1½ cups

1 envelope unflavored gelatin
1 cup Mayonnaise (page 92)
½ cup heavy cream, whipped
Salt and ground white pepper
Few drops of lemon juice

Sprinkle the gelatin over 3 tblsp cold water and heat gently over hot water, stirring until dissolved. Cool for 2 minutes, then stir into the mayonnaise, followed by the whipped cream. Season, adding the lemon juice to taste. Use immediately to mold or coat fish, shellfish or vegetables. This strength will withstand the heat of a cocktail party and summer weather.

LAST-MINUTE CHUTNEY

For curries, bread and cheese or cold meat when you want to add a quick fillip to a meal.

Makes 5 tblsp

3 tblsp plum or apricot jam, or blackberry jelly
1 clove garlic, crushed or finely chopped
1 small onion, grated
1 tsp coriander, fennel or dill seeds, as appropriate to the dish, crushed
1 dried chili, stalk removed, seeded and chopped, or pinch of cayenne
½ tsp wine vinegar
Salt and freshly ground black pepper

Heat all the ingredients together in a small pan. Transfer to a pot and leave to cool.

LEMON SAUCES

Lemon Mayonnaise is given on page 92 and Egg and Lemon Sauce on page 44. Make a lemon Chaudfroid (page 82); or make Poulette (page 64) using lemon-based stock, then dissolve ½ tblsp unflavored gelatin in it and use it as Chaudfroid.

LEMON MARINADE

I think of this as the French marinade, equally good for roasts of meat, chops, steaks and pieces of chicken or fish. It is one of the essential barbecue marinades and also makes a good baste.

Makes ½ cup
¼ cup olive oil
¼ cup lemon juice
2 bay leaves, crumbled
6 black peppercorns, crushed
1 clove garlic, crushed, with salt if necessary, or 1 tblsp finely chopped onion
½ tsp dried thyme or dried mixed herbs, or 2 tblsp finely chopped parsley

Mix all the ingredients together and use to marinate meat, fish or poultry for 4–12 hours. For lamb, omit the other herbs and use 1 tsp crumbled dried rosemary.

MAITRE D'HOTEL BUTTER

A classic garnish for fried fish or for broiled steaks or chops, this butter also adds style to steamed carrots and potatoes. Indeed, it is difficult to think of anything it cannot be served with. Also called "parsley butter," it can be made ahead in double quantities, and then formed into a roll. Wrap it in a butter wrapper and freeze it for up to 3 months. Cut off rounds with a serrated knife as needed. If wished you can chill the roll, then mark it from end to end with a fork. Flash freeze, then wrap and store. This will give each disk a patterned edge. The butter can also be whisked into sauces, in tiny pieces, just before they go to the table, to enrich them.

Tarragon Butter, Chive Butter and Watercress Butter can be made in the same way; see also Anchovy Butter (page 80), Green Butter (page 87) and Snail Butter (page 101).

Makes ¼ cup
¼ cup butter, at room temperature
½ tsp salt
Freshly ground black pepper
1 tsp finely chopped parsley
1 tblsp lemon juice

Cream the butter until soft, then beat in the other ingredients. Roll in a butter wrapper, then chill. Cut off rounds and arrange, at the last minute, on hot individual portions.

Colbert Butter is a classic for deep-fried fish, but goes well with broiled meat: to Maître d'Hôtel butter, add 1–2 tblsp meat jelly (from roast beef) or 1 tsp Meat Glaze (page 56–7), with a little finely grated lemon rind and a pinch of chopped fresh tarragon.

For **Green Peppercorn Butter**, beat in 1 tsp chopped green peppercorns; serve with fried or broiled fish.

For **Black Peppercorn Butter**, add 1 tsp crushed black peppercorns and add ½ tsp grated onion too; serve on broiled sirloin steaks.

For a piquant **Mustard Butter**, beat in ¾ tsp prepared English mustard, with a pinch of chopped chives; serve with broiled cod steaks or filet mignon.

Two butters for poached fish: for **Lemon Butter**, omit the parsley and include the grated rind of 1 lemon and about 1 tsp juice. For **Paprika Butter**, omit the parsley and lemon juice. Add 1 tsp finely chopped sweet red pepper and 1 tsp paprika; season well with black pepper then add a few drops of lemon juice to taste.

MAYONNAISE

The glossy coating of mayonnaise is the perfect summer partner to cold chicken or fish; as a sauce of character it can also turn simple ingredients – cold, cooked, leftover vegetables, for example, or hard-cooked eggs – into a proper dish. See also Aïoli (page 80), Jellied Mayonnaise (page 90) and the introduction to this section.

Makes 1 cup

2 medium-size egg yolks, at room temperature
½ tsp Dijon-style mustard
2–3 tsp lemon juice, or 1 tsp lemon juice and 2 tsp white
* wine vinegar*
Salt and freshly ground black pepper
1 cup olive oil

Put the egg yolks in a narrow-bottomed bowl with the mustard and 1 tsp lemon juice and add a little salt. Using a rotary or hand whisk or an electric beater at slowest speed, whisk the yolks until lemon-colored (if you took the eggs straight from the refrigerator, let them stand 5 minutes afterwards to complete the warm-up). Whisk until fluffy.

Pouring with one hand and whisking with the other, add ½ tsp oil and then another. Proceed very slowly with the first 2–3 tblsp of oil, adding only ½ tsp at a time, and making sure that each addition is absorbed before adding more. Once a thick emulsion has formed, you can go faster, adding more at a time. The final mayonnaise should be heavy and thick, clinging to the spoon without flopping. Whisk in the remaining lemon juice or vinegar and season to taste.

The flavor of mayonnaise depends on its oil. A rich greenish olive oil used as half the quantity will give it a Mediterranean feel. Half sesame or walnut oil with corn oil could also be used.

Mayonnaise keeps in the refrigerator for up to 1 week. Some people beat in 1 tblsp very hot water after finishing it – or heat the final addition of vinegar and whisk in. Cover the surface with plastic wrap to prevent a skin forming. Mayonnaise does not freeze, promptly curdling as it thaws. However, mousses, etc., containing comparatively small amounts of mayonnaise can be frozen successfully.

Commercial mayonnaise keeps, opened, in the refrigerator for 1 month. It is excellent but blander than the real thing: the next four additions will spark its taste.

For **Curry Mayonnaise**, melt 1 tblsp butter and cook 2 tsp curry powder for 1 minute. (Add this to the yolks at the beginning if making your own mayonnaise.) Alternatively stir into purchased mayonnaise and finish with ¼ cup heavy or light cream. This makes a soft sauce for a hard-cooked egg appetizer or for cauliflower. See also Coronation Sauce (page 83).

For **Angostura Mayonnaise**, whisk in 1 tblsp gin and 2 shakes Angostura bitters; this goes well with shrimp and other shellfish.

For **Lemon Mayonnaise**, whisk in the grated rind of 1 lemon plus 3 tblsp juice; good with plainly poached fish and cold chicken, but also with cold lobster.

For **Piquant Mayonnaise**, stir in ½ tblsp lemon juice, 1 tsp Worcestershire sauce, 1 tsp prepared mustard and 4 drops hot pepper sauce. Serve with poultry salads, hard-cooked eggs or pressed or smoked tongue. See also Mustard Chantilly (page 94) and Cocktail Sauce (page 83).

For **Herby Garlic Mayonnaise**, crush ½ garlic clove with salt and use this with the yolks to make the emulsion. Add 1 tblsp each chopped parsley, chives and fresh tarragon, with a little extra lemon juice. Serve with potato salad, cold vegetables or fish. See also Aïoli (page 80) and Sauce Verte (page 100).

For **Mayonnaise Niçoise**, add ¼ cup good tomato paste, 1 canned pimiento, blended to a purée, and a little chopped fresh tarragon. Serve with cold fish and hard-cooked eggs.

For a light, **Creamy Mayonnaise**, suitable for dressing coleslaw, use half the quantity of mayonnaise with an equal volume of plain yogurt, 1 tblsp prepared mustard and 1 tblsp sugar. See also Apple Mayonnaise (page 80).

For **Tarragon Mayonnaise**, delicious with cold chicken, make the mayonnaise with tarragon vinegar. Stir in 2 tblsp chopped tarragon, or garnish the dish with the fresh leaves.

MAYONNAISE IN A BLENDER

Using a blender cuts the agony out of mayonnaise-making – there is no need to worry about curdling. But the sauce it produces is much lighter and fluffier than true mayonnaise and it does not have the same gloss or rich smoothness. Consequently, it will not carry the same volume of additions. If you want to double the quantity for a party, use 2 yolks and 1 whole egg. This whole-egg mayonnaise can also be made with a hand-held whisk.

Makes 1 cup

1 medium-size egg
1 tblsp white wine vinegar or lemon juice
½ tsp Dijon-style mustard
Salt and freshly ground black pepper
1 cup olive oil

Put the egg in the blender with the vinegar or lemon juice and mustard and season lightly. Add 2 tblsp cold water, cover and blend on fast for 5 seconds. Add the oil slowly through the hole in the lid. Taste for seasoning and chill until needed.

MINT JELLY

This cool green jelly is the American favorite with roast lamb and chops.

Makes about 5 lb

5 lb tart apples, chopped but not peeled or cored
5 tblsp chopped fresh mint leaves
1 cup white wine or malt vinegar
About 7 cups sugar
Green food coloring (optional)

Put the apples in a large preserving kettle with water to cover – about 2 quarts. Stir in half the mint leaves and simmer for 40–45 minutes or until the fruit is soft and pulpy. Add the vinegar, then boil for a further 5 minutes.

Strain through a jelly bag, allowing about 12 hours. Do not press the bag, or the jelly will be cloudy. Measure the juice into the clean pan. Add 2 cups sugar to each 2½ cups juice. Stir over low heat until the sugar has dissolved, then bring to a boil and boil briskly, without stirring, for 10 minutes.

Check for set by spooning a little jelly onto a saucer. Put it in the refrigerator. It should set sufficiently so that you can push and crease it with your finger. Skim off any foam on the surface and add the remaining mint and the green coloring if using white vinegar. Stir well and pack into small jars with lids. When half set, stir each jar to suspend the mint leaves in the jelly. Store, away from light, for up to 1 year, but the jelly can be eaten as soon as cold.

Rosemary Jelly can be made the same way, using ¼ cup chopped rosemary instead of mint. When the jelly is half set, add a sprig of fresh rosemary to each jar. I use rosemary jelly for basting roast lamb and put the sprig in the bottom of the pan to flavor the sauce.

Parsley Jelly is made the same way: use ¼ cup for simmering plus 1 tblsp for the garnish. I use this for basting microwave-cooked lamb loin chops.

MINT SAUCE

The English enjoy mint sauce, made with fresh leaves, with lamb, though Americans prefer mint jelly. See also Chantilly Mint Sauce (page 82).

Serves 4–6

Large handful of fresh mint leaves, finely chopped
1 tblsp sugar
¼ cup vinegar

Put the mint in a mortar with the sugar and pound them, with a pestle, or blend together. Pour in ¼ cup boiling water and stir until dissolved. Add the vinegar and taste. More sugar can be added if wished.

MONTPELLIER BUTTER

This sauce, as elegant as the 18th century university town of Montpellier in South-East France from which it comes, is used as much for its appearance as for its piquant taste. Serve with party fish – sole, turbot and salmon – with fried flounder, or with hot vegetables such as broiled tomatoes or mushrooms for a hot appetizer.

Makes ⅔ cup

1 tsp finely chopped parsley
1 tsp finely chopped chives
2 tsp finely chopped watercress
1 tsp finely chopped fresh basil
1 clove garlic, crushed, with salt if necessary
2 canned anchovy fillets, drained and finely chopped
1 gherkin, finely chopped
2 tsp capers, finely chopped
½ cup butter, at room temperature
1 large hard-cooked egg yolk
2 tblsp olive oil
Salt and freshly ground black pepper

Chop the first 8 ingredients again together. Cream the butter in a blender, then add the chopped ingredients, with the hard-cooked egg yolk and the olive oil. Season to taste.

MUSTARD CHANTILLY

Serve with cold lobster or fish, or shrimp cocktails. See also Dill and Mustard Cream (page 112).

Makes 1 cup

¼ cup Mayonnaise, homemade if possible (page 92)
1 tblsp Dijon-style mustard
1 tblsp lemon juice
1 tblsp chopped capers
2 tsp finely chopped parsley
½ cup heavy cream, whipped
Salt and freshly ground black pepper

Stir all the ingredients together 2 hours before use and refrigerate, to allow the flavors to blend.

MUSTARD DIP

This Japanese dip can be a side sauce to sukiyaki or to omelettes, fried meat and dumplings.

Makes 6 tblsp

2 tsp mustard powder
3 tblsp light soy sauce
2 tblsp cider vinegar, or 1 tblsp lemon juice
1 tsp sesame oil (optional)

Mix all the ingredients together, adding 1 tblsp hot water if needed. A pinch of sugar can be added if liked. Serve in tiny bowls.

NUT SAUCES

Puréed nuts are one of the oldest ways of making sauces. My Skordalia (page 101) uses almonds – walnuts can be substituted – though this sauce can also be made without nuts. Pine nuts are classic for Pesto (right): almonds are a cheaper substitute. Balkan Tarator (page 105) contains walnuts, but hazelnuts are used in Turkey; see also Hazelnut and Almond Sauce (page 88), and the modern Cashew Cream (page 81) from California.

ORANGE PICKLE

Cold turkey is not my favorite dish, so I prepare orange pickle each year just before Christmas to make eating it worthwhile. The pickle is delicious, too, with goose or pork. See also Cumberland Sauce (page 86), a classic for cold meat, based on orange rind.

Makes 2 × 1 lb jars

6 oranges
1 tsp salt
2 cups sugar
1 tblsp honey
¾ cup malt vinegar
8 cardamom pods, crushed
1 in piece cinnamon stick, or ½ tsp ground cinnamon

8 black peppercorns, crushed
12 cloves, or ½ tsp ground cloves
8 allspice berries, or ¼ tsp mixed spice

Put the oranges into a pan in which they fit comfortably; cover with hot water, add the salt and heat gently. When boiling, turn down the heat and simmer for 50 minutes or until the orange peel is tender. Drain and cool.

In the same pan bring the sugar, honey, vinegar, spices and 2 cups water to a boil, stirring to dissolve the sugar; then simmer for 10 minutes. If you intend to strain out the spices, let the liquid infuse first for 20 minutes.

Meanwhile, slice the oranges thinly on a plate. Strain out the spices, if wished. Return the liquid to the pan and add the orange slices and juice. Bring to a boil, then simmer for 20 minutes. Remove from the heat and stand for 5 minutes.

Spoon the orange slices into 2 clean jars, pressing them down well. Spoon in extra liquid if needed. Cover with lids. The pickle can be eaten immediately, but will keep for 6 months. (For long storage, process in a boiling water bath.)

Reserve the spare vinegar – there will be about 2½ cups. It has a pleasant sweet-and-sour taste and can be used, in the proportion of half and half, with salad oil to make a dressing for chicory and other bitter leaves. It also makes a marinade for stewing beef. Season the dishes well with black pepper.

PESTO

Fresh, pungent basil is essential for this rich sauce from Genoa. One of the best of the pasta sauces, it involves no cooking. It can also be served with baked or new potatoes, steaks and chops, or stirred into vegetable soups. The Italian word "pesto" means to pound in a mortar – but a blender is faster. It is not worth making the sauce with dried basil; make it when the herb is in season and freeze it for up to 1 month. Walnuts can be substituted for pine nuts. The French version, "pistou," is without nuts.

Dresses ½ lb pasta

1 cup roughly chopped basil leaves, without stalks
2–3 cloves garlic, crushed, with salt if necessary
Salt
¼ cup roughly chopped pine nuts
6 tblsp freshly grated Parmesan or Romano cheese
½ cup olive oil
Freshly ground black pepper

Make the sauce about 45 minutes ahead, to allow the flavors to blend. Put the basil in the blender with the garlic, salt and pine nuts and purée. Add the cheese and half the oil and work to a thick paste, the consistency of mayonnaise. Add the remaining oil, if needed, to thin the paste. Taste and season; a few tblsp hot water from cooking pasta can be added to thin it. Use 2 tblsp to dress 1 portion pasta, or add 1 tblsp to each bowl of minestrone.

PIMIENTO CREAM

This pink cream can be served with baked potatoes or hot poached haddock. It is excellent made with bigarade – bitter or Seville – oranges when these are in season at the beginning of the year. For other pimiento sauces see Rusty Sauce (page 97) and Mayonnaise Niçoise (page 92).

Makes ½ cup

1 canned pimiento, drained
½ cup cottage cheese or cream cheese
Grated rind of 1 orange
Juice of ½ orange
1 tsp paprika
Salt and freshly ground black pepper

Blend the pimiento to a purée and add the next 4 ingredients. Season to taste.

POOR MAN'S CAVIAR

This dip or salad is eaten in the Balkans, the home of caviar, where it has this pleasant name, and throughout the Middle East. In Egypt a little tahini paste is added and the dish is called "baba ghannou," or "spoiled old daddy." As both names indicate, it is considered something of a delicacy though, like caviar itself, it can be an acquired taste. The purée can also be served as a sauce with hot fried food.

Makes 1 cup
2 large eggplants
1 large clove garlic, crushed, with salt if necessary
¼ cup olive oil
1 tblsp lemon juice
Salt
Chopped parsley

Heat the oven to 400°. Bake the eggplants for 45–60 minutes or until very soft. Alternatively, broil them until the skin is black on all sides and the pulp soft.

When cool enough to handle, cut them in half lengthwise and scoop out the flesh. Blend to a purée or mash to a pulp. Beat in the garlic and then the oil, a little at a time. Add half the lemon juice and season. Taste and add the remaining lemon juice if needed. Turn into a bowl and sprinkle with parsley.

RAITA

This is the Indian version of the Middle Eastern cucumber salad; see Cucumber and Yogurt Dip (page 86). Serve with curry.

Makes 2 cups
½ cucumber, peeled and chopped
Salt and ground white pepper
3 scallions, white and green chopped together, or ½ small onion, finely chopped or grated
½ small green pepper, seeds removed and finely chopped (optional)
1½ cups plain Yogurt, homemade if possible (page 106)

½ small green chili, stalk removed, seeded and finely chopped, or pinch of chili powder
1 tblsp finely chopped fresh coriander leaves or parsley

Spread out the cucumber in a colander and sprinkle with salt; leave 30 minutes to drain. Rinse under running cold water and drain well – if necessary blot with paper towels.

Stir the cucumber, scallions or onion and green pepper, if using, into the yogurt. Add the chili or chili powder; taste and season. Chill before serving, sprinkled with chopped coriander or parsley. If the curry is hot, I omit the green pepper and chilies and serve the raita in 3 small serving bowls. Sprinkle paprika mixed with a pinch of chili powder over one, ½ tsp ground cumin seeds mixed with black pepper over the second, and parsley over the third.

RAW TOMATO SAUCE

Called "salsa cruda" or "raw sauce" in Mexico and the Caribbean, this easy but spicy fresh sauce is as common on Mexican tables as salt and pepper. Like the familiar tomato ketchup, it is served with hard-cooked eggs, cold meat, cold or fried fish and shellfish. Try it, chilled, with hot Chinese noodles as an appetizer.

Makes 1 cup
½ lb very ripe tomatoes, skinned, seeded and finely chopped
½ small onion, finely chopped
1 clove garlic, crushed, with salt if necessary
1 serrano chili, or ½ red or green chili, stalk removed, seeded and finely chopped
Pinch of sugar
1 tblsp finely chopped fresh coriander or parsley
Salt and freshly ground black pepper

Stir all the ingredients together in a bowl. Taste and season. Chill for 30 minutes before serving.

For an excellent salad dressing, stir in ¼ cup olive oil and 1½ tblsp white wine vinegar; this goes well with all cold shellfish.

For **Blender Tomato Sauce**, a seeded green pepper can be used instead of the chili. Add a chopped celery stalk (or 1 tsp celery seeds), and double the parsley (or use chives). This makes a smoother dressing for sweetbreads and cold veal. Garnish with chopped chives.

RED WINE MARINADE

Ideal for beef or game. Salt is never included in marinades for either of these as it brings the meat juices to the surface rendering the final dish drier. Pork is rather a firm dry meat anyway, and does not seem to be affected. Blot the meat well before sealing it under a hot broiler or in hot fat, or it will ooze juices.

Marinates 3 lb meat

¼ cup olive oil
1 tblsp finely chopped onion
1 tblsp finely chopped parsley
10 black peppercorns, crushed
1 tblsp red wine or malt vinegar
½ cup red wine
1 bay leaf, crumbled
½ clove garlic, crushed or finely chopped (optional)
Pinch of dried oregano (optional)

Mix together all the ingredients and toss the meat. Leave for 4 hours, or overnight, turning the meat several times if possible. The marinade is ideal for beef and game. Optional extras are 2 tsp crushed coriander seeds (for venison or pork) or 1 tsp crushed juniper berries (for hare or pork).

REMOULADE

The knife grinder gives his name to this robust French sauce: a sharp knife was necessary for all the chopping. Serve it with hot, broiled fish or meat and also with cold roast beef, cold poultry or ham. It turns boring vegetables like turnips, which have few admirers, into quite a jolly salad. Without the anchovy but with 1 tblsp chopped shallot or onion added, it is widely known as sauce tartare.

Makes 1¼ cups

1 cup Mayonnaise, homemade if possible (page 92)
1 tblsp finely chopped fresh tarragon
1 tblsp finely chopped fresh chervil or chives
1 tblsp finely chopped parsley
1 tblsp Dijon-style mustard
1 tblsp chopped gherkins

1 tsp chopped capers
¼ tsp anchovy paste or 2 canned anchovy fillets, drained, chopped and pounded

Combine all the ingredients, then serve in a bowl or pitcher.

Sauce Gribiche probably started life as an emulsion of cooked egg yolks, but has become a variant of Rémoulade. Sieve the yolk of 1 large hard-cooked egg and beat into the sauce. Stir in the finely chopped egg white; serve with cold fish or shellfish.

RUSTY SAUCE

Known as "rouille," or rusty sauce, in France because of its red color, it is made with broiled, skinned sweet red peppers in Provence, but canned ones are quicker. Serve with hot food – broiled fish, a mixed fish stew or batter-fried vegetables. Accompanied by round slices from a French loaf, it is often served with Mediterranean fish soups – put the bread in a soup bowl, then add the sauce followed by the soup.

Makes 1¼ cups

3 tblsp 1-day-old bread crumbs
2 cloves garlic, crushed, with salt if necessary
2 canned pimientos, drained and coarsely chopped
1 hot red chili, fresh or dried, stalk removed and seeded (optional), or 2 tsp cayenne
Large pinch of paprika
½ cup olive oil
1–2 tblsp hot fish stock (page 11) or chicken stock (page 12)
Salt and freshly ground black pepper

Soak the bread crumbs in cold water for 5 minutes then squeeze out well. Put the bread crumbs and garlic in a blender with the pimientos, chili or cayenne and paprika and blend. With the blender running, pour in the oil through the hole in the lid, making sure each addition is absorbed before adding more. Add a little hot stock, season and serve tepid or warm.

Above: *This veal terrine for a summer buffet is glazed with Herby Aspic and exquisitely garnished with a tomato-skin rose, peas, pimiento-stuffed olives and "leaves" cut from cucumber peel.*

Right: *Hummus, the Greek chick-pea and tahini paste, makes a delicious before-dinner dip. Use strips of hot pitta (Arab pocket) bread to scoop it up.*

SATE SAUCE

Satés are delicious grilled bits of meat on wooden skewers – pork tenderloin, chicken or beef; the word actually means "steak." Peanut sauce is the most popular accompaniment. Garnish with little cubes of raw turnip – better than it sounds! The sauce can also be served as a dip with sticks of raw vegetables or small crackers.

Serves 4

Grated flesh of ½ fresh coconut, or 1⅓ cups unsweetened shredded coconut, or ¼ cup creamed coconut
1 cup salted peanuts
½ tsp turmeric
½ tsp curry powder
¼ tsp cayenne
2 tblsp sugar (optional)
1 tsp lemon juice
Salt

To make **Coconut Milk**, pour 1¼ cups boiling water over the fresh or shredded coconut. Leave for 30 minutes, then stir and press through a sieve – you will get about 1 cup milk. Alternatively, stir ¾ cup water into the creamed coconut.

Grind the peanuts coarsely in a blender or food processor. Put the coconut milk in a pan with the turmeric, curry powder, cayenne and sugar (no sugar for creamed coconut, but an extra pinch of salt). Bring to a boil, then stir in the peanuts. Cook gently, stirring, for 2 minutes. Add lemon juice and salt to taste and leave until cold.

Peanut Cream is quicker to make than Saté Sauce when you are in a hurry. Beat together in a bowl 2 tblsp peanut butter – smooth or crunchy as you like – with 2 tblsp lemon juice and ¼ cup water. This makes a pleasant dip, as well as a dressing for mixed chicken or cheese and nut salad, or banana and apple salads.

SAUCE VERTE

Green mayonnaise will enliven cold white fish, hard-cooked eggs or a potato salad. It is well worth making your own mayonnaise.

Makes 1¼ cups

6 spinach leaves, stalks removed, then chopped, or 2 tblsp frozen spinach
½ bunch of watercress, coarse stalks removed
2 tblsp coarsely chopped parsley
2 tblsp chopped chives
2 tblsp chopped fresh tarragon leaves, fennel fronds or dill
1 × Mayonnaise (page 92)
2–4 tblsp heavy cream, whipped
Salt and freshly ground black pepper

Blanch the spinach and herbs in boiling salted water for 2 minutes, then drain well. Squeeze gently in paper towels, then purée. Add this to the mayonnaise with the whipped cream and check the seasonings. Keep the surface covered with plastic wrap and serve immediately on removal, as the surface discolors slightly if allowed to stand. For this reason it is less good as a buffet sauce (or cover the surface with chopped herbs).

SHELLFISH BUTTER

Not for everyday occasions, this butter is economically made from left over shells. It can be stored in the freezer for up to 1 month. Crayfish and lobster shells can be used as well as the more common shrimp shells, provided you do not put large pieces of thick shell in the blender or food processor: you will break the blades. Serve with all kinds of fish, including shellfish, or quenelles. The butter can also be added to Béchamel (page 25) or a fish Velouté (page 74) before serving to enrich the sauce.

Makes 6 tblsp

Shells, heads and legs from 1 lb shrimp, crayfish or lobster, any shellfish coral reserved
½ cup butter
Salt and freshly ground black pepper

Remove any coral from between the back legs and dry the shells on a baking sheet in the bottom of a low oven for 15 minutes, taking care they do not toast. Break up large, hard shells with a hammer on a board. Grind the shells in a food processor or blender (lobster shells can be put through an old-fashioned meat grinder).

Put the ground fishy mess (excluding the coral) into the top pan of a double boiler over simmering water and add the butter and 2 tblsp water. Cover and simmer gently for 10 minutes. Line a sieve with cheesecloth and turn the mixture into it over a bowl. When the first liquid has dropped through, twist the cheesecloth down hard on the shells, scraping the outside of the bundle with a spoon. Collect the butter in a pot, season to taste, stir in any coral and chill before serving.

SKORDALIA

A purée of softened bread, garlic and oil, this creamy Greek sauce is one of the oldest in existence. Delicious with deep-fried vegetables and batter-covered fish, it is traditionally served on Clean Monday, the kite-flying day preceding Shrove Tuesday at the beginning of Lent. Skordalia can also be eaten with cooked legumes, for example the Egyptian brown bean called "ful mesdames," and it makes a good side dip for tempura and fondue bourguignonne. A little cooked, mashed potato is sometimes used instead of soaked bread.

Makes 1 cup
1 cup 1-day-old white bread crumbs
½ cup ground almonds
3 cloves garlic, crushed, with salt if necessary
Salt
½ cup olive oil
1 tblsp lemon juice
Freshly ground black pepper

Soak the bread in a little cold water, then squeeze out. Put the bread, almonds, garlic and salt in a blender or food processor and purée. With the blender running, add the oil through the hole in the lid in a thin stream, making sure each addition is absorbed before adding the next. Beat in the lemon juice and season to taste. Chill for 30 minutes before serving. The sauce will keep, covered, in the refrigerator for 1 week.

A more sophisticated, richer version can be made by stirring 1 cup 1-day-old bread crumbs and ½ cup ground almonds, plus a little parsley and lemon juice to taste, into Aïoli (page 80).

SNAIL BUTTER

Garlic-scented butter, beloved of the French, is served with snails "à la bourguignonne:" it does not, of course, contain snails. The butter makes an excellent topping for broiled fish, clams or mussels served hot on the shell, and is ideal for spooning into hot, baked potatoes.

Makes ½ cup
½ cup butter, at room temperature
2–3 cloves garlic, crushed, with salt if necessary
1 shallot, finely chopped, or 1 tblsp chopped onion
3 tblsp finely chopped parsley
1–2 tsp lemon juice
Salt and freshly ground black pepper

Beat the butter until soft, and add the garlic. Beat in the shallot or onion, if using, and the parsley. Taste and add lemon juice and seasoning.

Garlic Butter, for spreading on French bread to heat (10 minutes in foil in the oven at 350°) is made the same way. For a strong flavor use ¼ cup butter and up to 3 garlic cloves, plus 1 tsp chopped shallot or onion and 1 tsp chopped parsley. For a dinner party you may prefer to blanch the garlic cloves (5 minutes in boiling water) first: use 3 garlic cloves as blanching tames the flavor quite considerably.

Overleaf: *As an accompaniment to the festive turkey, the red berries of Cranberry Whole Berry Sauce echo the Christmas holly.*

SOY AND GINGER DIPPING SAUCE

This basic marinade or dip can be used for almost any Chinese or Oriental-style meal. Serve it with dumplings, or "dim sum," with sukiyaki and as a dip for Mongolian hot pot – bites of meat and vegetables cooked at the table in boiling oil. See also Hoisin Sauce (page 89), Mustard Dip (page 94) and Chili Dip (page 82).

Serves 4

3–4 tblsp soy sauce
1–2 tblsp dry sherry wine
2–3 scallions, chopped
2 thin slices fresh ginger root, chopped
Pinch of sugar

Mix all the ingredients together and serve in small bowls.

TAHINI CREAM

This cream is eaten throughout the Middle East as a dip accompanied by strips of warm pocket bread, or as a salad and sometimes as the sauce for a hot main course. It also makes a dressing for a simple salad of tomatoes and mild Bermuda onion rings or hard-cooked eggs. Tahini is a paste of sesame seeds, obtainable from Greek Stores and health food shops. Other Middle Eastern dips containing tahini are Hummus (page 90) and the Egyptian baba ghannou (see Poor Man's Caviar, page 96).

Makes 1 cup

1–3 cloves garlic, crushed, with salt if necessary
½ cup tahini paste
Salt
2–4 tblsp lemon juice
2 tblsp finely chopped parsley

Add the garlic to the tahini in a bowl, with salt if necessary, and stir in the smaller quantity of lemon juice. Taste: more lemon juice can be added if wished. If the paste has the right balance of oil and acid but is too stiff, stir in 1 tblsp water. Sprinkle the surface with parsley and serve.

A creamier version can be made by stirring in ½ cup plain Yogurt, homemade if possible (page 106).

TAPENADE

This caper and anchovy paste or dip is known throughout France by its Provençal name, which comes from the local word for a caper – "tapéno." Unlike the many ancient sauces from this part of the world, tapenade, invented at the Maison Dorée in Marseilles, is only about 100 years old. It can be used to stuff the egg whites left over when the yolks have been removed or to fill tomato cases; or spread it on toast, then cut into fingers as a canapé. Garnish with extra olives if you are using it as a dip.

Makes ½ cup

4 large hard-cooked egg yolks
4 ripe olives, pitted
2 canned anchovy fillets, drained and roughly chopped
2 tblsp canned tuna fish, drained
2 tsp capers, chopped
½ tsp Dijon-style mustard
1 tblsp olive oil, plus 1 tblsp oil from the can of tuna
Freshly ground black pepper

Put all the ingredients in the blender. Purée until smooth then taste and season. If wished, the hard-cooked egg whites can be chopped and added to the paste.

TARATOR

I discovered this walnut cream sauce, a specialty of Georgia in the Caucasus, when I was first married – we used to play the game of opening the cook book blind, putting down a finger and eating whatever was there on Sunday. This was one of our best discoveries, which we first ate with a cold poached tail of salmon (using the stock in the sauce). In Georgia it is served with hot, fried chicken, but I find it most useful as a dressing for cold poached chicken, which it transforms. Make the sauce 1–2 days in advance to allow it to mature. This quantity serves 4–6.

Makes 2 cups

2 slices brown bread, without crusts
2 cloves garlic, crushed, with salt if necessary
Salt
1 cup chopped walnuts
1 cup chicken stock (page 12) or fish stock (page 11)
Freshly ground black pepper
1 tblsp lemon juice (optional)

Soak the bread in cold water for 5 minutes, then squeeze out. Put the bread, garlic, salt, walnuts and stock in a blender and purée to a fine cream. Taste, season and add lemon juice if wished. Leave 1–2 days to mature.

TARTARE

Mayonnaise flavored with herbs, onions and pickles is generally known as "tartare sauce;" widely available in bottles it is just the thing for topping hamburgers (see Rémoulade, page 97). This is French "sauce tartare," made from an emulsion of hard-cooked egg yolks with olive oil blended into the yolks in the same careful way as mayonnaise. Indeed it is considered a type of mayonnaise and is probably its original form. Serve sauce tartare with fried fish or deep-fried shellfish in batter.

Makes ¾ cup

3 large hard-cooked egg yolks
1 large raw egg yolk
1 tsp Dijon-style mustard
1 tsp lemon juice or white wine vinegar
½ cup olive oil
1 tsp chopped capers
1 tsp chopped gherkins
1 tblsp chopped parsley or chives
Salt and freshly ground black pepper

Sieve the hard-cooked yolks into a bowl and whisk in the raw yolk until smooth. Whisk in the mustard and lemon juice or vinegar.

Whisking just as you would for mayonnaise, add the olive oil very slowly, until an emulsion is formed. Stir in the capers, gherkins and parsley or chives. Season to taste.

TOMATO ASPIC

One of the quickest and easiest of cold dressings, this can be used as a coating for cold cooked vegetables or chicken, or to suspend vegetable pieces in a mold. Ideal for appetizers, it is a slimmer's salad dressing and can also be used to dress vegetables: whisk it vigorously just before it sets.

Makes 1 cup

½ cup tomato juice or 2 tblsp tomato paste made up to this volume with water
½ cup chicken stock, from a bouillon cube if wished
½ envelope unflavored gelatin
2 tblsp white wine or sherry
Salt and freshly ground black pepper
1 tsp onion juice (optional)
1 tsp lemon juice (optional)

Warm the tomato juice and chicken stock together. Sprinkle the gelatin over the white wine or sherry in a cup and stir over hot water until dissolved, then stir into the tomato juice. Taste and season, adding the onion and/or lemon juice if wished, according to the salad. Chill to set.

TUNA MAYONNAISE

This distinctive fish mayonnaise adds zip to bland food and gives substance to a fish cocktail when you do not have quite enough seafood. In Italy it is most famous with cold, poached veal in "vitello tonnato." It is excellent with a warm chick-pea salad.

Makes 1½ cups

5 oz canned tuna fish in oil
1 tsp capers
5 canned anchovy fillets, drained and roughly chopped
2 tblsp lemon juice
2 large egg yolks
1 cup olive oil
Freshly ground black pepper

Put the tuna with its oil in the blender, add the capers and anchovies and purée. Blend in the lemon juice and add the egg yolks, one at a time. With the blender running, add the olive oil a little at a time through the hole in the lid, checking each addition is absorbed before adding more. Taste and season with pepper. More capers and anchovies can garnish the dish this sauce accompanies.

WATERCRESS CREAM

Serve with cold roast chicken, cold poached vegetables such as green beans and zucchini, fish (hot or cold) or hard-cooked eggs. Garnish with watercress.

Makes 1 cup

½ bunch watercress, coarse stalks removed
1 large shallot or ½ onion, chopped
1 tblsp lemon juice
½ cup Mayonnaise, homemade if possible (page 92)
Pinch of cayenne or 1 tsp prepared English mustard
½ cup heavy cream, or plain Yogurt, homemade if possible (right)
Salt and freshly ground black pepper

Blend the watercress, shallot or onion and lemon juice to a purée. Stir into the mayonnaise and add the cayenne or mustard. Whip the cream and fold in, or add the yogurt. Taste and season.

YOGURT

Homemade yogurt is more versatile than store-bought. This one has the consistency of half-whipped cream but is less fattening and cheaper. It will heat without separating and can be used for cream in most circumstances. I always keep it in the house.

Makes 3 cups

3 cups milk
½ cup skimmed milk powder
2–3 tblsp plain yogurt

Boil the milk gently for 2 minutes to sterilize it, then let it stand for 20 minutes to cool a little (or stand the saucepan for 10 minutes in a sink of cold water). Make a paste with the milk powder and yogurt.

Stir the milk into the paste and pour into jars (if using a machine) or into a thermos flask, or stand the bowl, covered with plastic wrap, in a warm place. The first batch may take 5 hours to set. Later batches (saving 2–3 tblsp of each one to start the next) will be quicker. Chill the yogurt for 2 hours before making additions. It will keep for 5 days in the refrigerator, becoming more acid at the end of a week. After 3 months start a new batch.

For **Yogurt Dressing** for a salad, add to 1 cup yogurt 1 tblsp lemon juice, seasoning and 1 tblsp chopped chives or scallion tops.

For **Sweet Yogurt Dressing**, stir in 3–4 tblsp clear honey or white sugar to taste; some people like light brown sugar because it offers texture, especially when the dressing is used on fruit salads.

Salad Dressings

The dressing makes a salad; in seconds, it transforms plain green leaves or vegetables into a dish, enhances the flavor of fruit and adds that special touch to the simplest arrangements. Choose from this selection for anything from a summer buffet to a quick home lunch. There are a dozen or more each for tomato salad, celery, tossed green leaves or potato salad. Famous names like Green Goddess Dressing and Thousand Island Dressing are included, as well as new ideas to dress appetizers, side salads or a salad to follow the main course. There are some surprises, too, in a Chinese dressing or one from India, as well as new versions of American classics.

SALAD DRESSINGS

Dressings point up the natural flavor of the ingredients used in salads – usually plain, raw vegetables. They often also add a contrasting accent: a sweeter or more sour flavor, and occasionally a different, or crisper texture. Simple combinations generally work best.

Salad dressings sometimes serve as **marinades**. Potatoes, for example, can be dressed several hours ahead to allow the flavors to permeate the salad. Most dressings, however, are best added at the last moment. Assemble the dressing and vegetables separately, then toss just before serving. Caesar Cardini, the inventor of Caesar salad, explained the best way to do this: simply to roll each leaf over in the dressing until lightly coated.

Plain salt is enough to dress radishes, raw new lima beans and the new season's walnuts. Lemon juice with seasoning sets off ripe avocados, while olive oil with salt and freshly ground black pepper is often all that is needed for tomatoes or cooked legumes. Never hesitate to serve any salad in plain Vinaigrette (page 126); also sometimes known as French dressing, it is simple but subtle. The proportions are 3–4 parts oil to 1 part acid (lemon juice or vinegar); beat together until an emulsion forms.

The type of **oil** you select will immediately add character to your vinaigrette's flavor. First pressing, virgin olive oil, green and olive-flavored, is the strongest, but all olive oils add personality to a green salad containing nothing but lettuce, and are good for robust vegetables like potatoes. Sunflower and corn oils are blander and do not overpower delicate flavors. Peanut, sesame, hazelnut and walnut oils are all distinctive (and the latter 2 are expensive luxuries). If wished, a stronger oil can be mixed with a blander one.

The **acid** in a vinaigrette may be vinegar – cider, sherry, white or red wine, and occasionally malt – lemon juice, which is sharper, or vinegar steeped with herbs (tarragon is the most popular), chilies or even raspberries. The best rule is to taste the oil or vinegar (or both) once you have planned the dish and decide whether the flavor will add to or detract from the combination.

Fresh herbs are a salad's glory. If you cannot grow them, buy them and keep the stems in a pot of water, leaves covered with a plastic bag, in the refrigerator, where they will often last a week. A soupçon of **garlic** adds flavor, but avoid little raw pieces. One solution is to wipe the cut clove around the salad bowl, pressing to transfer the juices. Another is to use a crusher or chop and crush the garlic to a paste, Middle East style, with salt and a flat knife. **Onion juice** is milder; grate the onion, then press through a sieve, or turn the onion on a lemon squeezer and add the juice.

One way to add crisp texture is to include **croûtons** (page 120) of fried bread – hot or cold – in the salad, not in the vinaigrette. Another possible addition is the **chapon** from the south of France, thin rings cut from a slightly stale French loaf, wiped with garlic and olive oil. They go well with green salad, and are occasionally spread with Roquefort or an anchovy paste such as Tapenade (page 104).

Really fresh **vegetables** or **fruit** are essential for a perfect salad. Make sure green leaves are dried perfectly – a dish towel is fine for this; a salad spinner is quicker, but don't overload or overspin. Then crisp them, covered, for 1 hour in the bottom of the refrigerator. Vegetables should be cut up as near as possible to the time they are served.

Salads need not be raw. Parboiled vegetables, zucchini, for example, will often absorb the dressing better; they should be soft enough to eat, but retain something of their crisp texture. Salt cucumbers and leave them for 30 minutes to drain. Wash off the salt, drain and pat dry. Cooked and cooled vegetables are often served with coating sauces like Mayonnaise (page 92) or aspic (see Tomato Aspic, page 105). Vegetables à la greque are cooked and served cold in the same sauce, which acts as a marinade then a dressing (see Tomato and Coriander Bouillon, page 72).

I have included **salad creams** or **boiled dressings**, those old-fashioned creams which are cooked then cooled. With milk as the base, they are thickened with flour and enriched with egg. The same creamy texture can be achieved by using sour cream, petits suisses cheeses or plain yogurt.

Yogurt made at home (page 106) has more body than most store-bought versions (which can usually be substituted). The heavy, creamy texture of homemade yogurt has something of the charm of mayonnaise without the calories; it makes a good base for other ingredients as it does not separate as easily as commercial yogurts. Use instead of heavy or sour cream; the results, of course, will be lighter and less rich.

Salad Dressings

ANCHOIADE

Serve with raw vegetables as a Provençal appetizer, or pour over chilled celery hearts. It also makes a relish for cold beef.

Makes ¾ cup
2 oz canned anchovy fillets, drained
3 cloves garlic, crushed, with salt if necessary
1 tsp white wine vinegar
Freshly ground black pepper
½ cup olive oil

Process together the first 3 ingredients until smooth. Season, then add the oil through the hole in the blender lid, little by little until absorbed.

BAGNA CAUDA

The Italian name of this dip means "hot bath;" serve it in a fondue pot with a burner beneath. It is a specialty of Piedmont in the north, where it may include a white truffle – even more expensive than the black variety! It also makes a good dip for raw vegetables, particularly celery and Belgian endive, and a dressing for pasta.

Makes 1 cup
4 cloves garlic, crushed, with salt if necessary
2 oz canned anchovy fillets, finely chopped, with oil reserved
3–4 tblsp olive oil
½ cup butter
Salt and freshly ground black pepper

Mash the garlic and anchovies to a paste. Make up the oil from the anchovy can to ¼ cup and put into a small flameproof pot. Add the butter and heat to simmering point. Add the anchovy paste and stir until smooth. Taste and season with pepper: extra salt should be unnecessary.

BASIL AND HONEY VINAIGRETTE

For tomatoes, cold cooked zucchini and other vegetables.

Makes 1¼ cups
1 cup olive or light salad oil
1 clove garlic, crushed, with salt if necessary
1 tblsp honey
¼ tsp mustard powder
2 tblsp lemon juice
2 tblsp chopped fresh basil
2 tblsp chopped parsley
¼ tsp salt
¼ tsp paprika

Blend all the ingredients for 2 minutes, then chill. The dressing will keep, covered, in the refrigerator for up to 2 days.

BASIL AND TOMATO SAUCE

For hard-cooked eggs and fish.

Makes ¾ cup
3 ripe tomatoes, skinned, seeded and chopped
Salt
3 tblsp chopped fresh basil
¼ cup good olive oil
1 clove garlic, crushed, with salt if necessary
2 tsp lemon juice
Freshly ground black pepper

Put the tomato flesh in a sieve and sprinkle lightly with salt. Leave to drain for 30 minutes. Meanwhile, put 1 tblsp basil to soak in the olive oil.

Strain the oil, discarding the basil. Add the garlic and lemon juice and beat with a fork. Season to taste. Put the tomato flesh in a bowl and sprinkle with the vinaigrette. Add the remaining basil leaves and use immediately.

BUTLER'S DRESSING

A cooked egg dressing for green salads and mixed potato salads. The yolks are puréed then creamed with the oil, rather than used raw as in mayonnaise – though the final consistency is much the same. In the 19th century this was made by the butler in his pantry, just before the salad was served, rather than in the kitchen.

Makes 1 cup
2 large hard-cooked egg yolks
Salt and freshly ground black pepper
1 tblsp Dijon-style or prepared English mustard
1–2 tblsp white wine vinegar or tarragon vinegar
2 tblsp olive oil
2–3 scallions, finely chopped (optional)
6 tblsp light cream or sour cream

Mash the yolks well and season, stirring in the mustard. Stir in the vinegar, oil and the scallions if wished. If a light dressing is needed, whisk in the cream. ¼ cup chopped watercress or fresh mint can be added; use only ½ tblsp mustard. Alternatively, for a spicier dressing, add 2 tsp Worcestershire sauce or a little cayenne.

BUTTERMILK DRESSING

Use to dress a green salad.

Makes ½ cup
½ cup buttermilk
2 tsp white wine vinegar or lemon juice
Small pinch of grated lemon rind
Pinch of chopped fresh tarragon or chives
Salt and freshly ground black pepper

Mix all the ingredients together; season to taste.
    Buttermilk dressing can be used, in the proportion of 1:4, to dilute cottage cheese dressings and Mayonnaise, to make them lighter and thinner.

CAESAR DRESSING

An American classic, this dressing for hearts of romaine lettuce was invented in Mexico by Caesar Cardini. Americans flocked over the border during Prohibition to his restaurant in Tijuana in search of forbidden liquor and carried back this recipe which quickly became celebrated. Croûtons (page 120) can be included in the salad just before the egg is added.

Makes ¾ cup
1 clove garlic, split and crushed
7 tblsp olive oil
2 tblsp lemon juice
1½ tblsp Worcestershire sauce
1 tblsp white wine vinegar
Salt
Freshly ground black pepper
1 medium-size egg

Leave the garlic in the olive oil for 2 hours to infuse. Alternatively, if you want the dressing almost immediately, you could warm the oil slightly in a pan to bring out the garlic flavor. Let it stand for 10 minutes.
    Beat the oil (discard the garlic), lemon juice, Worcestershire sauce, wine vinegar and salt in a bowl to form an emulsion. Add pepper to taste.
    Just before serving, boil the egg for 1 minute: this should set the outside, while leaving part of the white and yolk raw. Cut off the top of the egg and scoop around the inside, rapidly mixing the raw and set portions. Pour the vinaigrette over the salad and toss the lettuce to coat. Quickly pour in the egg. Toss again and serve.

CARAWAY DRESSING

Serve, Scandinavian-style, with sliced beets.

Makes 6 tblsp
1 tsp caraway seeds
1 tsp salt
1½ tblsp vinegar
2 tsp sugar

Crush the seeds and pour on 3 tblsp boiling water. Mix in the remaining ingredients and stir until the sugar has dissolved. Leave for 1–2 hours before straining. If you are cooking the beets at home, dress while warm, immediately after peeling, then cool in the dressing.

Dill seed dressing is made in the same way.

CELERY SEED DRESSING

Good on vegetables and on fruit for an appetizer, this is based on vinaigrette. For a richer dressing, see Sour Cream Dressing (page 124).

Makes 1 cup

½ tsp celery seeds
¼ cup sugar
½ tsp mustard powder
½ tsp salt
½ tblsp grated onion
½ cup vegetable or corn oil
2 tblsp white wine vinegar

Purée all the ingredients in a blender until thick and frothy. Toss with the salad just before serving. The same dressing can be made with poppy seeds; use up to 1 tblsp.

CHIFFONADE DRESSING

To make a "chiffonade," salad leaves are rolled up tightly lengthwise then sliced across, to be unraveled as thin green strips. Sorrel was formerly sliced like this and served in clear soups, from which this style of garnish acquired its French name, which means a "rag" of cloth. Nowadays lettuce is much more commonly treated this way and a chiffonade of lettuce is often put at the bottom of the glass under the seafood in a shrimp cocktail. It is also used around a dish as a garnish; for the latter purpose, it has its own classic vinaigrette. Chiffonade dressing is often also used to toss other green salads.

Makes 1¼ cups

½ cup olive oil
2 tblsp tarragon, white wine or cider vinegar
1 tblsp chopped scallion or chives
1 tblsp chopped parsley
1 tblsp finely chopped gherkins, green pepper or green olives
1 tblsp finely chopped onion (optional)
1 medium-size hard-cooked egg, finely chopped
Salt and freshly ground black pepper

Beat the olive oil and vinegar together to make an emulsion. Beat in the remaining ingredients; taste and season. Toss shredded lettuce or a green salad just before serving.

COLESLAW DRESSING

This traditional, old-fashioned dressing is cooked then cooled and appeals to those who do not like oil. Besides dressing raw cabbage, it goes well with cold cooked celeriac. Make a double quantity: it keeps well in the refrigerator and freezes for up to 1 month. See also Apple Mayonnaise (page 80), Creamy Mayonnaise (page 92) and Salad Cream (page 123).

Makes 1¾ cups

1 tblsp flour
1 tblsp sugar
1 tsp mustard powder
1 tsp salt
Pinch of cayenne
3 tblsp vinegar
1 tblsp butter
1 medium-size egg yolk
1 cup heavy cream, evaporated milk or sour cream

Mix the first 5 ingredients in a small, heavy-based saucepan. Stir in the vinegar and cook, stirring, until the mixture boils. Off the heat beat in the butter and yolk, then the cream. Whisk until light and fluffy. If the dressing is too thick or too sweet, thin down with extra vinegar.

COTTAGE CHEESE DRESSING

For cold, mixed vegetables or lettuce.

Makes ½ cup
½ cup cottage cheese
3 tblsp buttermilk or milk
1 tsp chopped scallion
1 tsp finely chopped parsley
Salt and freshly ground black pepper
Pinch of cayenne

Blend the cottage cheese and buttermilk or milk until smooth. Stir in the other ingredients, seasoning to taste, and chill.

Make the dressing sour-sweet by stirring in 2 tblsp fine-cut marmalade and 3 tblsp lemon juice: good for coleslaw and grated carrot salad.

CURRY VINAIGRETTE

For tomatoes, pears, Belgian endive and cold cooked zucchini. See also Mem Sahib's Dressing (page 121).

Makes ¾ cup
1 tblsp curry paste or powder
1 tblsp lemon juice
1 tsp finely chopped shallot or white part of scallion
6–8 tblsp olive oil
2 tblsp wine vinegar
Salt and freshly ground black pepper

Put the curry paste or powder in a bowl and stir in the lemon juice and shallot or onion. Beat in the oil and vinegar alternately with a fork. Season to taste and serve immediately, or beat again before serving. Use within 24 hours.

For potato salad, add 1 tblsp chopped mango or fruit chutney and 1 chopped hard-cooked egg.

DAIRY CHEESE DRESSING

For green salads, vegetables and fruit.

Makes ¾ cup
1 (3 oz) package cream cheese
½ tsp prepared English mustard
1½ tblsp white wine vinegar or lemon juice
½ tsp grated onion
¼ cup salad oil, light cream or buttermilk
2 tblsp finely chopped parsley
Salt and freshly ground black pepper

Mash the cheese with the mustard and vinegar or lemon juice until smooth. Stir in the remaining ingredients, seasoning to taste.

For a Northern European sauce, suitable for cucumbers, fish or cold meat, use cream or buttermilk instead of oil and stir in 3 tblsp grated or prepared horseradish.

Petits suisses cheeses make a good variation of this. Mix 3 petits suisses with 2 tblsp tarragon vinegar and ½ tsp sugar. Stir in 2 tsp chopped fresh tarragon or chives and garnish with more herbs. Serve over ripe apricots, peaches or melon as an appetizer.

DILL AND MUSTARD CREAM

A favorite of King Frederick Augustus III of Saxony when served with herrings, it was originally a marinade for raw fish, but also makes a good dressing for potato salad. See also Dill and Sour Cream Sauce (page 87).

Makes 1 cup
½ cup sour cream
5 oz pot of Dijon-style mustard
2 tblsp white wine vinegar
1 tblsp lemon juice
½ cup coarsely chopped fresh dill, plus extra to garnish
1 tsp black peppercorns, coarsely ground

1 tsp allspice berries, coarsely ground
1 tblsp sugar
Salt and ground white pepper
Thinly sliced onion rings for garnish

Combine the first 9 ingredients, seasoning to taste. Garnish the salad with extra fresh dill and onion rings.

EGGLESS THICK DRESSING

Evaporated milk makes a good thick dressing that can be substituted for mayonnaise over hard-cooked eggs, tomatoes and other salad ingredients.

Makes 1 cup

1 tsp prepared mustard, mild or hot
½ tsp salt
1 tsp sugar
½ cup evaporated milk
½ cup olive oil
2–3 tblsp white wine vinegar or lemon juice

Mix the mustard, salt and sugar in a bowl and stir in the evaporated milk. Whisk in the oil, a little at a time. Finally, whisk in the vinegar or lemon juice; this has the effect of thickening the dressing.

A pinch of cayenne or 1–2 tblsp prepared horseradish can be added, with 1–2 tsp more lemon juice to taste.

EGG VINAIGRETTE

Vinaigrette "à l'oeuf" is an interesting variant for a green salad – try one made with garden cress and lettuce, or chicory.

Makes ½ cup

2 large eggs, hard-cooked for 6 minutes only: the yolks should be firm but not dry
1 tsp Dijon-style mustard
Salt and freshly ground black pepper
1 tblsp white wine vinegar
3 tblsp olive oil

Mash the yolks with the mustard until smooth and season. Stir in the vinegar and then the oil. Chop the egg white finely and add.

GARLIC SALAD DRESSINGS

Most salad dressings of Mediterranean derivation contain garlic, so consult the index. The most famous garlic dressing is Aïoli (page 80) and the much cruder Catalan version All-i-oli, which means "garlic and oil," which is just what it is!

GREEN GODDESS DRESSING

This celebrated American dressing, named after a play starring the English actor George Arliss, was invented at the Palace Hotel in San Francisco, later destroyed in the earthquake and fire in 1906. The original recipe contained no cream. Serve it with shellfish, fish and vegetable salads; excellent with potato salad.

Makes 1½ cups

2 canned anchovy fillets, drained and chopped
¾ cup Mayonnaise, homemade if possible (page 92)
1 clove garlic, crushed, with salt if necessary
1 tblsp lemon juice
1 tblsp tarragon or white wine vinegar
2 tblsp scallion tops, finely chopped
2 tblsp finely chopped parsley
4–6 tblsp sour cream
Salt and freshly ground black pepper
2 tsp chopped fresh tarragon or chives (optional)

Mash the anchovies to a paste and add to the mayonnaise with the garlic. Stir in the lemon juice, vinegar, scallions and parsley. Beat in the sour cream and season to taste. Garnish with chopped herbs if wished. Whipped cream can replace the sour cream; add a few extra drops of lemon juice.

Overleaf: *The taste and texture of raw vegetables at their very best is enhanced by the two classic summer salad dressings, Mayonnaise and Vinaigrette.*

GREEN-GREEN DRESSING

The double green of lime and avocado gives this dressing its name, and its thick rich flavor. Serve it with green salad to accompany steaks in a mustard or fiery sauce, roll it up in ham or try it with shrimp, fish, sliced tomatoes or mixed potato and celery salad.

Makes 1 cup

1 ripe avocado
2 tblsp lime juice (or lemon juice)
½ tsp salt
2 tblsp heavy cream
Few drops of hot pepper or Worcestershire sauce

Halve the avocado, discard the seed and scoop out the flesh, scraping all the dark green layer from inside the skin. Mash with the lime juice until smooth. Stir in the remaining ingredients and chill.

GREEN PEPPER CREAM

A cool contrast for tomatoes or grated carrots.

Makes 1¼ cups

2 green peppers
1 cup whipping cream
2 tblsp lemon juice
¼ tsp paprika
Salt and ground white pepper

Broil the peppers, turning them over until the skins are charred. When cool enough to handle rub off the skins. Discard stalks and seeds and chop finely.

Whip the cream until stiff, and stir in the lemon juice and paprika. Fold in the peppers and season. For extra color you could use a small sweet red pepper or one of the new yellow varieties.

HERB DRESSING IN ONE MINUTE

Herbs express the freshness of summer – though many can be grown in pots on a windowsill throughout the year. This selection, Paul Bocuse's, will go with most salads.

Makes ¾ cup

1 clove garlic, unpeeled but split
2 tblsp lemon juice
1 tsp salt
⅛ tsp freshly ground black pepper
Up to ½ cup olive oil
1 tblsp finely chopped parsley
1 tblsp finely chopped fresh tarragon
1 tblsp finely chopped chives
1 tblsp finely chopped fresh chervil or basil

Wipe the cut sides of the garlic around the bowl to be used (discard the garlic). Stir together the lemon juice, salt and pepper. Beat in the olive oil with a fork until the dressing thickens and emulsifies. Stir in the herbs and serve immediately: rebeat if it has to wait. Use within 24 hours. See also Tarragon Dressing (page 124).

A southern selection of herbs, for tomatoes, celery or artichokes, includes equal quantities of parsley, marjoram, basil and chives.

For **Minty Vinaigrette** to dress peas, pears, oranges, melon, carrots, cauliflower and even tomatoes: use 3 tblsp wine vinegar, ½ tsp Dijon-style mustard, 2 tblsp chopped fresh mint, 1 tblsp chopped parsley and 6 tblsp olive oil.

HERB DRESSINGS

Herbs are listed under their own names: see the Basil dressings on page 109, Dill and Mustard Cream (page 112), Dill and Sour Cream Sauce (page 87), Tarragon Dressing (page 124), Ravigote (page 122), Herby Garlic Mayonnaise (page 92) and Herby Yogurt Dressing (right).

HONEY SWEET AND SOUR DRESSING

Serve over crisp romaine lettuce or shredded white cabbage or bok choy. It also goes well on cold cooked green beans. In the Middle East a few drops of orange-flower water are added to dress leaves.

Makes ¾ cup

½ cup oil
2 tblsp white wine or cider vinegar
2 tblsp clear honey
1–2 tblsp lemon juice
Salt and freshly ground black pepper

Combine the first 3 ingredients, adding lemon juice and seasoning to taste.

HONEY AND YOGURT DRESSING

This slightly sweet dressing is good with cucumber salad – garnished with fresh dill – or with roast lamb. Pour it over sliced tomato salad or raw carrot strips.

Makes ½ cup

1 clove garlic, crushed, with salt if necessary
½ cup plain Yogurt, homemade if possible (page 106)
1 tblsp lemon juice
1 tsp clear honey
Salt and freshly ground black pepper
1 tblsp chopped fresh mint (optional)
2 tsp toasted sesame seeds (optional)

Stir the garlic into the yogurt, with the lemon juice and honey. Taste and season. Stir in the mint or sesame seeds, if wished. The dressing can be thinned with 2–3 tblsp half-and-half and used to toss a green salad.

For **Herby Yogurt Dressing**, omit the honey and lemon juice and stir in 2 tblsp chopped fresh herbs; add chives for a sauce for roast chicken or for fried eggplants or zucchini.

HOT BACON DRESSING

A dressing made with hot bacon fat instead of oil is very good served on bitter salads such as Belgian endive, chicory and spinach, or spinach and raw mushroom salad. With onion and mustard added it goes well with potato and raw celery salads. If the fat is insufficient, add a little butter. Walnut oil is a luxury, but makes a delicious addition, traditional for this type of dish in some of the winegrowing regions of France.

Makes ½ cup

3 slices bacon, cut into matchstick strips
2 tblsp butter or walnut oil (if necessary)
½ medium-size onion, finely chopped (optional)
2 tblsp wine vinegar
2 tsp Dijon-style mustard (optional)
Salt and freshly ground black pepper

Fry the bacon over low heat until it gives up its fat and the shreds are crisp, being careful not to burn it: add the butter or oil if needed. Fry the onion, if using, in the fat until soft.

Pour the fat over crisp green salad and toss. Add the vinegar and mustard, if using, to the pan and stir to deglaze. Season to taste. Pour over the salad, toss again and serve immediately before the fat has time to congeal.

HOT SALAD DRESSINGS

Hot salad dressings may sound unlikely, but there are a few. The Hot Bacon Dressing above has the effect of slightly wilting the vegetables on which it is poured; with bitter leaves like spinach or raw mushrooms this makes them slightly more palatable. They do not, of course, go to the table hot, unlike Bagna Cauda (page 109), which is served in a fondue pot on a burner and offers a contrast of hot, rich dip and crisp raw vegetables. For salads à la greque vegetables are cooked in their dressing (see Tomato and Coriander Bouillon (page 72), but are then served cold.

Above: *Blue cheese – see Roquefort Cream – makes a luscious dip for a wide selection of vegetables, and also a creamy salad dressing.*

Left: *Green-green Dressing makes a wonderful sauce or dip for raw, crunchy vegetables. Chill them well for maximum crispness and contrast.*

ITALIAN DRESSING WITH CROUTONS

Crisp vegetables and croûtons add welcome texture to this red vinaigrette for green salad. Without the croûtons it goes well with corn. See also Parmesan Dressing (page 122).

Makes 1½ cups

1 clove garlic, crushed, with salt if necessary
¼ cup red wine vinegar
1 tsp salt
½ tsp freshly ground black pepper
¼ tsp paprika
¾ cup good olive oil
1 tblsp chopped sweet red pepper
1 tblsp chopped green pepper
½ tblsp chopped parsley
½ tblsp chopped chives or finely chopped onion

For the croûtons:
2 tblsp oil
3 slices thick bread, without crusts, diced
Salt and freshly ground black pepper
1 tsp paprika, or 2 tblsp grated Parmesan cheese

Add the garlic to the vinegar with the salt, pepper and paprika. Whisk in the oil with a fork.

To make **croûtons** heat the oil, then toss the bread dice over medium heat until golden brown. Drain on paper towels, then season and toss with paprika or grated Parmesan.

Before serving whisk the vinaigrette again, and add the chopped vegetables and herbs. Add the croûtons to the salad with the dressing and toss.

KETCHUP POUR OVER

"Shake, oh shake the ketchup bottle, None will come and then a lot'll," said Ogden Nash. Here is an instant sauce for raw or parboiled cauliflower florets or cold cooked zucchini.

Makes 1 cup
¼ cup tomato ketchup
2 tblsp oil
¼ cup red wine vinegar
¼ cup sugar
¼ cup steak chili-tomato sauce, or ½ tsp Chinese chili sauce
Dash of hot pepper sauce (for chili-tomato)
Pinch of garlic salt
Dash of Worcestershire sauce
Freshly ground black pepper

Mix all the ingredients together; season to taste.

LEMON SALAD DRESSINGS

Lemon juice brings out the flavor of most vegetables. It makes a characterful Vinaigrette or Lemon Cream Dressing (both page 126), an excellent Mayonnaise (page 92) and the less fattening Yogurt Dressing (page 106).

LIME OR LEMON DRESSING

Use to dress ripe avocados, a green salad or fruit for an appetizer.

Makes 1 cup

5 tblsp frozen lime or lemonade concentrate
5 tblsp clear honey
5 tblsp salad oil
1 tsp celery seeds or poppy seeds

Mix all the ingredients; leave 1 hour to blend. Then beat again before using.

LOW CALORIE DRESSING

Made without oil, this can replace Vinaigrette to dress green salads. For other low calorie dressings, see Buttermilk Dressing (page 110), Tomato Aspic (page 105), Tomato Dressing (page 125) and Mock Mayonnaise (right).

Makes ⅔ cup
¼ cup lemon juice
Pinch of sugar
Pinch of salt

Mix the lemon juice with 6 tblsp water, add the sugar and season; this is slimming and economical.

For a Chinese-style **Soy Salad Dressing** combine ¼ cup lemon juice with ¼ cup warmed meat jelly from under the roast, or warmed Meat Glaze (page 57). Stir in 2 tblsp soy sauce and a pinch of sugar. Taste – seasoning should be unnecessary. Use to dress a tomato salad.

MAYONNAISE

Mayonnaise is listed with Cold Savory Sauces, on page 92. There are many mayonnaise-based salad dressings, so consult the index. Chief among them are Green Goddess Dressing (page 113), Russian Dressing (page 123) and Thousand Island Dressing (page 125). Other mayonnaise-based sauces are Aïoli (page 80), Chantilly Mint Sauce (page 82), Curry Mayonnaise (page 83), Jellied Mayonnaise (page 90), Rémoulade (page 97) where you will also find the popular version of Sauce Tartare and Sauce Gribiche, and Tuna Mayonnaise (page 106).

MEM SAHIB'S DRESSING

An unusual spicy cream for cold cooked green beans, raw cauliflower florets, sliced tomatoes or fruit for an appetizer. You can substitute ½ tsp curry paste or powder for the first 4 spices.

Makes 1 cup
½ (8 oz) package cream cheese
1 tsp grated onion
Small pinch each of ground cloves and cinnamon
Tiny pinch of grated nutmeg
¼ tsp ground cumin
1 tsp coriander seeds, coarsely ground
½ tsp sugar
¼ cup light cream
Salt and freshly ground black pepper
Chopped fresh coriander or flat parsley (cilantro) for garnish (optional)

Beat the cream cheese until soft and blend in the onion, spices and sugar. Gradually stir in the cream until you have the consistency you want: a thin cream for pouring over salads, a thick one over halved peaches or melon balls. Season. Stand for 1 hour to blend the flavors. Serve, garnished with the herbs, if wished – they are such a pretty shape you may prefer to lay them around the edge of the dish.

MOCK MAYONNAISE

Use this creamy jellied buttermilk as a dieters' dressing for vegetables.

Makes 1¼ cups
¼ cup white wine vinegar
1 tsp mustard powder
1½ tsp sugar (or liquid artificial sweetener)
½ envelope unflavored gelatin
1 cup buttermilk
1 tsp grated onion
Salt and freshly ground black pepper

Bring the vinegar, mustard and sugar (or sweetener) to a boil. Off the heat stir in the gelatin until dissolved. Cool 2 minutes, then stir into the buttermilk with the onion, and season to taste. Chill. Whisk before serving.

ORANGE VINAIGRETTE

Marmalade enhances the orange taste of this dressing and adds an element of sweet-and-sour to it. Use to dress beets, and orange and onion, or orange and ripe olive salad. It is also good with watercress, chicory and Belgian endive.

Makes ½ cup

Grated rind and juice of ½ orange
2 tblsp fine-cut marmalade
¼ cup olive oil
1 tsp lemon juice
Salt and freshly ground black pepper

Mix all the ingredients together, seasoning to taste: the lemon juice counteracts the sweetness of the marmalade.

A **Plain Orange Vinaigrette** can be made without marmalade or lemon juice. Use the juice of 1 orange and add ⅛ tsp prepared mustard and a pinch of sugar; season well with black pepper. This shows off small, baby carrots or a carrot salad.

Try **Orange Yogurt** too, with the juice of 1 orange and ½ cup plain yogurt.

PARMESAN DRESSING

A touch of cheese goes well with lettuce hearts, tossed green salads and many mixed salads.

Makes 1 cup

6 tblsp olive oil
2 tblsp white wine vinegar
½ cup Mayonnaise, homemade if possible (page 92)
½ clove garlic, crushed, with salt if necessary
½ cup grated Parmesan cheese
Salt and freshly ground black pepper

Stir the olive oil and vinegar into the mayonnaise, adding them alternately. Stir in the garlic. Add the Parmesan and season to taste.

For a creamier version, replace the oil and vinegar with 6 tblsp sour cream; substitute 2 tsp cider vinegar for the wine vinegar.

PEACH PUREE

For mixed salads, chicken with vegetables, cheese with celery and ham – anything enhanced by a fruity dressing.

Makes ½ cup

2 large ripe peaches
1 tblsp tarragon or white wine vinegar
Freshly ground black pepper
2 tsp chopped chives for garnish

Pour boiling water over the peaches, count to 10, then skin. Blend the flesh with the vinegar until smooth. Season with pepper and garnish with chives.

Pear Purée, for watercress and cheese salads, can be made the same way. Purée the flesh of 2 pears with 2 tsp lemon juice and beat in 2–4 tblsp heavy or sour cream, then season.

RAVIGOTE

Serve this green, piquant herby vinaigrette with jellied chicken, hot or cold boiled beef, hot sweetbreads and brains, poached fish and cold, cooked vegetables; the French name means "reinvigorating." I eat it most often in the center of a cold globe artichoke, where it replaces the hairy choke. In Spain a side dish of vinaigrette is also served with the artichoke for dipping the outside leaves: this is called "con dos salsas," or "with two sauces."

Makes ¾ cup

3 tblsp olive oil
½ cup wine vinegar
1 tsp very finely chopped scallion
1 tsp capers, chopped (optional)
1–2 tblsp mixed finely chopped parsley, chives and fresh tarragon, or parsley alone
Salt and freshly ground black pepper
Pinch of cayenne

Beat the olive oil and vinegar together with a fork, then stir in the remaining ingredients. Taste and season. Beat again before serving.

ROQUEFORT CREAM

France's most distinguished cheese – the best blue cheese in the world – makes a good salad dressing. For a simple sauce for green and mixed vegetable salads, just mash 2 oz cheese into ½ cup Vinaigrette (page 126). For pears or watercress, the addition of plain yogurt or sour cream improves the color. Other powerful blue cheeses, such as Stilton, Gorgonzola and the cheaper Danish Blue could be substituted.

Makes 1 cup
2–3 oz Roquefort cheese
1–1½ tblsp white wine vinegar (less for sour cream)
¼ cup olive oil
¼ cup plain Yogurt, homemade if possible (page 106), or sour cream
Freshly ground black pepper

Mash the cheese with the vinegar, then stir in the oil and yogurt or sour cream. Taste and season with pepper: it should not need salt.

RUSSIAN DRESSING

Use this decorative spicy pink American mayonnaise for coating hard-cooked eggs, chicken or shellfish for an appetizer, or for a buffet party. It also perks up summer sandwiches, giving zest to supermarket ham or cold roast chicken. The sharp pickles that probably gave it its name have been replaced by colorful vegetables from the American South.

Makes 1 cup
1 cup Mayonnaise, homemade if possible (page 92)
2 tblsp finely chopped sweet red pepper
2 tblsp finely chopped green pepper
1 celery stalk, finely chopped
1 tblsp tomato paste
1 tblsp Worcestershire sauce
Dash of hot pepper sauce, or pinch of chili powder

Chop all the vegetables together until very fine, then mix into the mayonnaise. Add the tomato paste and hot seasonings and taste to check.

The lazy way to make this is to add a slurp of tomato ketchup and a splodge of cream to bought mayonnaise.

For **Cossack Dressing**, more recherché, more Russian and fit for smoked trout and summer dinner parties, add a pinch of mustard powder when making the mayonnaise, then 1½ tsp Worcestershire sauce and 1 tblsp grated onion when done. Stir in 1 tblsp red caviar just before serving.

SALAD CREAM

For hard-cooked eggs, sliced tomatoes, raw celery or cooked celeriac and crunchy apple or raw onion salads. Cooked salad dressings, with milk and eggs, have gone out of fashion in these days of commercial bottled sauces. Nevertheless, they are good to eat – and economical. See also Coleslaw Dressing (page 111).

Makes 1 cup
2 tblsp flour
1 tblsp sugar
Salt and ground white pepper
½ tsp mustard powder
¾ cup milk
1 medium-size egg yolk
3 tblsp white wine vinegar
1 tblsp butter, in tiny pieces, or heavy cream

Mix the first 4 ingredients in a small, heavy-based saucepan, then stir in the milk and yolk. Cook over low heat, stirring, for 1–2 minutes. Off the heat beat in the vinegar, then the butter or cream. Taste and season. Chill before use. The cream can be added just before serving. The dressing can be made richer by stirring in extra sour cream; add chopped chives.

SESAME SEED DRESSING

This dressing is both sour-sweet and nutty, and goes well on vegetables such as cold cooked zucchini. See also Tahini Cream (page 104).

Makes 1 cup
2 tblsp sesame seeds
3 tblsp cider vinegar
1 tblsp soft brown sugar
2 tblsp soy sauce
2 tblsp sesame or corn oil
Freshly ground black pepper

Crush the sesame seeds, if possible, by pounding them in a mortar with a pestle. Combine with the other ingredients and stir. Taste for seasoning.

SOUR CREAM DRESSING

For cooked corn, celeriac or artichoke bottoms or for raw, grated or baby carrots.

Makes 1½ cups
¼ cup beef stock, made by boiling Brown Bone Stock (page 14) or good canned consommé or broth to reduce it by half
1 cup sour cream
2–4 tblsp Mayonnaise, homemade if possible (page 92)
1 shallot, finely chopped, or 1 tsp grated onion
1–2 tblsp chopped parsley, or mixed parsley and chives
Salt and freshly ground black pepper

If the stock or consommé jellies when cold, warm it slightly and use when syrupy. Stir it into the sour cream. Stir in the other ingredients and season to taste. Chill.

For a quicker dressing, stir ½ tsp grated onion or ½ crushed garlic clove into the sour cream and add a pinch of sugar and one of the following: ½ tsp celery or dill seeds, a little chopped fresh dill or chopped fennel fronds. Suitable for fish and most vegetables.

SYDNEY SMITH'S SALAD DRESSING

The 19th century English cleric and wit, "the Smith of Smiths," wrote this recipe in verse, ending with the phrase: "I have dined today." Serve with green salad.

Makes 1 cup
2 small potatoes, boiled in their skins, cold
Yolks of 2 medium-size eggs, boiled for 8 minutes; the yolks should not be dry
½ tsp finely chopped onion
1 tblsp Dijon-style mustard
1 tsp salt
2 tblsp white wine vinegar
¼ tsp anchovy paste, or 1 canned anchovy fillet
¼ cup good olive oil

Peel the potatoes, chop roughly and process. Add the remaining ingredients, pouring the oil through the hole in the blender lid to make a smooth emulsion. Freshly ground black pepper wasn't included in the original; add to taste.

TARRAGON DRESSING

Tarragon vinegar preserves the exquisite flavor of the herb; use white wine vinegar and steep the sprigs in it for 2 months before using. Since tarragon partners chicken so well, this is the ideal vinegar for making mayonnaise to serve with cold chicken – which also goes well with hard-cooked eggs and fish. The vinaigrette can be used to toss mixed green salads or new peas, or combination salads containing cheese or chicken. Garnish with fresh leaves when available.

Makes ½ cup
2 tblsp tarragon vinegar
6 tblsp olive oil
1 tblsp chopped fresh tarragon (optional)
Salt and freshly ground black pepper

Mix together all the ingredients, seasoning to taste. For a creamier dressing for cucumber, substitute ½ cup light cream for the olive oil. Add a pinch of sugar to taste.

A richer version is made with cream. Sour ½ cup light cream, or heavy cream, whipped until stiff, with the vinegar, then soften with 1 tsp of sugar.

THOUSAND ISLAND DRESSING

The islands of the title are in the St Lawrence Seaway, on the Canadian border. However this dressing, which owes much to Russian Dressing, is almost certainly of commercial origin and belongs more to the American West Coast. Although it is worth making your own mayonnaise, it is also a good way of cheering up the store-bought version. 19th century Thousand Island Dressing did not contain mayonnaise at all, but was a pink vinaigrette colored with paprika or tomato paste. Serve it with green or mixed salads, shrimp or potato salad.

Makes 1½ cups
2 tblsp chopped celery
2 tblsp chopped dill pickle
1 cup Mayonnaise (page 92)
1 tblsp tomato paste or tomato ketchup
1–2 tblsp white wine vinegar (less if using ketchup)
½ clove garlic, crushed, with salt if necessary
2 tsp Worcestershire sauce
Salt and freshly ground black pepper

Chop the celery and pickle together until very fine (or process together with the vinegar for a totally smooth dressing). Stir the ingredients together, seasoning to taste.

TOFU DIP OR SALAD DRESSING

Tofu is the Japanese name for soybean curd; its silky-white texture gives a smooth dressing. Serve, sprinkled with parsley, as a dip, or as a substitute for mayonnaise with chicken salad, celery or mixed green salad.

Makes ½ cup
¼ cup tofu
1 tblsp lemon juice
2 tblsp oil
Pinch of salt
½–1 tsp light soy sauce (optional)
½ clove garlic, crushed, with salt if necessary (optional)
Pinch of dill seeds or celery seeds (optional)
1 tblsp finely chopped parsley

Process the first 4 ingredients together until smooth and chill. Soy sauce, garlic, and dill or celery seeds can be added to vary the flavor. Sprinkle with parsley.

TOMATO DRESSING

An oil-less dressing for cold cooked green beans and hard-cooked eggs.

Makes ½ cup
1 large hard-cooked egg yolk
1 tblsp tarragon or white wine vinegar
½ tsp grated onion
½ tsp Worcestershire sauce
½ cup tomato juice
Salt and freshly ground black pepper
Chopped fresh dill or basil (optional)

Mash the yolk to a paste with the vinegar and grated onion. Work in the remaining ingredients, seasoning to taste and adding the herbs. Chill before serving.

VINAIGRETTE

Often called "French dressing" outside France, this is one of the simplest sauces – but can make or mar a salad. Small, well-judged additions make a significant difference. Rule one is to be generous with the oil, which should be 3–4 times the volume of the acid. Rule two is to make sure the salad itself is not wet, leaking juices (from tomatoes for instance) that could dilute the dressing and spoil the effect. Rule three is taste and season. Vinaigrette can be used with practically every kind of salad, raw and cooked. It is however most frequently used for tossing green leaves.

Makes ⅔ cup

1 clove garlic (optional)
½ tsp prepared English or Dijon-style mustard (optional)
2 tblsp lemon juice or vinegar
1 tsp salt
⅛ tsp of freshly ground black pepper
Up to ½ cup olive or salad oil

If using garlic, either split it and then rub the cut side around the salad bowl, pressing well (then discard), or, alternatively, crush it, with a pinch of salt and a flat knife blade if necessary. Make a paste in the bottom of the bowl with the garlic and mustard, if using. Stir in the lemon juice or vinegar, and season to taste with salt and pepper.

Beat in the oil with a fork until the dressing thickens and emulsifies. Firm ingredients such as cooked potato or legumes and peaches or apricots can be marinated in vinaigrette for several hours.

If the dressing has to stand, rebeat it just before serving, then toss the salad and serve. Do not let delicate leaves stand in the dressing for longer than necessary: they will wilt and lose their freshness. Fresh herbs can be added in season: see Herb Dressing in One Minute (page 116).

The dressing can be stored, in or out of the refrigerator, for a week or more in a securely topped bottle, so it can be made in quantity. Because it separates, shake the bottle hard before use each time to re-form the emulsion.

For **Sweet Vinaigrette**, to dress bitter salad vegetables like Belgian endive and chicory, or for mixed kidney and other bean salads, or to serve with duck, goose or grated carrots, use lemon juice and stir in a good pinch of sugar.

For **Mustard Vinaigrette**, stir in 1½ tsp Dijon-style mustard, plus 1 tblsp heavy cream: good with green beans, all cooked legumes and lentils and also apple or cheese salads.

For **Onion Vinaigrette**, include a little chopped Bermuda onion in a sweet or mustard vinaigrette: good with beets, or orange and ripe olive salad.

For **Lemon Cream Dressing**, use 1 tblsp lemon juice, 3 tblsp oil and 3 tblsp heavy cream: for avocados, beet or apple salad.

WALNUT OIL VINAIGRETTE

A luxurious dressing for lettuce and green salads, pears or honeydew melon – even beets. Include some chopped nuts in the salad. It is also good with legumes – navy and flageolet beans.

Makes ½ cup

2 tsp Dijon-style mustard (optional)
2 tblsp cider or white wine vinegar
6 tblsp walnut oil
Salt and freshly ground black pepper

Stir the mustard, if using, and vinegar together; add the oil and beat with a fork to an emulsion. Season to taste; beat again before serving.

For green beans (or green bean and tomato salad) use red wine vinegar and add 1 tsp finely chopped shallot or scallion.

Hazelnut oil, plus hazelnuts, can be used the same way.

The flavor of walnut oil combines very successfully with bacon, and crisply fried pieces can be substituted for the chopped walnuts. I like Hot Bacon Dressing (page 117) made with walnut oil, which cleverly combines the two.

Sweet Sauces

Hot and cold sauces for ice cream and banana splits, hot, sweet fondues in which to dip cake or cubes of fruit on long forks: this selection of sweet sauces will double or treble your range of easy desserts. It includes Coffee Liqueur Sauce, Apricot Nectar and Spiced Mango Sauce, as well as the classic accompaniments for dishes like crêpes Suzette and Poires Belle Hélène. There are also fruit sauces to transform cake slices or hot puddings, fruit syrups for every purpose and creamy or crunchy toppings for fruit salad. Sweet fillings for crêpes are here, plus sauces for soufflés and mousses, and classic pastry creams and custards, cake toppings and fillings.

CREAMS AND CUSTARDS

Whipped cream is one of the simplest and loveliest of all accompaniments to desserts. Sweeten it, or increase its volume and add to its lightness with beaten egg white (see Chantilly Cream, page 134). Sour cream, petits suisses cheeses, Crème Fraîche (page 138) or sweetened cream cheese are popular alternatives.

Crème Anglaise (page 137), or vanilla **custard**, holds pride of place as the homemade cream; it is good as a hot pouring sauce and delicious cold, especially flavored with kirsch. Its only challenger as an accompaniment to fruit is vanilla ice cream, the best of which is based on egg custard. Make Crème Anglaise with egg yolks and milk (or light or heavy cream). The chilled version can be enriched with whipped cream. Alas, its reputation suffers because substitutes are more common than the real thing. **Custard powder** is a pale shadow of genuine custard – mere colored cornstarch – even though it is beloved by schoolchildren. I first met Crème Anglaise at a dinner party in Paris at the age of 20 and was amazed to find this sophisticated, chilled kirsch-scented custard was my national sauce. We ate it at every dinner party I gave for the next 3 months.

To make Crème Anglaise – or any custard – first **scald** the milk: bring it almost to a boil (until tiny bubbles appear around the edge). Flavorings are often **infused** in the milk. Include them while it heats, then leave in the hot liquid, covered, for 20 minutes to transmit flavor. A vanilla bean (which can be washed and reused several times) gives a better flavor than vanilla extract (which is derived from the bean and in turn tastes better than chemically made essence). Alternatives are a cinnamon stick or a thinly pared strip of lemon or orange rind.

Making custard takes patience, although heating the milk first, as described above, helps to shorten the cooking time. Cook in a double boiler (page 19) over simmering – not boiling – water, stirring methodically with a wooden spoon around sides and bottom. A tiny amount of cornstarch can be included as an instant thickener. If serving immediately or chilling, pour into another container. If you want to keep the custard warm, arrest cooking (by plunging the base of the pan into cold water) then return to the boiler, off the heat. To cool custard successfully, you must cover the surface with plastic wrap or a butter wrapper, to stop a skin forming. Store it in the refrigerator for 2–3 days or freeze (leaving ½ in headspace) for up to 3 months.

Crème Pâtissière, or confectioner's custard (page 138) is similar but easier to make. Because it contains flour, there is no risk of curdling and so it can be made over direct heat which is quicker and less bothersome. Crème Pâtissière is wonderfully useful because it is firm when set – it will not ooze too much when cut into and will support the weight of fruit in a pastry case, so is ideal for tarts.

I always use **vanilla sugar** for custards and desserts. Just put a vanilla bean in a jar of granulated (or confectioners') sugar and leave to mature for a few weeks. Use the ready-flavored sugar for cooking and save time on infusing. You can also use it for last-minute sprinkling. Another popular flavoring is **citrus rind**. The colored part of orange or lemon peel – called "zest" – contains a strong oil. The traditional way to extract the oil is to rub the peel vigorously with a sugar cube until it is saturated. Use the sugar as part of the measured quantity in a recipe. For cooking, pare off thin strips of rind with a potato peeler and use for flavoring (discard after boiling). Grated rind dissolves into the food; the tiny holes of a nutmeg grater are best for this, though you can use a larger, cheese grater. Freshly bought oranges or refrigerated oranges grate most easily. Ones that have been kept for several days at room temperature are too soft. **Julienne strips**, pared rind which is cut into thin matchstick shreds, can be used for looks as well as flavor. Before adding them to the liquid, blanch for 5 minutes in boiling water to reduce their bitterness; refresh them under cold running water.

The most useful filling for firm layer cakes, nut tortes and meringues is **buttercream.** My French Crème au Beurre (page 138) is made with softened butter and egg yolks, which are lightly cooked when hot sugar syrup is poured on them. It takes many flavors. It is easiest to make with an electric mixer. Soft when first made, it gradually firms up as it chills. Use it before it gets cold: it pipes very successfully.

Buttercream is also ideal for sticking chocolate scrolls, chopped nuts and sugar strands to cakes and meringues.

Sweet Sauces

SYRUPS

Indispensable for fruit, syrup is made by boiling sugar and water together, when the nature of the sugar changes. The thickness of the syrup depends on the proportion of sugar to water. For fruit salad you will need ¾ cup syrup per 1 lb fruit.

Since syrup is made hot but used cold, it is well worth making to store. For convenience, make stronger syrups and dilute them when necessary. In summer I keep light canning syrup (see below) in the refrigerator and heavy syrup in the freezer: it takes up little room and never freezes hard, so a little can be scooped out whenever you need it.

Sugar Syrup

The basic method of making sugar syrup does not change, but the quantity of sugar may vary from 1 part sugar to 4 parts water to the reverse, giving thin or thick syrup. A thinner syrup may be boiled to make it thicker. This light syrup is useful for storing and general purposes.

Makes 3 cups
1 cup sugar
Flavoring (optional, see below)

Put the sugar and 2½ cups water in a heavy-based saucepan. Heat gently, stirring, until the sugar has dissolved. Add any flavoring and boil for 2 minutes. Strain and use hot, or cool and chill.

Flavor the syrup while cooking with one of the following: a thinly pared strip of orange or lemon rind, 2 whole cloves, a piece of vanilla bean, cardamom seeds or 2 crushed cardamom pods, a 2 in cinnamon stick or a head of elderberry flowers tied in cheesecloth (this gives a muscat flavor). The chilled syrup can be flavored with 3 tblsp Marsala, 2 tblsp kirsch fantasie or 1 tblsp orange-flower water.

Poaching and fruit salad syrup: use this with fresh fruit and as a moisturizer, for example when making icings. Sugar quantity to water: ½ cup per 2½ cups.

Light canning syrup for preserving apricots, pears, peaches and mandarin oranges. Sugar quantity to water: 1 cup per 2½ cups. Dilute it with water, lemon or orange juice, etc., for fruit salad.

Medium canning syrup for preserving plums and tart berries. Sugar quantity to water: 1½ cups per 2½ cups. It also makes excellent sorbets: just add orange or lemon juice to taste and freeze.

Heavy syrup for pouring over pastries (see Rose-water Syrup, page 153). Sugar quantity to water: 2 cups per 2½ cups. Add this syrup to taste to fruit purées for sorbet and ice cream (it gives a softer texture) and freeze.

Dunking syrup is used for dipping beignets, small doughnuts and deep-fried fruit. The syrup should be very cold, the food very hot. Drain on paper towels before serving. Sugar quantity to water: 4 cups per 2½ cups. Don't make syrup for dunking in quantities below 1 quart – it is not successful. Any leftover syrup can be strained and used diluted for another purpose.

Sugar may also be boiled to change its opacity and consistency when cool again. Cooked to a lower temperature, **boiled sugar** forms fudge when cold; at a higher one it makes caramel, which sets hard when cold. Made caramel must be used immediately if you want a glossy, hard coating for pastry or a dessert. To make **caramel**, boil the syrup until it turns golden-brown, then arrest cooking: to check the rise in temperature you will need to do more than simply take the pan off the heat. Sometimes the base of the pan is plunged into cold water, but, for a syrup, add a cold liquid to it (see Caramel Syrup, page 134). The extra liquid melts the caramel again, giving the sauce the taste of caramel without its consistency.

Sieved jam is used for **fruit glazes** for flans and tarts. Glazes have both color and flavor, improving the appearance of the tart and also keeping the fruit moist. Apricot glaze is the most useful, though red jam is used for red fruit. Put ¼ cup jam (avoiding fruit lumps) with 1 tsp lemon juice and 6 tblsp water in a pan and stir until dissolved. Sieve, if wished, to remove bits of fruit, then paint the glaze over the fruit while it is still hot; serve the tart cold. For a hot tart, sprinkle a little sugar on the glaze and slip the tart under a hot broiler for 2 minutes.

ALI BABA SAUCE

An exotic, thick Middle Eastern topping. Serve at room temperature with plain, stewed apples or hot baked apples, and also with creamy grain puddings.

Makes 1½ cups
1/4 cup butter, softened
1 tblsp clear honey
1/4 tsp ground apple pie spice or cinnamon
Finely grated rind of 1 lemon
1/2 lb fresh dates, skinned, pitted and finely chopped
   (about 1 cup)
1/2 cup finely chopped blanched, toasted almonds
1–2 tblsp lemon juice

Cream the butter, honey, spice and lemon rind until pale and fluffy, then stir in the dates and almonds. Sharpen to taste with lemon juice, then stir in 1–2 tblsp hot water to make a thick cream. Serve at room temperature. The sauce can be frozen for up to 3 months. Bring back to room temperature before serving.

ALMOND SAUCES
See Frangipane (page 140) and Praline (page 152).

APPLE SAUCE, NORMANDY-STYLE

A hot sauce for steamed puddings, ice cream, vanilla cream or deep-fried triangles of Camembert served as an appetizer, it is equally successful cold. Serve hot or cold with roast pork, duck or goose: it cuts the fattiness of the meat. See also Apple Mayonnaise (page 80).

Makes 1 cup
1 tblsp unsalted butter
1/2 lb tart apples, sliced and sprinkled with 1 tblsp lemon
   juice
Thinly pared strip of lemon rind
Sugar to taste
2–3 tsp Calvados or applejack

Melt the butter in a heavy-based saucepan over low heat. Add the apples and lemon rind; lay a piece of butter wrapper on top. Cover the pan and cook gently, stirring occasionally, until the apples are very soft and pulpy.

Drain off any liquid and discard the lemon rind. Purée the apples in the blender or through a nylon sieve, then return the purée to the rinsed-out pan. Add sugar to taste (less to accompany meat or poultry). Simmer gently for 5 minutes until the sauce is reduced and thickened. Stir in the Calvados (for a sweet sauce) and serve hot or warm with a dessert. It is worth making this sauce in quantity, as it will freeze (leaving ½ in headspace) for up to 9 months.

Serve the following hot sauces with desserts: For **Apple and Walnut Sauce**, omit the Calvados and stir in 2 tblsp coarsely chopped walnuts and a pinch of ground mace. For **Cinnamon Apple Sauce**, use a 2 in stick of cinnamon instead of lemon rind. For **Apple and Date Sauce**, stir 1/3 cup chopped, pitted dates into the unsweetened purée and sharpen with lemon juice.

For **Apple and Sour Cream Sauce**, to serve cold with a compote of peaches, apricots or dried fruits, omit the Calvados. Fold in 2 tblsp each sour cream and bland mayonnaise. Chill before serving.

APRICOT LIQUEUR SAUCE

Serve hot with ginger, orange or chocolate puddings, hot vanilla or chocolate soufflés, or baked bananas. Try it also over creamy grain puddings or molds and baked egg custard.

Makes 1 cup
16 oz canned apricot halves in syrup
2 tblsp frozen orange juice concentrate
2 tblsp sugar
1 tblsp arrowroot
1–2 tsp Amaretto di Saronna, Grand Marnier or apricot
   brandy

Drain the apricots, reserving 3 tblsp syrup, and purée in the blender. Pour the purée into a small heavy-based saucepan and add the orange juice and

1 tblsp sugar. Blend the arrowroot with the reserved syrup and add to the pan. Bring slowly to a boil and simmer for 5 minutes, stirring constantly, until the sauce has cleared and thickened. Off the heat stir in the liqueur and more sugar, if wished. Serve hot.

For **Peach Liqueur Sauce**, use canned peach halves or slices.

APRICOT NECTAR

The exquisite flavor of dried apricots pairs well with pie pastry. Try this cold sauce with apple pie, or mince pie, or with plum pudding instead of Brandy Butter (page 132). It makes an excellent layer in a meringue cake.

Makes ¾ cup
½ lb(1⅓ cups) dried apricots, soaked overnight in water
  to cover
Finely grated rind and juice of 1 orange
Clear honey to taste
½ cup heavy cream, whipped

Simmer the apricots in their soaking liquid with the orange rind until tender: cool slightly. Drain the apricots, reserving the liquid, and purée in the blender with the orange juice. Add a little reserved syrup if necessary, but do not thin too much. Sweeten with honey to taste and leave until cold. Fold in the whipped cream and chill.

For **Tipsy Apricot Cream**, add 2–3 tsp Noyau or Amaretto di Saronna. For **Apricot Yogurt Sauce**, replace the cream with plain yogurt, homemade if possible (page 106).

BANANA SAUCES

See Whipped Banana Topping (page 161) and Strawberry and Banana Sauce (page 160).

BLACKBERRY KIR

French Resistance hero Canon Kir, later Mayor of Dijon, invented the drink named after him by combining

two of Burgundy's products, cassis – black currant liqueur – and white wine. Add fruit to make a heady cold sauce for tapioca, baked egg custard or ice cream. Serve it hot with creamy rice pudding.

Makes 2 cups
1 tblsp butter
1 tblsp cornstarch
¼ cup crème de cassis
¾ cup dry white wine
¾ lb (3 cups) fresh or frozen blackberries
Lemon juice to taste

Melt the butter in a heavy-based pan, then remove from the heat. Blend the cornstarch and cassis and stir into the butter. Stir in the wine and blackberries. Bring slowly to a boil, stirring constantly, until the sauce has thickened; simmer for 3–5 minutes. Stir in lemon juice to taste. Serve hot, or cool, covered, and then chill.

BLACK CURRANT PUREE

An attractive cold sauce to pour over vanilla and other pale molded creams, cold baked custard or ice cream-filled crêpes or meringues. Black currants are an ideal fruit for the freezer. With their good color and flavor they store well and make welcome sauces out of season. Store sugared washed berries in 1 cup packs, leaving ½ in headspace. Commercial frozen fruit is also good.

Makes about 1 cup
1 lb (2 pints) black currants, stripped from their stalks
½ cup sugar, or to taste
2 tblsp Grand Marnier or other orange-flavored liqueur
  (optional)

Put the black currants into a heavy-based saucepan with half the sugar and 2 tblsp water. Cover and simmer gently until tender. Cool slightly, then purée in the blender. Sieve the purée into a bowl and add more sugar to taste. Stir in the liqueur, if using, and chill.

BLUEBERRY SAUCE

A sauce from Vermont to serve hot over pancakes, waffles or steamed pudding, or cold as a topping for cheesecake or molded creams. It can also be stirred into yogurt. Bilberries can be substituted.

Makes 1 cup
¼ cup sugar, or more to taste
2 in cinnamon stick
2 tsp cornstarch
1 lb (2 pints) fresh or frozen blueberries
Finely grated rind and juice of 1 lemon

Put the sugar and cinnamon in a small heavy-based saucepan. Blend the cornstarch slowly with ½ cup water and stir in; bring to a boil, stirring. Add the blueberries. Cook over low heat, stirring frequently, until the berries just begin to burst.

Stir in the lemon rind and juice and add more sugar to taste. Discard the cinnamon.

For **Blueberry Split Sauce**, swirl in ½ cup sour cream just before serving.

For **Spiced Blueberry Sauce**, add ¼ tsp ground apple pie spice with the cinnamon stick.

BRANDY BUTTER

Sometimes called "senior wrangler sauce" – after the candidate securing the highest marks in Cambridge University's mathematical exams – or "King George's Sauce" – after George III – this cold brandy butter is the classic accompaniment to plum pudding and mince pie. See also Hard Sauce (page 143).

Makes 1 cup

½ cup unsalted butter, at room temperature
½ cup granulated or confectioners' sugar, sifted
6 tblsp brandy

Beat the butter until pale and creamy, then gradually beat in the sugar. When most of the sugar has been incorporated, beat in the brandy – a little at a time to prevent curdling – alternating it with the remaining sugar. Beat until the sauce is light and fluffy. Pile into a bowl and serve with a spoon.

For **Cumberland Rum Butter**, use light brown sugar and beat in the finely grated rind of 1 lemon, 1 tsp lemon juice and a large pinch of grated nutmeg; use dark rum instead of brandy. This sauce is traditionally served at christenings in the North of England, packed into small pots as a spread for the crackers called water biscuits.

BRANDY CREAM

A rich, velvety sauce; serve hot with festive plum puddings, mince pies and crêpes, or coffee gelatin. See also Brandy Butter (left).

Makes about 1 cup
4 large egg yolks
½ cup heavy cream
½ cup brandy
2 tblsp sugar

Combine the egg yolks, cream, brandy and sugar in the top of a double boiler. Add 2 tblsp water. Set over barely simmering water and cook, stirring constantly with a wooden spoon, for about 8 minutes or until the sauce has thickened slightly. Do not boil or it will turn lumpy. Serve at once or keep warm over hot water.

BRITTLE TOPPING

Brittle adds crunch to sundaes; sprinkle it over ice cream or whipped cream on top of fruit salads to add texture. It is easiest to use a candy thermometer, but if you are judging by eye, prepare a large bowl of cold water and immerse the base of the pan when the syrup has turned golden-brown to stop further cooking.

Makes 1½ cups

1 cup sugar
1 cup roughly chopped unsalted (cashews, skinned peanuts or hazelnuts, walnuts, almonds, or a mixture)
1 tblsp butter
Few drops of vanilla

Line a small jelly roll pan with foil and oil it. Heat the sugar and 5 tblsp water in a heavy-based pan over low heat, stirring with a wooden spoon until dissolved. Bring slowly to a boil; boil for 10–15 minutes without stirring, or until the syrup turns a deep golden-brown or reaches 375° on a candy thermometer.

Remove from the heat and stir in the nuts, butter and vanilla. Continue stirring until the bubbling ceases, then pour into the oiled pan.

When cold and set, snap the brittle into pieces with your hands. Put in a strong plastic bag and crush into fragments with a rolling pin or hammer. Store the brittle in an airtight container: it will keep for 1 month. Use as a topping, sprinkled over ice cream or cream.

BURNT HONEY CREAM

This cold sauce is good with hot apple pie and crêpes, or fruit salad.

Makes 1 cup
½ cup sugar
¼ cup clear honey
½ cup heavy cream

Heat the sugar with 2 tblsp water in a small heavy-based pan over low heat, without stirring, until dissolved. Bring to a boil and boil rapidly until the syrup turns a rich caramel color.

Immediately remove from the heat and stir in 2 tblsp water – wear a glove and stand well back as it will splutter! Return to low heat and stir until the caramel has dissolved. Heat gently without stirring until the syrup reaches 240° on a candy thermometer; at this temperature a small sample dropped into cold water will form a soft ball. Add the honey and stir until blended. Leave until cold.

Whip the cream until soft peaks form. Fold the honey syrup through the cream. Chill.

BUTTER SAUCES
Sweet butter sauces will be found under Brandy Butter (left) and Hard Sauce (page 143).

BUTTERSCOTCH SYRUP

Serve hot with baked apples or pears, pancakes, waffles, and steamed or baked puddings.

Makes 1 cup
½ cup unsalted butter, diced
⅔ cup firmly packed brown sugar
¼ cup light corn syrup
1 tblsp lemon juice

Heat the butter, sugar and syrup gently in a heavy-based saucepan, stirring occasionally, until dissolved. Bring to a boil, then remove from the heat and stir in the lemon juice. Serve at once.

For **Walnut or Almond Butterscotch Sauce**, add 2 tblsp coarsely chopped nuts with the lemon juice.

CARAMEL SAUCE

A quick sauce for vanilla or chocolate ice cream or plain crêpes.

Makes 1½ cups
⅔ cup firmly packed brown sugar
1 large egg, lightly beaten
⅛ tsp salt
3 tblsp Madeira wine, or ¼ tsp vanilla

Cook the sugar in a heavy-based saucepan with ½ cup water over low heat, stirring occasionally, for 5 minutes. Gradually pour the hot syrup in a thin stream onto the beaten egg, whisking constantly. When all the syrup has been incorporated, whisk in the salt and Madeira or vanilla. Serve at once, or keep warm over hot water.

CARAMEL SYRUP

Invented by the most famous of French chefs, Carême, caramel makes a distinctive cold syrup for macerating fresh fruit: orange slices, pineapple pieces, melon balls or grapes. It can also be used to glaze fruit tart toppings, or poured over a dish of baked apples or pears.

Makes about 1 cup
1 cup sugar
Flavoring (optional, see below)

Heat the sugar in a heavy-based saucepan with ½ cup water, without stirring, until dissolved; add any whole flavorings. Bring to a boil and boil briskly, without stirring, until the syrup turns a caramel color.

Immediately remove from the heat and add 2 tblsp water. Wear a glove and stand well back as it will splutter! Return to low heat and stir until the caramel has dissolved. Set aside to cool. Add any liquid flavorings when the syrup is cold. Discard whole flavorings before using.

Whole flavorings: flavor the syrup, before boiling, with a strip of orange or lemon rind, 2 whole cloves, a split vanilla bean or 2 in piece of cinnamon stick.

Liquid flavorings: pep up the cold syrup with a little stem ginger syrup, orange-flower water, brandy or liqueur.

CHANTILLY CREAM

This lightly whipped and sweetened cream can be served with virtually any dessert. The name comes from the dairy region north of Paris, which traditionally supplies the capital; the magnificent Château Chantilly is the home of the Condés, one of the French royal houses, for whom this cream was almost certainly invented. Serve the cream with any hot fruit dessert or fruit salad, with rich cakes and as a filling for vacherins and other meringues: it has a lighter consistency than Crème au Beurre. The Austrian "Schlagsahne" or beaten cream is made in the same way, but a stiffly beaten egg white is folded in at the end. This increases its volume, making it less rich, and also more economical.

Makes 1½ cups
1 cup heavy cream, well chilled
1–2 tblsp vanilla sugar (page 128) or granulated sugar
  (optional)

Pour the cream into a chilled bowl and beat slowly until foamy. Gradually increase speed to medium and continue beating, adding the sugar if using, until the cream is light and just thick enough to hold its shape. The quantity of sugar depends upon how the cream is to be used: it may be omitted.

The cream is usually but not always flavored with vanilla. If wished, use a few drops of vanilla extract or 1–2 tblsp brandy, rum, liqueur or kirsch, folded in just before serving. One of the most delicious combinations is cream and kirsch. *Kirschwasser* is a powerful, colorless *eau de vie*, made from cherries. The best comes from Switzerland and the Black Forest region of South Germany and adjacent parts of France and is horribly expensive. For cooking, a second-grade kirsch is perfectly permissible; this is often labeled "kirsch fantasie."

A lighter Chantilly Cream can be made by substituting ¼ cup milk for the same quantity of cream.

CHERRY JUBILEE

One of the most famous alcoholic sauces, this hot cherry sauce is poured over portions of vanilla ice cream. It is also good with crêpes. For a cold version, see Heady Cherry Sauce (page 143).

Makes 1½ cups
¼ cup brandy
1 lb canned, pitted Bing cherries
⅛ tsp ground cinnamon
2 tsp arrowroot
2 tblsp kirsch or cherry brandy

Warm the brandy in a cup over hot water. Meanwhile, drain the cherry syrup from the can into a heavy-based saucepan, reserving the cherries, and add the cinnamon. Boil until reduced by one-quarter.

Blend the arrowroot with 2 tblsp water, add a little hot syrup and stir back into the pan. Simmer, stirring, until the sauce has cleared and thickened slightly. Add the cherries and simmer for 2 minutes. Remove from the heat.

Pour in the warmed brandy and set light to it – hold the match just above the side of the pan and stand well back, as the flames will shoot up for a few seconds. When the flames die down, stir in the kirsch (see note under Chantilly Cream) or cherry brandy. Serve at once.

CHOCOLATE FONDUE

The perfect hot sauce for dipping bananas, ladyfingers or cubes of pineapple on long-handled forks, it allows you to experience chocolate sauce in all its luxury – almost equivalent to the childhood treat of cleaning out the chocolate bowl with a finger.

Makes 1 cup

8 (1-oz) squares semisweet or sweet chocolate, in pieces
½ cup heavy cream
Pinch of grated nutmeg
½ tsp ground cloves
½ tsp ground cinnamon
Pinch of ground mace or mixed spice
¼ cup coffee liqueur, dark rum or brandy

Melt the chocolate with the cream in a fondue pot on the stove. Add the spices and stir until smooth. Stir in the alcohol and serve, over a table burner if possible.

CHOCOLATE MARQUISE

A dark, glossy French coating for cream puffs, éclairs, pastry cakes and nut tortes; the quantity given will cover a 9 in diameter cake. The icing sets, but is not too hard to cut with a spoon. See also Ganache (page 141). Serve it cold as a side sauce with a fruit mousse, strawberries, ice cream or nut meringues.

Makes 1 cup

14 (1-oz) squares semisweet or bittersweet chocolate, in pieces
5 tblsp sugar

Put the chocolate pieces in the top pan of a double boiler over hot – not boiling – water and leave until melted, stirring occasionally.

Meanwhile, heat the sugar gently in a small heavy-based saucepan with 1 cup water, stirring until dissolved, then bring to a boil and boil for 5 minutes without stirring.

Stir the syrup into the chocolate a little at a time. Put the pan over direct heat and simmer gently for 5 minutes, or until the sauce has thickened to the consistency of light cream. Use immediately if you wish to coat a cake, torte or meringues.

CHOCOLATE SAUCE BELLE HELENE

A thick, creamy chocolate sauce for pouring, hot, over poached pears filled with vanilla ice cream in the classic French dessert, Poires Belle Hélène – the dish honors the heroine of Offenbach's tuneful and mildly indecent operetta, a Paris success de scandale in 1864. Try the sauce over other fruit and ice cream combinations; sprinkle chopped nuts on top. See also Chocolate Fudge Sauce (page 141) and Cocoa Sauce (page 136).

Makes 1 cup

4 (1-oz) squares semisweet or sweet chocolate, in pieces
3 tblsp heavy cream
1 tblsp unsalted butter, in tiny pieces
2–3 drops of vanilla

Put the chocolate and ½ cup warm water into a heavy-based saucepan. Melt, stirring, over very low heat. Stir in the cream. Bring slowly to a boil and simmer, stirring, for 1–2 minutes. Off the heat stir in the butter and vanilla. Serve hot.

For **Chocolate Custard**, make Crème Anglaise (page 137), using 2 tblsp sugar only and stir in 2 (1-oz) squares semisweet or sweet chocolate, grated. This is excellent cold poured over light layer cakes.

CINNAMON FRAPPE

Cinnamon has an affinity for black currants and blueberries and is also good with stewed blackberry and apple and poached pears. Serve this frozen cream in small pots.

Makes 1 cup
1 cup heavy cream, chilled
1 tsp ground cinnamon
5 tblsp sugar

Add 1 tblsp cold water to the cream and whip until soft peaks form. Mix the cinnamon and sugar and gently fold in. Turn into ramekins or small pots and freeze for 1–2 hours. If freezing longer, allow the cream to soften 20 minutes in the refrigerator before serving.

CITRUS FLUFF

A light, tangy topping to serve cold with fruit salads. See also Orange Yogurt (page 148).

Makes 2½ cups
Finely grated rind and juice of 1 large lemon or 2 limes
2 large eggs, separated
¼ cup sugar

Put the lemon or lime rind and juice in the top of a double boiler with the egg yolks and sugar and beat lightly together. Set over hot – not boiling – water and beat for 15 minutes or until thick and pale. Remove from the heat, pour into a bowl and cover with plastic wrap. Leave until cold.

Using clean dry beaters, beat the egg whites until they form stiff peaks. Fold the egg whites into the citrus custard. Serve at once.

COCOA SAUCE

Serve hot, with a hot chocolate steamed pudding, well-drained poached pears or crêpes.

Makes 1¼ cups
1½ tblsp cocoa powder
2 tblsp brown sugar
1 tsp arrowroot
1 tblsp butter, in tiny pieces
Large pinch of ground cinnamon or instant coffee powder, or a few drops of vanilla (optional)

Blend the cocoa and sugar to a paste with 3–4 tblsp warm water. Slowly stir in 1 cup more warm water. Bring to a boil, stirring, and simmer for 8–10 minutes.

Blend the arrowroot with 1 tblsp water and add a little hot sauce, then stir back into the pan. Simmer, stirring, until the sauce clears and thickens slightly. Stir in the butter and flavoring, if used.

For **Milky Cocoa Sauce**, use warm milk not water.

COCONUT CREAM

This non-dairy cream is especially good served cold over fresh and dried fruit compôtes. Creamed coconut can be bought in cans or packages and adding water is a quick way to make coconut cream; the end result is rather sweeter than the "milk" made from a fresh nut (page 100).

Makes about 1 cup
⅓ cup creamed coconut, in pieces
1–2 drops of vanilla (optional)

Put the coconut pieces into a bowl and slowly beat in about ½ cup warm water. Continue beating until smoothly blended and creamy. Beat in the vanilla, if using.

COCONUT LIME OR LEMON SAUCE

This frothy, tropical-tasting cold cream goes well on orange or pineapple slices. Or eat it alone as a dessert!

Makes 3 cups

½ package lime- or lemon-flavored gelatin (sufficient to make 1 cup gelatin)
Finely grated rind and juice of ½ lime or 1 lemon
1 cup heavy cream
2 tblsp sugar
⅔ cup grated fresh coconut or shredded coconut

Put the gelatin in a small pan with 1 cup water. Stir over low heat until dissolved, add the rind and juice, then cool until thickened, but not set. Process or whisk until light and frothy.

Whip the cream with the sugar until thick, then fold in most of the coconut. Fold this into the gelatin mixture. Serve with the remaining coconut sprinkled on top.

COFFEE LIQUEUR SAUCE

Serve this hot sauce with mixed coffee and chocolate ice creams, with hot chocolate desserts or use when reheating cold crêpes under the broiler. See also Coffee and Hazelnut Cream (page 143), Instant Coffee Cream (page 144) and Mocha Mousseline (page 145).

Makes 1 cup

1 cup hot strong black coffee
2 tblsp sugar, or to taste
2 tsp arrowroot
2 tblsp coffee liqueur

Pour the coffee into a small heavy-based saucepan. Add the sugar. Blend the arrowroot with 2 tblsp water and add to the pan. Bring to a boil and simmer, stirring, until the sauce has cleared and thickened slightly. Remove from the heat and stir in the liqueur. Serve at once or keep warm over hot water.

CREME ANGLAISE

England's most famous sauce is the vanilla-flavored pouring sauce known as custard in its own country. It can be served warm or cold. Correctly made, it is delicious with fruit desserts, baked and steamed puddings, hot charlottes and sweet pies, with cold tarts and as a topping for trifles. As a precaution against curdling, 1 tsp cornstarch can be included. The real thing is far superior to its many imitations.

Makes about 2 cups

1½ cups milk
2 in piece of vanilla bean, split, or ½ tsp vanilla extract
¼ cup sugar
1 tsp cornstarch (optional)
4 large egg yolks

Scald the milk with the vanilla bean if using, then cover and infuse (off the heat) for 10–15 minutes. Remove the bean.

Combine the sugar (and cornstarch if using) and egg yolks in the top of a double boiler off the heat. Whisk until the mixture is pale, creamy and thick enough to fall in a satiny ribbon from the whisk when the beaters are lifted. Whisk in the hot milk, a little at a time.

Set on the double boiler over hot – not boiling – water and stir for about 10 minutes, until the sauce is thick enough to coat the back of the spoon. Do not allow the custard to approach simmering point, or it will curdle and turn lumpy.

Remove from the heat and stir in the vanilla extract, if using. Transfer immediately to a pitcher and serve. If keeping the sauce warm, plunge the base of the pan into a bowl of cold water (to arrest cooking) then return to the top of the boiler: the sauce can be kept warm over warm water for up to 30 minutes.

If serving cold, transfer to a bowl and cover the surface with plastic wrap or a butter wrapper. Leave until cold then chill. The custard can be refrigerated for 2–3 days and frozen (leaving ½ in headspace) for up to 3 months.

Vanilla is the classic flavoring, but any of the following can be added instead: 1 tblsp kirsch, Cognac, orange or coffee liqueur, rum or instant coffee powder.

CREME AU BEURRE

French buttercream, made with syrup, holds its shape well and is ideal for filling or topping and piping fancy cakes or pastries and nut meringues. It can also be rolled inside crêpes for heating under the broiler. It will keep for 5–6 days in the refrigerator and can be frozen for up to 3 months.

Makes 2 cups
4 large egg yolks
½ cup sugar
1 cup unsalted butter, at room temperature
2–3 tsp vanilla (optional)

Whisk the yolks. Heat the sugar gently with ½ cup water in a heavy-based saucepan, stirring until dissolved. Bring to a boil, then boil without stirring until the syrup reaches 240° on a candy thermometer. At this temperature a small sample dropped into cold water will form a soft ball. Remove from the heat.

Whisking all the time, pour the syrup onto the yolks in a thin stream. Whisk until cool, pale and mousse-like.

Cream the butter until it is the same consistency as the yolk mixture. Beat it gradually into the yolks, then beat in the vanilla or flavoring of your choice and any food coloring.

For **Lemon Buttercream**, add 1 tsp grated lemon rind and 2–3 tblsp lemon juice. Make **Orange Buttercream** the same way, with orange rind and juice, adding a few drops of orange food coloring, if wished. For a liqueur buttercream, stir in 2 tblsp kirsch, brandy or Cointreau. These combine well with citrus rinds: use them to replace the juice.

For **Chocolate Buttercream**, melt 4 (1-oz) squares semisweet chocolate over hot water, then cool until just beginning to set; stir into the buttercream. More quickly, stir in ¼ cup cocoa powder.

For **Coffee Buttercream** dissolve 2 tblsp instant coffee powder in 1 tblsp boiling water. Cool and stir in.

For **Praline Buttercream**, stir in ½ cup crushed Praline (page 152).

For **Fruit Buttercream**, stir in ½ cup strawberry or raspberry purée and add ½–1 tblsp kirsch. This is excellent layered into angel cake.

CREME FRAICHE

This slightly sharp "chilled" cream, sold commercially in France, is the perfect foil to soft summer fruit and the cuisine minceur substitute for thick cream in many savory recipes. Serve it, too, with any hot fruit dish.

Makes 1½ cups
1 cup heavy cream
½ cup buttermilk or sour cream

Combine the heavy cream and buttermilk or sour cream in a heavy-based saucepan and heat gently to 90°; at this temperature it will still feel slightly cool to the touch. Pour into a bowl, cover and leave to thicken in a warm place for 8 hours. Stir well, then chill before using. The crème will keep, covered, in the refrigerator for about 1 week.

CREME PATISSIERE

Also called "confectioner's custard," this creamy, thick custard is used as a base for fruit in pastries and is a popular filling for light layer cakes. It does not run when cut and is firm enough to support the weight of fruit in an open fruit tart. It keeps, covered, for 2–3 days in the refrigerator, and will freeze for up to 3 months.

Makes 2 cups
2 cups milk
1 vanilla bean, split
2 tblsp flour
4 tsp cornstarch
3 tblsp sugar
4 large egg yolks
1 tblsp butter

Scald the milk with the vanilla bean in a heavy-based saucepan. Cover and leave to infuse off the heat for 20 minutes. Remove the vanilla bean, wash and dry it and reserve for re-use.

Mix the flours and sugar. Add the yolks and whisk until thick and pale.

Slowly stir in the milk. Pour the mixture back into the milk pan. Bring slowly to a boil, stirring. Simmer very gently for 20 minutes, stirring frequently to prevent scorching. Remove from the heat and beat in the butter. Beat for 1–2 minutes more, then turn the crème into a bowl. Cover the surface with wax paper or plastic wrap and leave until cold.

Stir in any one of the following flavorings after the butter: 2–3 tblsp kirsch, rum, orange-flavored liqueur or instant coffee powder (dissolved in the same volume of water), 4–6 tblsp melted semi-sweet chocolate, 1 cup ground nuts or 2 tblsp Praline (page 152), plus a few drops of almond extract or ½ cup fruit purée. For a stronger vanilla flavor, stir in vanilla extract to taste.

Crème St Honoré, used to fill cream puffs, is made by lightening Crème Pâtissière with beaten egg whites: beat 2 large egg whites with 1 tblsp sugar until very stiff and fold into the cold crème.

CUSTARD

Custards are made of milk or cream and sugar, thickened with yolks. Crème Anglaise (page 137) is the best-known pouring custard, while Crème Pâtissière (left) is an ideal custard for a filling. See also Frangipane (page 140) and Sherry Custard (page 156).

EGG NOG SAUCE

Pour this hot sauce over hot steamed puddings or crêpes.

Makes about 1 cup

3 large egg yolks
1 tblsp light brown sugar
½ cup heavy cream
¼ cup brandy
Tiny pinch of grated nutmeg

Cream the egg yolks and sugar together with a wooden spoon in the top of a double boiler, off the heat, until thick and pale. Slowly stir in the cream and brandy. Flavor with nutmeg.

Set over hot – not boiling – water and cook for about 10 minutes, stirring all the time, until the sauce has thickened. Serve at once, or keep warm over hot water.

FLUFFY BUTTER SAUCE

A cold sauce for steamed puddings, sweet pies and waffles.

Makes about 1½ cups

2 tblsp unsalted butter, at room temperature
2 cups confectioners' sugar, sifted
¼ cup heavy cream
2 large egg whites
2–3 tsp amontillado or cream sherry wine, rum or port wine, or a few drops of vanilla

Beat the butter until very soft and creamy, then gradually beat in the sugar. Beat in half the cream, 1 tblsp at a time. Beat the egg whites until stiff peaks form, then fold them into the creamed butter mixture with the remaining cream. Fold in the sherry or other flavoring. Pile into a bowl or sauce-boat and chill.

FOAMING BUTTER SAUCE

The perfect hot sauce for steamed sponge puddings – or plum pudding, for a change.

Makes 1½ cups

½ cup unsalted butter, softened
1½ cups confectioners' sugar, sifted
1 large egg, separated
1 tsp vanilla, 1 tblsp brandy, or 2 tblsp port or amontillado or cream sherry wine

Whisk the butter and sugar in the top of a double boiler, off the heat, until pale and fluffy. Whisk in the egg yolk. Slowly whisk in the vanilla or alcohol. Set over hot – not boiling – water and cook for about 5 minutes, stirring all the time, until slightly thickened.

Using clean, dry beaters, beat the egg white until stiff. Lightly fold into the sauce. Serve hot or very cold, but do not reheat.

FONDUE SAUCES

Delicious hot sauces for dipping ladyfingers, cubes of pineapple, halved apricots or pieces of sponge cake on long forks: see Chocolate Fondue (page 135), Fruity Fondue (right) and Spoom (page 157).

FRANGIPANE

An Italian invention introduced to France over 300 years ago, this perfumed almond custard is used to fill crêpes, choux pastries and fruit tarts. Frangipane will keep for 5–6 days in the refrigerator, and can be frozen for up to 3 months.

Makes about 2 cups

1 cup milk
1 large egg
1 large egg yolk
½ cup sugar
2 tblsp flour
3 tblsp butter
Few drops of almond extract
Few drops of orange-flower water or vanilla
¾ cup finely crushed macaroons or ground almonds
2 tblsp kirsch (optional)

Scald the milk. Meanwhile, combine the egg, egg yolk and sugar in the top of a double boiler. Whisk over hot – but not boiling – water until the mixture is thick enough to fall in a satiny ribbon when the beaters are lifted. Whisk in the flour, a little at a time. Whisk in the milk.

Pour the mixture into a clean heavy-based saucepan. Stir over very low heat until it starts to stiffen, then beat vigorously for 2–3 minutes, taking care the paste does not scorch on the bottom of the pan. Off the heat, beat in the butter and flavorings, then the macaroons or almonds and kirsch, if using. Cover the surface with wax paper or plastic wrap and leave until cold.

FRUIT SAUCES

Hot and cold fruit sauces are listed under the type of fruit. Sauces not in the Sweet Sauces, or not listed under their fruit are: Gooseberry Sauce and Rhubarb Sauce (page 49), Golden Lemon Sauce (page 142), Heady Cherry Sauce (page 143), Port Wine Plum Sauce (page 149), Melba Sauce (page 145), Redberry Sauce (page 152), Spiced Mango Sauce (page 157) and Whipped Banana Topping (page 161).

FRUIT SUNDAE SAUCE

A colorful cold sauce with a fresh flavor to pour over ice cream, chilled soufflés, meringues and molded creams.

Makes about 1 cup

1 lb (2 cups) blackberries, raspberries or strawberries, or a mixture of these
Sifted confectioners' sugar, to taste
Dash of kirsch, maraschino, light rum or orange juice

Hull any strawberries used. Purée the fruit in the blender, then press through a nylon sieve to remove seeds. Sweeten to taste with confectioner's sugar and flavor with liqueur or orange juice. Chill before serving.

FRUITY CREAM CHEESE

A cold, creamy dressing for fruit salads or chilled compotes, it is also delicious in crisp pastry cases, or as a cake topping. If using a cream cheese, choose a brand which is "stabilized" or has 30% or less fat, so that it will not turn grainy when beaten.

Makes about 1½ cups

½ lb fresh soft fruit, such as apricots, plums, peaches, raspberries, strawberries, blackberries or bananas
1 tsp lemon juice
½ lb (1 cup) Fromage blanc, Quark or a cream cheese
1–2 drops of almond or vanilla extract
¼ cup confectioners' sugar, or to taste

Prepare and chop the fruit, then purée with the lemon juice in the blender. If using cream cheese, beat it until very soft and creamy. Using a fork, slowly blend in the fruit purée and extract, then sweeten to taste with confectioners' sugar. Chill until ready to serve.

This sauce can be made with puréed, drained canned or poached fruit and the sugar omitted.

FRUITY FONDUE

A zingy, hot sauce for dipping cubes of fruit or firm sponge cake on long-handled forks. It also makes a good pouring sauce for raisin puddings, and traditional hot puddings like brown Betty.

Makes 1 cup
½ cup unsweetened pineapple juice
½ cup unsweetened orange juice
2 tblsp confectioners' sugar
1½ tblsp cornstarch
Finely grated rind and juice of 1 lemon or ½ lime
1–2 tblsp kirsch

Heat the pineapple and orange juices with the sugar in a fondue pot on the stove. Blend the cornstarch with 2 tblsp water, add a little hot juice and return to the pan. Add the lemon or lime rind and juice and bring to a boil, stirring. Simmer for 2–3 minutes or until thickened and smooth. Remove from the heat, stir in the kirsch and serve, over a table burner if possible.

For **Pineapple Orange Sauce**, for pouring, add ½ cup finely chopped pineapple (fresh or canned) to the thickened sauce and heat through before adding the kirsch. Serve over ice cream or hot fritters.

FUDGY CREAM

A wickedly rich, hot sauce for spooning over chocolate or nut ice cream or frozen yogurt, waffles, crêpes and creamy grain puddings.

Makes 1¾ cups
½ cup butter, diced
⅔ cup firmly packed light brown sugar
½ cup sugar
1 cup evaporated milk
1 tblsp dark rum (optional)

Dissolve the butter and sugars in a heavy-based saucepan over medium heat. Stir in the milk, bring slowly to a boil and simmer for 5 minutes, stirring occasionally. Off the heat stir in the rum, if using. Serve hot or warm: the sauce stiffens as it cools.

For **Chocolate Fudge Sauce**, melt 4 (1-oz) squares semisweet chocolate, coarsely grated, with the sugars.

For **Nutty Fudge Sauce** or **Raisin Fudge Sauce**, stir ½ cup chopped nuts or ⅓ cup raisins into the sauce at the end.

GANACHE

The most luxurious of chocolate icings; use it for topping and filling coffee and chocolate cakes and tortes of all sorts. It also pipes well. This quantity will fill and cover an 8 in cake. Ganache also makes a soft dip for unhulled strawberries while barely warm – and a luxurious sauce for ice cream and hot chocolate soufflés when hot.

Makes about 2 cups

8 (1-oz) squares semisweet or sweet chocolate, in pieces
1 cup heavy cream
1 tblsp dark rum

Put the chocolate and cream in a heavy-based saucepan and heat gently, stirring from time to time, until the chocolate has melted. Remove from the heat and cool until beginning to thicken. Add the rum and whisk for several minutes until the cream becomes very fluffy and lightens in color. It sets firmly once chilled, so use it for filling or piping before it sets – and make sure your timing is right if you want to use it as a dip for strawberries.

Left over ganache can be rolled into balls and coated with cocoa or chocolate sprinkles to make unusual chocolate truffles.

GINGERED HONEY

Serve hot with old-fashioned steamed puddings, or cold with greengage mousse, swirled into yogurt, or with wedges of honeydew melon for an appetizer. The coriander seeds add a distinctive flavor.

Makes ⅔ cup

1 tblsp chopped stem ginger
1 tblsp stem ginger syrup
½ cup clear honey
Finely grated rind and juice of ½ lemon
1 tblsp butter
1 tsp coriander seeds (optional)

Put the chopped ginger, ginger syrup, honey, lemon rind and juice, and butter into a small, heavy-based pan. If using coriander, tie the seeds in a piece of cheesecloth and crush with a rolling pin, then add to the pan. Heat gently, stirring frequently, until the sauce has blended; do not boil, or it will become thick toffee. Discard the coriander, if used, and serve the sauce hot or cold.

GINGER SYRUP SAUCE

A delicious cold syrup for melon, pears or citrus salads.

Makes about ⅔ cup

½ cup sugar
Grated rind and juice of ½ lemon
1 tblsp finely chopped stem ginger
1–2 tblsp ginger wine or stem ginger syrup

Put the sugar into a heavy-based saucepan with ½ cup water. Heat gently, stirring occasionally, until the sugar has dissolved, then boil gently for 2 minutes. Off the heat stir in the lemon rind and juice and chopped ginger. When cold, stir in the wine or syrup to taste. Chill before serving.

GOLDEN LEMON SAUCE

A hot, rather buttery, lemon custard for hot raisin puddings.

Makes about 1¼ cups

1 tblsp cornstarch
½ cup sugar
2 tblsp butter
Finely grated rind and juice of 1 lemon
Tiny pinch of grated nutmeg (optional)

Mix the cornstarch and sugar in a small heavy-based saucepan. Gradually stir in 1 cup water. Bring slowly to a boil and simmer, stirring, for 2–3 minutes until thickened and smooth. Off the heat stir in the butter, and lemon rind and juice. Flavor to taste with nutmeg, if using.

For tangy **Lemon 'n' Lime Sauce**, use the grated rind and juice of 1 lime and 1 tblsp lemon juice instead of the whole lemon.

GREEN PEPPERCORN SYRUP

Pepper, surprisingly, brings out the flavor of fresh fruit — a sprinkling of freshly ground black pepper over strawberries and cream, for instance, is very effective and certainly makes a talking point. Try this hot, savory syrup with poached pears or strawberries; just heat the fruit through, no more, in the syrup. See also Curry Sour Cream (page 157).

Makes 1 cup

1 cup sugar
Juice of 2 oranges
Juice of 1 lemon
Finely pared rind of 1 orange
1 tblsp green peppercorns, rinsed

Stir the sugar in a pan over medium heat with 1 tblsp water until it dissolves, then cook over high heat until it turns golden brown. Quickly add the orange and lemon juices, standing back as it will splutter!

Add ¾ cup water and the orange rind and stir until the caramel has dissolved, then boil until the syrup has reduced to 1 cup. Fish out the orange rind and add the peppercorns. Heat through for 1 minute with the fruit.

HARD SAUCE

Hard sauces, the American term for cold, sweet-flavored butters, are popular served with rich, hot fruit and ginger puddings, or baked apples and bananas because they melt on top! Best known is Brandy Butter (page 132). Hard sauces can also be used as a spread for plain cookies, or an icing on sponge and coffee cakes. Despite the name, a hard sauce should be soft enough to spoon or spread. It can be chilled until very firm, then cut into fancy shapes.

Makes 1 cup
½ cup unsalted butter, at room temperature
½ cup granulated or confectioners' sugar, sifted
2–3 tblsp Grand Marnier, kirsch or other eau-de-vie

Beat the butter until pale and creamy, then gradually beat in the sugar. When most of the sugar has been incorporated, beat in the liqueur a little at a time to prevent curdling, alternating it with the remaining sugar. Beat until the sauce is light and fluffy. Pile into a bowl and serve with a spoon.

For **Orange or Lemon Butter**, beat in the finely grated rind of 1 orange and 1–2 tblsp juice. Omit the liqueur.

For **Vanilla Butter**, use vanilla sugar or flavor with vanilla extract.

For **Spice Butter**, use brown sugar and beat in 1–2 tsp ground cinnamon or apple pie spice and ⅛ tsp of ground cloves. Omit the liqueur.

For **Fruit Butter**, use confectioners' sugar and omit the liqueur. Beat in ¼ cup heavy cream and ½ cup crushed or mashed strawberries, raspberries or bananas.

HAZELNUT CREAM

Ideal for sandwiching small meringues, this cream also makes a rich, thick topping for strawberries and other soft fresh fruit or for coffee desserts. Double the quantity for refrigerator cakes such as layered ladyfingers.

Makes 1½ cups
½ cup hazelnuts
3 tblsp sugar
¼ cup butter
3 tblsp Grand Marnier or frozen orange juice concentrate
½ cup heavy cream

Toast the hazelnuts at 225° for about 15 minutes (do not let them color too much). Rub off the skins, if necessary, in a dish towel. Grind finely in a food processor or nut grinder. Add the sugar and blend briefly, then blend in the butter. Beat in the Grand Marnier or orange juice concentrate. Whip the cream until soft peaks form, then fold in the hazelnut purée. Chill.

For **Coffee and Hazelnut Cream**, use a coffee liqueur instead of the orange liqueur or juice.

HEADY CHERRY SAUCE

Serve cold with banana splits, sponge cake and ice cream. For a hot alcoholic sauce, see Cherry Jubilee (page 134).

Makes 1½ cups
1 lb (1 pint) pitted cherries
½ cup sugar
¼ cup kirsch, maraschino or Amaretto
2 tsp arrowroot

Simmer the cherries, covered, in a heavy-based saucepan with the sugar, liqueur and ¼ cup water for 5 minutes. Blend the arrowroot with 2 tblsp water, stir in a little hot juice and return to the pan. Bring slowly to simmering point and cook, stirring constantly, until the sauce has cleared and thickened slightly. Remove from the heat and leave until cold.

HONEY SAUCES

See Burnt Honey Cream (page 133) and Gingered Honey (page 142).

INSTANT COFFEE CREAM

An easy sauce, quickly made from pantry ingredients; it can be used hot or cold for jazzing up ice cream, plain chocolate desserts or yogurt.

Makes 1 cup

1 cup evaporated milk
2 tblsp instant coffee powder
1 tblsp cornstarch
1–2 drops of vanilla
Sugar (optional)

Stir the milk and coffee in a small heavy-based saucepan, until the coffee has dissolved. Blend the cornstarch with 2 tblsp milky coffee, then return to the pan. Bring to a boil, stirring, and simmer for 1–2 minutes, until thick and smooth. Off the heat, stir in the vanilla and add sugar, if wished. Serve hot or cold.

For **Coffee and Nut Sauce**, add ½ cup coarsely chopped walnuts, almonds, pecans or toasted, skinned hazelnuts.

ITALIAN MERINGUE

This is softer than baked meringue – the egg whites are cooked by the hot syrup. Swirl over cold tarts, fruit desserts, angel cakes, cup cakes and other light sponges. This quantity will coat an 8 in cake.

Makes 1½ cups

1 cup sugar
¼ tsp cream of tartar
3 large egg whites

Heat the sugar and cream of tartar gently with ½ cup water in a heavy-based saucepan, stirring until the sugar has dissolved. Increase the heat and boil without stirring until the syrup reaches 240° on a candy thermometer; at this temperature a little dropped into cold water will form a soft ball.

While the syrup is boiling, beat the egg whites until soft peaks form. When the syrup reaches the right temperature, pour it, in a thin stream, onto the egg whites, beating all the time. Continue beating until the meringue is cool and shiny, then use at once.

For **Coffee Meringue Topping**, add 1 tblsp instant coffee powder with the water.

JAMMY JAMMY

Old-fashioned, hot and sticky, this sauce makes sponges and baked or steamed puddings irresistible.

Makes 1 cup

¼ cup jam or marmalade
Finely grated rind and juice of ½ lemon
1 tblsp arrowroot
1 tblsp kirsch or brandy (optional)

Melt the jam slowly with 1 cup water in a small heavy-based saucepan, stirring. Add the lemon rind and juice and simmer for 3–4 minutes. Blend the arrowroot with 1 tblsp water. Add a little hot liquid and stir back into the pan. Simmer gently, stirring, until the sauce has cleared and thickened. Off the heat stir in the kirsch or brandy, if using. Serve at once.

LEMON SAUCES

Lemon-flavored sauces are Golden Lemon Sauce (page 142), Coconut Lemon Sauce (page 137), Citrus Fluff (page 136), Lemon Sabayon Sauce (page 156) and Pâtissier's Lemon Sauce (page 148). Firmer sauces are Lemon Butter (page 143) and Lemon Buttercream (page 138).

MAPLE CREAM

For pancakes, waffles and ice cream; serve hot or cold.

Makes 1¼ cups
½ cup maple syrup
½ cup heavy cream
¼ cup butter
½ cup chopped hazelnuts, pecans or walnuts

Put the maple syrup, cream and butter in a small heavy-based saucepan and stir over low heat until blended. Bring to a boil and simmer for 6–7 minutes, until the sauce is syrupy. Off the heat stir in the nuts. Serve at once or leave until cold; stir again before serving.

Black **Treacle Cream** and **Molasses Cream** can be made the same way.

MAPLE AND ORANGE PANCAKE SAUCE

This hot sauce is delicious over waffles and coffee-flavored desserts.

Makes 1 cup
½ cup maple syrup
⅓ cup firmly packed brown sugar
¼ cup butter
Grated rind and juice of 2 oranges

Put the maple syrup into a small heavy-based saucepan with the sugar, butter and orange rind and juice. Stir over low heat until smoothly blended and warmed. Serve at once.

MELBA SAUCE

A vibrant purée, this was invented by Escoffier, celebrated French chef at the Savoy Hotel, London, who poured it over peaches on vanilla ice cream and created Peach Melba in honor of the Australian opera singer Dame Nellie Melba. This chilled purée can also be used over strawberries or a pyramid of cream puffs, and is good with cold mousses or frozen vanilla yogurt.

Makes 1½ cups
1 lb (2 pints) raspberries
6–8 tblsp confectioners' sugar, sifted

Purée the raspberries in the blender, then sieve into a small pan. Add sugar to taste and stir over a low heat until the sugar has dissolved. Leave until cold, then chill.

For a thicker sauce, omit the sugar. Melt ¼ cup currant jelly and add the sieved purée. Blend 2 tblsp cornstarch with 1 tblsp water and stir into the purée. Simmer gently, stirring, until thickened slightly. Cool then chill.

MOCHA MOUSSELINE

The port of Moka on the Red Sea, now silted up, was the port exporting all coffee to Europe until the end of the 17th century. Its name is given to coffee and chocolate mixtures like this hot sauce. Serve it with coffee or chocolate desserts.

Makes 1 cup
1 large egg
1 large egg yolk
2 tblsp sugar
2 tsp instant coffee powder
2 tsp cocoa powder

Put the whole egg and yolk in the top of a double boiler with the sugar. Dissolve the coffee and cocoa in 2 tblsp hot water and add. Whisk over hot – not boiling – water until thick and mousse-like. Serve at once.

The sauce can be made with 2 tblsp sherry, wine or fruit juice instead of coffee and cocoa.

Above: *A traditional apple pie is served with rich, vanilla-flavored custard sauce – Crème Anglaise.*

Right: *Frothy, hot Sabayon is the French name for Italian zabaione; pour it over a fruit pudding – or into a custard glass and eat it just as it is!*

Far right: *Send delicate French crêpes flaming to the table soaked in Suzette Sauce – a combination of butter, orange and liqueur.*

MOCK CREAM

This excellent – and less expensive – alternative to real dairy cream is good for emergencies. It can safely be used in gelatin desserts or ice cream and is delicious spooned over soft fruit. Without the sugar it can be used in savory mousses.

Makes 1 cup

½ cup unsalted butter, diced
½ cup milk
1 tsp unflavored gelatin
1–2 tsp sugar (optional)

Heat the butter and milk very gently in a heavy-based saucepan, until the butter starts to melt. Remove from the heat and stir until melted.

Sprinkle the gelatin over 2 tsp water in a heatproof bowl. Stir in a little of the buttered milk, adding the sugar (for a sweet cream only). Set the bowl over a pan of simmering – not boiling – water and stir until the gelatin has dissolved. Stir in the remaining buttered milk.

Pour into a blender and purée for 30 seconds. Spoon into a bowl, cover and chill for 8 hours before using.

NUT SAUCES

Praline flavoring (page 152) – almonds in caramel – can also be made with other nuts. For creams, see Hazelnut Cream (page 143), Frangipane (page 140) and Walnut Cream (page 161). Other nut sauces are Walnut or Almond Butterscotch Sauce (page 133), Coffee and Nut Sauce (page 144) and Nutty Fudge Sauce (page 141).

ORANGE YOGURT

A tangy, chilled sauce for fruit compotes or salads, hot pears and sponge puddings. See also Citrus Fluff (page 136) and Suzette Sauce (page 160).

Makes 1½ cups

4 oranges
1 tblsp lemon juice
2 tblsp clear honey
1 cup plain Yogurt, homemade if possible (page 106)

Finely grate the rind from the oranges and reserve. Thickly peel the oranges, taking care to remove every scrap of bitter white pith. Remove the sections by cutting in between the membrane. Remove any seeds, then roughly chop the flesh.

Purée the chopped orange sections with the orange rind, lemon juice, honey and yogurt in the blender until smooth. Pour into a pitcher and chill before serving.

PATISSIER'S LEMON SAUCE

Adding a lemon sauce is a very successful way of flavoring whipped cream without curdling it. Use the lemon cream to layer cakes, tortes and large meringues. Without the cream, the sauce jellies slightly: with its good flavor of lemons use it to fill cream puffs, sweet rolls or layered flaky pastry. Or serve it hot as a pouring sauce for sponge pudding. Double the quantity if omitting the cream.

Makes 1½ cups

1 large egg
⅔ cup sugar
Grated rind and juice of 1 lemon
2 tblsp flour
1 cup heavy cream, whipped (optional)

Whisk together the egg, sugar and lemon rind until foamy. Measure the lemon juice and make it up to ½ cup with water. Beat this into the egg mixture, alternately with the flour.

Pour the mixture into a small, heavy-based saucepan and bring to a boil over low heat, stirring constantly. Cook, stirring, for 3–5 minutes until smooth and thick. Serve hot, as it is, or leave until cold. If wished, fold in the whipped cream before using.

PEACH SAUCE

A hot sauce to spoon over ice cream-filled meringues or sweet soft cheese desserts. See also Peach Liqueur Sauce (page 131).

Makes about 1 cup
6 large, ripe peaches
Few drops of lemon juice
3 tblsp brandy or rum
1 tblsp maraschino
Vanilla sugar (page 128) or confectioners' sugar, to taste

Cover the peaches with boiling water, leave for 1 minute, then slip off the skins. Halve, pit and chop the peaches, sprinkling with a little lemon juice to prevent browning.

Purée the peaches with the brandy or rum and maraschino in a blender, then pour into a small heavy-based pan. Sweeten to taste with sugar and heat gently, stirring, until the sauce is warmed through. (Do not allow the sauce to boil or it will lose its fresh flavor.)

Nectarines can be used instead of peaches; peel off their skins with a knife.

PINEAPPLE SAUCE

Serve hot with hot chocolate soufflés and deep-fried beignets or fritters. See also Fruity Fondue (page 141).

Makes 1¼ cups
¾ cup unsweetened pineapple juice
2 tblsp sugar
2 tsp arrowroot
1 tsp lemon juice
1 cup skinned, cored and finely chopped fresh pineapple
1–2 tblsp white rum or kirsch (optional)

Bring the pineapple juice and sugar to a boil in a small heavy-based saucepan. Blend the arrowroot with 2 tblsp water, add a little hot liquid and stir back into the pan. Simmer, stirring, until the sauce has cleared. Add the lemon juice and pineapple and stir until heated through. Off the heat add the rum or kirsch, if wished. Serve hot.

If preferred, make the sauce with 1 cup canned crushed pineapple. Drain off the syrup and make up to ¾ cup with water; use in place of the pineapple juice. Add sugar to taste as pineapple syrups are usually heavily sweetened.

For **Pineapple and Balm Sauce**, stir in finely chopped fresh lemon balm, to taste, just before serving.

For **Pineapple and Kumquat Sauce**, add ¼ cup thinly sliced and seeded kumquats with the chopped pineapple.

PLUM SAUCES
Plums can be used for Damson Cheese (page 87) and for a delicious sauce with port wine (see below).

PORT WINE PLUM SAUCE

Serve this rich and red sauce hot to liven up the plainest sponge or batter pudding. It is also delicious cold, with vanilla or hazelnut ice cream, or yogurt.

Makes about 1 cup
½ lb red plums, halved and pitted
2 tblsp sugar, or to taste
½ cup tawny port or red wine
Finely grated rind and juice of ½ lemon
2 in piece cinnamon stick
3 whole cloves

Heat the plums slowly in a heavy-based saucepan with 2 tblsp sugar, the port or red wine, lemon rind and juice and spices. Simmer, covered, for 5 minutes, until very soft. Taste and add more sugar, if liked. Discard the spices before serving.

For **Prune Sauce**, use chopped and pitted semi-dried prunes instead of plums.

Overleaf: *For summer fruit and summer weather, Crème Fraîche, Crème Pâtissière and heavy cream are unsurpassed.*

PRALINE

Scatter this crunchy nut topping over soft mousses and custards, vanilla pudding, ice cream or frozen yogurt, or creamy cakes for a good texture contrast. It can also be sprinkled on cream poured over fruit salads. Praline is worth making in quantity as it keeps well for several weeks in an airtight container. See Praline Buttercream (page 138).

Makes 1 cup
½ cup sugar
1 cup whole, unskinned almonds, lightly toasted

Put the sugar with ¼ cup cold water into a small heavy-based saucepan and heat very gently until dissolved. Increase the heat and cook until the syrup turns a deep caramel color. Add the toasted almonds and mix well, then immediately pour onto an oiled foil-lined baking sheet; leave until cold.

Break the cold praline into pieces with the end of a rolling pin. Put in a strong plastic bag and crush finely with the rolling pin, or grind in an electric mill.

RASPBERRY SAUCES

Most famous of the raspberry sauces are Melba Sauce (page 145) and Redberry Sauce (below). See also Fruit Sundae Sauce (page 140) and Spoom (page 157).

REDBERRY SAUCE

A delicious silky-smooth purée to serve cold with meringue and ice cream desserts, molded creams or creamy grain puddings, slices of cheesecake or soft sponges. It can also be served, well chilled, as a summer dessert soup, accompanied by cream – called "Kissel" in North East Europe and "Rødgrød" in Denmark.

Makes 2 cups

1 lb (2 pints) raspberries
1 lb (2 pints) red currants, stripped from the stalks
½ cup sugar, or to taste
¼ cup potato flour, or 1 tblsp cornstarch
Finely grated rind of 1 orange

Purée the fruit in the blender, then press through a nylon sieve into a heavy-based saucepan. Add sugar to taste. Stir over low heat until dissolved. Blend the flour or cornstarch with 1 tblsp water, then stir in 2–3 tblsp warm purée. Return to the pan and bring slowly to simmering. Keep the heat low and stir constantly to prevent scorching. Stir in the orange rind. Simmer 1–2 minutes until thickened and smooth. Leave until cold. Serve at room temperature or chilled.

Try other fruit combinations: strawberries and raspberries, blackberries and black currants, or peaches and cherries. Add a little port wine or liqueur when cold. If using frozen fruit, thaw and drain well, or the sauce will be watery.

RED WINE SYRUP

Traditionally a whole bottle of claret was used to poach fruit such as pears. Use this spiced red wine syrup to steep less-than-perfect peaches for serving hot (or cold). It is also good with prunes. The syrup can be boiled down to a syrupy glaze and used to coat pears: include a little red food coloring.

Makes 2½ cups

1 cup granulated sugar, or 1⅓ cups firmly packed brown sugar
1 in piece stick cinnamon, or pinch of ground cinnamon
Thinly pared strip of orange rind
Seeds of 2 cardamom pods, or pinch of ground cardamom
1½ cups light red wine

Put the sugar, cinnamon, orange rind and cardamom in a large saucepan with ½ cup water. Bring to a boil. Simmer for 15 minutes (with any fruit needing 30–45 minutes cooking). Add the red wine and simmer for a further 15 minutes (more, if needed, for obstinate, woody pears). Strain out whole spices.

If wished, the fruit can be removed and the syrup boiled to reduce to a smaller quantity of thicker syrup for pouring cold over cold fruit.

RHUBARB SAUCE

The Rhubarb Sauce given on page 49 is suitable for desserts.

RICH RUM CREAM

Especially good, chilled, over apple, pear or peach pies and tarts and chocolate puddings.

Makes about 2 cups

1 cup milk
2 large egg yolks
½ cup sugar
Finely grated rind of ½ lemon
4–6 tblsp dark rum
½ cup heavy cream

Scald the milk in the top pan of a double boiler over direct heat. Beat the egg yolks and sugar together until pale and thick, then slowly stir in the hot milk. Pour the mixture back into the pan. Place over hot – not boiling – water and stir until the custard is thick enough to coat the back of the spoon. Do not allow the custard to approach the boil or it will turn lumpy.

Strain the custard into a bowl, then stir in the lemon rind and rum. Cover the surface with plastic wrap or wax paper and leave until cold.

Whip the cream until it will hold its shape. Stir 2 tblsp of the cream into the rum custard, then fold in the rest. Chill.

ROSE-WATER SYRUP

Use this delicious cold syrup from the Middle East for dunking hot sweet beignets and other deep-fried pastries, and pour it over sweets wherever honey is specified. It gives Greek baklava its special taste. It is also good with cold milky and yogurt desserts. Add a few spoonfuls to a fruit salad for a mysterious Middle Eastern flavor.

Orange-flower water can be used in the same way. Both these flavorings were used in the West in medieval times for flavoring creams, and indeed until the early 19th century. It was Carême, France's most distinguished chef, who banished these subtle Middle Eastern flavorings and made the simpler flavors of fruit – orange and lemon – popular for custards.

Makes 3 cups

1½ cups sugar
2 tblsp rose-water

Heat the sugar gently with 1½ cups water in a heavy-based saucepan, stirring until dissolved. Bring to a boil, then cook for 8 minutes until syrupy. Off the heat stir in the rose-water, then cool and chill. It keeps, covered, in the refrigerator almost indefinitely.

RUM AND RAISIN SAUCE

Serve hot with banana splits, fried apple rings or fritters, cold with small cakes. See also Rich Rum Cream (left) and Raisin Fudge Sauce (page 141).

Makes 1½ cups

⅔ cup raisins
1 cup firmly packed brown sugar
Small pinch of salt
¼ cup dark rum
Few drops of lemon juice

Simmer the raisins in ½ cup water for 10 minutes, until soft. Add the sugar and salt and stir until dissolved. Simmer for 10 minutes. Stir in the rum and lemon juice to taste and serve hot. The sauce becomes fudgy when cold and may need more lemon juice.

Left: *Baste a classic French savarin ring generously with Savarin Rum Syrup, and allow the yeast cake to soak it up before serving with fresh fruit in the middle.*

Above: *Cold pears on ice cream are served in a coating of hot Chocolate Sauce Belle Hélène for a classic French sweet.*

SABAYON

Serve this foaming wine sauce warm over hot fruit charlottes, steamed puddings and fritters, or with pear pie. The name is a French corruption of "zabaione" and Marsala is the wine traditionally used. It can be replaced by a mixture of orange-flavored liqueur and water. Sabayon can also be served in glasses as a dessert in its own right, with crisp cookies. Do not let it stand, but eat it immediately. It is liable to collapse, when its volume is considerably reduced. There is also a cold wine version, bulked by whipped cream: Wine Foam (page 161).

Makes 1 cup
3 large egg yolks
3 tblsp sugar
½ cup Marsala

Put the egg yolks, sugar and Marsala into the top of a double boiler. Set over hot – not boiling – water and whisk until the sauce becomes thick and creamy. Serve warm or it will collapse.

For **Lemon Sabayon Sauce**, use sweet white wine with the finely grated rind and juice of 1 lemon.

SAUTERNES SAUCE

In 19th century France this was called "chaudeau sauce" – hot water sauce – because it was cooked over hot water, rather like Sabayon (above). However, it is less fluffy with a consistency similar to custard. It is made with the luscious sweet white wine of Bordeaux. Look for a Sauternes bottled in clear (not green) glass; this indicates the wine is very sweet. Drink the rest with the dessert. Serve the sauce hot with hot apple tart, pear pie or pastry turnovers. It is also good with hot baked sponge puddings, especially those with a fruity layer.

Makes 2 cups
3 large eggs
6 tblsp sugar
2 cups Sauternes or other sweet white wine
1 tblsp amontillado or cream sherry wine

Beat the eggs lightly together in the top of a double boiler, off the heat, with a wooden spoon. Add the sugar, then beat until thick and pale. Gradually stir in the wine and sherry.

Set over hot – not boiling – water and cook for about 10 minutes, stirring constantly, until thick enough to coat the back of the spoon. Do not boil, or it will turn lumpy. Serve at once or keep warm over hot water.

SAVARIN RUM SYRUP

The history of this rum syrup goes back to the early 18th century: King Stanislaw Lesczynski of Poland poured rum over his favorite cake – a sweet yeast cake called Kugelhupf – and named it "Ali Baba," after the hero in his favorite book, The Thousand and One Nights. The title was later shortened to "baba." Stanislaw lost his throne and was exiled to Lorraine in France, where the king, Louis XV, was his father-in-law. The French were delighted with the new idea and set to work to improve on it. Invented in the 1840s, the cake and the rum syrup with which it was saturated was named after the French gourmet Brillat-Savarin. Use the syrup, well-laced with alcohol, while still warm for basting a 9 in savarin ring or several babas. It can also be used to moisten other cake layers.

Makes 2 cups
1 cup sugar
Finely grated rind of 1 lemon
½ cup dark rum

Heat the sugar gently with 1½ cups water in a heavy-based saucepan, stirring until dissolved. Bring to a boil and boil for 4–5 minutes without stirring. Off the heat stir in the lemon rind and rum. Use for soaking cakes while it is still warm.

For **Vanilla Syrup**, omit the lemon rind and rum. Add a split vanilla bean to the sugar and increase the water to 2 cups.

SHERRY CUSTARD

Superb, chilled, with raspberries, strawberries, fruit tarts or as a dessert topping.

Makes 1½ cups
3 large egg yolks, lightly beaten
½ cup sugar
½ cup pale cream sherry
½ cup heavy cream

Combine the egg yolks and sugar in the top of a double boiler and whisk until thick and creamy. Slowly stir in the sherry. Set over hot – not boiling – water and stir until the custard is thick enough to coat the back of the spoon. Do not allow it to approach the boil or it will turn lumpy. Strain into a bowl, cover with plastic wrap or wax paper and leave until cold.

Whip the cream until it holds its shape, then fold into the sherry custard. Chill.

SOUR CREAM SAUCE

Completely simple, but many prefer it to cream itself; for all fruit desserts.

Makes 1 cup
1 cup sour cream
4–6 tblsp granulated or brown sugar
2 tsp finely chopped fresh mint, or 2–3 drops of vanilla

Stir the sour cream until smooth, then stir in the sugar and mint or vanilla. Serve at once or chill.

Surprising as it may sound **Curry Sour Cream** is also a success with fresh fruit. Replace the sugar and mint with 3 tblsp mild vinegar, ¼ tsp curry powder and 1 tsp sugar and mix into the sour cream.

SPICED MANGO SAUCE

This cold sauce is particularly good with individual rice puddings or custards and angel cake. It can also be swirled into yogurt.

Makes 1 cup
2 large ripe mangoes, skinned, seeded and roughly chopped

1 tsp lemon juice
Large pinch of ground cinnamon
1–2 tsp confectioners' sugar
1 tblsp orange liqueur (optional)

Purée the mango flesh with the lemon juice in a blender. Pour into a bowl and stir in the cinnamon. Sweeten to taste with confectioners' sugar and add the liqueur, if using. Cover and chill.

A 16-oz can well-drained mango slices can be used instead of fresh; omit the sugar.

SPOOM

This hot fruity froth makes a lovely fondue sauce, or can be eaten alone as a dessert – it is so light the volume doesn't matter. It is also delicious with milky grain puddings. Spoom is one of the few ways of using frozen strawberries, which are otherwise rather sad when thawed. Thaw frozen fruit thoroughly and drain well or the purée will be very thin. As it holds its volume when cold, spoom makes an economical and unusual sauce for summer fruit. Match the fruit in the sauce to the fruit you are serving.

Makes 5 cups

1 cup unsweetened, thickish fruit purée, from plums,
   cherries, strawberries, black currants, etc.
½ cup sugar
1 tsp lemon or orange juice
1 large egg white

Put the purée in a heatproof bowl with the sugar and add lemon or orange juice to taste. Heat through in the top of a double boiler.

Beat the egg white until stiff. Fold the white into the purée, then beat until the mixture is thick and foamy and increased in volume like a soufflé, and stiff enough to hold peaks. Serve at once or leave until cold.

For cold **Fruit Foam**, from southern Germany, combine the ingredients (no need to beat the white first) and beat to a foam. Serve at once over angel cake or any cold dessert. This is a very useful sauce as it works with a thin fruit purée, and one fruit poured over a different one is delicious when you have no cream or ice cream. It also makes a change!

Above: *Strawberries and red currants make a special Fruit Sundae Sauce for vanilla ice cream and strawberries.*

Left: *Chocolate Marquise is poured over chocolate and vanilla ice creams, layered with chopped nuts, for a special treat.*

Right: *Three hot sauces for ice cream. Left, Butterscotch Syrup;* right, *Caramel Sauce;* in the center, *sieved Heady Cherry Sauce.*

STRABERRY CREAM

A chilled cream that makes the best of less-than-perfect berries. Pour it over peaches, raspberries, molded creams or a combination fruit sundae.

Makes 1¼ cups
1 lb (1½ cups) strawberries, hulled
3 tblsp currant jelly
Finely grated rind of 1 orange
2 tblsp orange juice
½ cup sour cream, or plain Yogurt, homemade if possible
   (page 106)

Purée the strawberries in a blender, then sieve into a bowl. Combine the jelly, orange rind and juice in a small saucepan and stir over low heat until the jelly has melted. Stir into the strawberry purée. Blend in the sour cream or yogurt and chill.
   For **Strawberry and Banana Sauce**, replace half the strawberries with 2 small, firm bananas.
   For **Brandied Strawberry Sauce**, use heavy instead of sour cream; stir in 1–2 tblsp brandy.

SUZETTE SAUCE

The perfect finish for sweet crêpes, this warm sauce is named for a star at the Comédie Française in Paris who was the "petite amie" of British King Edward VII. A number of chefs, including Henri Charpentier, claim to have invented it. The sauce is also delicious over ice cream or fritters. Van Der Hum is a South African liqueur, made from a small citrus fruit, like a tangerine.

Makes 1 cup
½ cup unsalted butter, diced
½ cup sugar
Finely grated rind and juice of 3 tangerines or 1 orange
2 tblsp Van Der Hum, Grand Marnier or other orange-
   flavored liqueur
1 tblsp brandy

Combine the butter, sugar, tangerine or orange rind and juice, liqueur and brandy in a small heavy-based saucepan or skillet. Stir over low heat until the sugar has dissolved, then boil for 1 minute or until the sauce is syrupy. Serve warm. Traditionally ready-cooked crêpes are reheated at the table in the sauce.

SYLLABUB

A famous medieval wine cream, good by itself and delicious on all chilled fruit. Do not let it stand overnight – it separates.

Makes about 1¾ cups
2 tblsp sweet sherry wine
2 tblsp brandy
¼ cup sugar
Thinly pared rind and juice of ½ lemon
1 cup heavy cream

Combine the sherry, brandy and sugar in a large bowl. Add the lemon rind and juice, stir well, then cover and leave to stand for 2–3 hours for the flavors to blend.
   Discard the lemon rind and beat the mixture until the sugar has dissolved. Slowly beat in the cream and continue beating until the syllabub is light and fluffy and thick enough to hold soft peaks. Serve at once or chill for up to 2 hours.

VANILLA FOAM

A superior "white sauce," chilled, then lightened with egg whites, it goes well with fruit and is quicker and cheaper than Crème Anglaise.

Makes 1½ cups
2 tblsp unsalted butter, at room temperature
1 cup confectioners' sugar
2 tblsp flour
1 large egg, separated
½ tsp vanilla

Beat the butter until pale and creamy. Mix the confectioners' sugar and flour, then beat half into the butter, followed by the egg yolk. Stir in the remaining sugar mixture, followed by ½ cup water.

Pour into a small heavy-based saucepan and stir over low heat until smooth and thickened. Pour into a bowl and stir in the vanilla. Cover the surface with plastic wrap or a butter wrapper and leave until cold. Just before serving beat the egg white until stiff and fold in.

If wished the sauce can be flavored with 2 tblsp sweet sherry or port wine or 1 tblsp orange liqueur instead of vanilla.

WALNUT CREAM

This combination of walnuts and cream is simply made: it makes a delicious filling for coffee meringues and nut layer cakes. Other walnut sauces include Apple and Walnut Sauce (page 130) and Walnut Butterscotch Sauce (page 133).

Makes 1½ cups
2 large egg yolks
½ cup vanilla sugar (page 128), or same quantity granulated sugar and ¼ tsp vanilla
½ cup heavy cream
1¾ cups finely chopped walnuts

Whisk the egg yolks and sugar together until creamy. Whip the cream until stiff peaks form, then beat into the sugar mixture. Beat in the chopped walnuts.

WHIPPED BANANA TOPPING

A fluffy, slightly sweet whip to spoon, cold, over strawberries or peaches, or over a moist walnut, chocolate or coffee-flavored cake.

Makes 1 cup
1 large banana
Few drops of lemon juice
1 large egg white
Pinch of salt
¼ tsp kirsch, or 1 drop of vanilla

Mash the banana with the lemon juice. Beat the egg white until frothy. Add the salt and continue beating until stiff peaks form. Beat the mashed banana until smooth, then gradually beat it into the egg white. Add the kirsch or vanilla and beat a little longer until the banana is smoothly incorporated and the mixture holds its shape.

The mixture can be frozen; serve **Banana Frappé** while still icy, scooped over a hot plum compote, or a fruit pie.

WINE FOAM

Unlike the classic hot Sabayon, this cold version is stable – it contains arrowroot and cream – and can be stored in the refrigerator for a few days. Serve over poached pears and fresh fruit salads, or with light sponge cakes.

Makes 1¼ cups
3 large egg yolks
¼ cup sugar
Pinch of arrowroot
½ cup white wine or dry sherry wine
½ cup heavy cream, lightly whipped

Combine the egg yolks, sugar, arrowroot and wine in the top of a double boiler. Set over hot – not boiling – water, and whisk until very thick. Remove from the heat and whisk until cool, then place the container in a bowl of ice cubes and continue whisking until cold. Fold in the whipped cream.

WINE SAUCES

Sauces based on wine include Sabayon (page 156), Sauternes Sauce (page 156) and Syllabub (left). See also Port Wine Plum Sauce (page 149).

WHAT GOES WITH WHAT

Hot Meat

Beef roasts
Béarnaise (page 24)
Beef stock gravy (page 25)
Bourguignonne (page 28)
Brown sauce (page 29)
Chasseur (page 31)
Chestnut sauce (page 32)
Demi glace (page 40)
Espagnole (page 45)
Herby onion gravy (page 51)
Horseradish cream (page 89)
Light gravy (page 54)
Madeira sauce (page 55)
Meat glaze (page 56–7)
Poivrade (page 63)
Port wine sauce (page 64)
Red currant jelly glaze (page 65)
Red wine sauce (page 66)
Rich gravy (page 66)
Sour cream gravy (page 69)
Soy glaze (page 69)

Beef steaks
Sauces listed for beef roasts
Anchovy butter (page 80)
Anchovy hot butter (page 21)
Béarnaise (page 24)
Colbert butter (page 91)
Black peppercorn butter (page 91)
Creamy mustard sauce (page 36)
Devil sauce (page 41)
Lyonnaise (page 55)
Maître d'hôtel butter (page 91)
Mustard butter (page 91)
Oyster and soy sauce (page 62)
Teriyaki sauce (page 72)
Truffle sauce (page 73)

Boiled ham, tongue and veal
Apricot glaze (page 21)
Béchamel (page 24)
Bigarade (page 26)

Caper sauce (page 30)
Cherry sauce (page 32)
Cider sauce (page 33)
Creamy mustard sauce (page 36)
Green fields sauce (page 50)
Green peppercorn sauce (page 50)
Gumbo (page 51)
Mustard sauce (page 60)
Orange glaze (page 61)
Parsley sauce (page 63)
Poulette (page 64)
Raisin sauce (page 65)
Suprême (page 71)
Velouté (page 74)
Watercress sauce (page 75)
Whiskey cream (page 75)
White wine sauce (page 76)

Braised meat
Agrodolce (page 20)
Apricot and lamb tagine (page 22)
Creole sauce (page 37)
Curry sauce (page 40)
Espagnole (page 45)
Gumbo (page 51)
Korma curry sauce (page 53)
Lyonnaise (page 55)
Mole poblano (page 58)
Raisin sauce (page 65)
Vindaloo curry sauce (page 74)

Dips and relishes for meat
Aïoli (page 80)
Anchoïade (page 109)
Angostura mayonnaise (page 92)
Banana raita (page 81)
Cashew cream (page 81)
Chili dip (page 82)
Chili tomato sauce (page 32)
Coconut sambal (page 83)
Colbert butter (page 91)
Cucumber relish (p. 86)
Cucumber and yogurt dip (page 86)
Devil sauce (page 41)
Green-green dressing (page 116)

Guacamole (page 88)
Hazelnut and almond sauce (p. 88)
Herby garlic mayonnaise (page 92)
Hoisin sauce (page 89)
Horseradish cream (page 89)
Mustard dip (page 94)
Peanut cream (page 100)
Pesto (page 95)
Poor man's caviar (page 96)
Raita (page 96)
Saté sauce (page 100)
Skordalia (page 101)
Soy and ginger dipping sauce (104)
Sweet and sour, Chinese style (p. 71)

Hamburgers
Anchovy butter (page 80)
Barbecue baste, oriental style (p. 22)
Barbecue hot baste (page 23)
Barbecue mustard baste (page 23)
Bordelaise (page 28)
Chili dip (page 82)
Chili tomato sauce (page 32)
Devil sauce (page 41)
Hoisin sauce (page 89)
Hot tomato sauce (page 89)
Mustard butter (page 91)
Mustard dip (page 94)
Raw tomato sauce (page 96)
Rémoulade (page 97)
Tartare (page 105)

Kabobs, broiled foods and bastes for the microwave oven
Apricot glaze (page 21)
Barbecue baste with ginger and soy (page 22)
Barbecue baste Oriental style (page 22)
Barbecue hot baste (page 23)
Barbecue mustard baste (page 23)
Barbecue red baste (page 23)
Chili tomato sauce (page 32)
Chinese sparerib sauce (page 33)
Cumberland sauce (page 86)

Devil sauce (page 41)
Lemon marinade (page 91)
Mustard glaze (page 60)
Orange glaze (page 61)
Parsley jelly (page 93)
Red currant jelly glaze (page 65)
Sesame sauce (page 67)
Teriyaki sauce (page 72)

Lamb chops and noisettes
Sauces listed for lamb roasts
Anchovy hot butter (page 21)
Apricot glaze (page 21)
Barbecue mustard baste (page 23)
Chasseur (page 31)
Hazelnut and almond sauce (p. 88)
Maltaise butter (page 55)
Parsley jelly (page 93)
Pesto (page 95)
Raw tomato sauce (page 96)

Lamb roasts
Bread sauce (page 28)
Celery sauce (page 31)
Cup of coffee sauce (page 37)
Espagnole (page 45)
Herby brown sauce (page 29)
Herby onion gravy (page 51)
Light gravy (page 54)
Mint butter (page 57)
Mint jelly (page 93)
Mint sauce (page 93)
Mustard glaze (page 60)
Port wine sauce (page 64)
Red currant jelly glaze (page 65)
Red wine sauce (page 66)
Rosemary jelly (page 93)
Springtime green sauce (page 70)
Turkey gravy (page 74)

Liver and kidneys
Beef stock gravy (page 25)
Bigarade (liver) (page 26)
Black currant sauce (liver) (page 27)
Bordelaise (page 28)
Bourguignonne (page 28)
Brown sauce (page 29)
Chasseur (page 31)
Chili tomato sauce (page 32)
Creamy mustard sauce (kidneys)
  (page 36)
Creole sauce (page 37)
Deviled cream (page 41)

Herby onion gravy (page 51)
Lyonnaise (liver) (page 55)
Madeira sauce (page 55)
Marsala sauce (liver) (page 56)
Meat glaze (pages 56–57)
Piquant brown sauce (liver) (p. 63)
Port wine sauce (page 64)
Raspberry purée (liver) (page 65)
Rich gravy (page 66)
Robert (liver) (page 66)
Teriyaki sauce (page 72)
Tomato amatriciana (page 72)
Winter tomato sauce (page 76)

Meatballs
Egg and lemon sauce (page 44)
Emergency tomato sauces
  (page 44)
Lyonnaise (page 55)
Mustard sauce (page 60)
Tomato amatriciana (page 72)
Tomato sauce (page 73)
Winter tomato sauce (page 76)

Pork chops and medallions
Sauces listed for pork roasts
Bordelaise (page 28)
Calvados cream (page 30)
Creamy mustard sauce (page 36)
Lyonnaise (page 55)
Marsala sauce (page 56)
Pesto (page 95)
Rémoulade (page 97)
Teriyaki sauce (page 72)

Pork roasts
Apple mayonnaise (page 80)
Apple sauce Normandy-style (130)
Beef stock gravy (page 25)
Brown sauce (page 29)
Cider sauce (page 33)
Damson cheese (page 87)
Espagnole (page 45)
Herby onion gravy (page 51)
Light gravy (page 54)
Mustard sauce (page 60)
Orange pickle (page 94)
Piquant brown sauce (page 63)
Prune sauce (page 65)
Raisin sauce (page 65)
Red wine marinade (page 97)
Robert (page 66)
Sage and onion sauce (page 67)
Soy glaze (page 69)

Hot Duck, Turkey and Game

Duck, goose and turkey
Beef stock gravy (page 25)
Bigarade (page 26)
Black currant sauce (page 27)
Bread sauce (page 28)
Brown sauce (page 29)
Cherry sauce (page 32)
Chestnut sauce (page 32)
Cranberry relish (page 84)
Cranberry spicy jelly (page 84)
Cranberry whole berry sauce (p. 84)
Damson cheese (page 87)
Herby onion gravy (page 51)
Hoisin sauce (page 89)
Light gravy (page 54)
Orange sauce (page 62)
Piquant brown sauce (page 63)
Prune sauce (page 65)
Raspberry purée (page 65)
Red currant jelly glaze (page 65)
Turkey gravy (page 74)

Game birds, hare and venison
Agrodolce (page 20)
Beef stock gravy (page 25)
Bigarade (page 26)
Bordelaise (page 28)
Bread sauce (page 28)
Brown sauce (page 29)
Buttered crumbs (page 29)
Calvados cream (page 30)
Chasseur (page 31)
Chestnut sauce (page 32)
Demi glace (page 40)
Espagnole (page 45)
Madeira sauce (page 55)
Poivrade (page 63)
Port wine sauce (page 64)
Rich gravy (page 66)
Red wine marinade (page 97)
Sour cream gravy (page 69)

Rabbit
Agrodolce (page 20)
Brown sauce (page 29)
Chasseur (page 31)
Creole sauce (page 37)

Hot Chicken and Veal

Chicken

Allemande (page 20)
Almond sauce (page 20)
Aurore (page 22)
Barbecue baste with ginger and
    soy (page 22)
Barbecue hot baste (page 23)
Barbecue mustard baste (page 23)
Barbecue red baste (page 23)
Béchamel (page 24)
Beurre noisette (page 26)
Bread sauce (page 28)
Celery sauce (page 31)
Chasseur (page 31)
Chili tomato sauce (page 32)
Chinese sparerib sauce (page 33)
Cream cheese sauce (page 36)
Cream sauce (page 36)
Creole sauce (page 37)
Curry cream sauce (page 40)
Curry sauce (page 40)

Egg and lemon sauce (page 44)
Fines herbes (page 48)
Foaming wine sauce (page 48)
Green peppercorn sauce (page 50)
Guacamole (page 88)
Gumbo (page 51)
Hazelnut and almond sauce
    (page 88)
Herby onion gravy (page 51)
Hollandaise (page 52)
Horseradish cream (page 89)
à la King (page 53)
Korma curry sauce (page 53)
Light gravy (page 54)
Mole poblano (page 58)
Mornay (page 58)
Mushroom sauce (page 59)
Mushroom and wine cream
    (page 59)
Mustard sauce (page 60)
Oyster and soy sauce (page 62)
Parsley sauce (page 63)
Poulette (page 64)
Rich gravy (page 66)

Springtime green sauce (page 70)
Suprême (page 71)
Tarragon sauce (page 72)
Teriyaki sauce (page 72)
Velouté (page 74)
Watercress cream (page 106)

Veal

Allemande (page 20)
Béchamel (page 24)
Calvados cream (page 30)
Chive sauce (page 63)
Deviled cream (page 41)
Fines herbes (page 48)
Green fields sauce (page 50)
Mushroom and wine cream
    (page 59)
Mustard sauce (page 60)
Newburg sauce (page 61)
Orange cream (page 61)
Orange sauce (page 62)
Paprika sauce (page 62)
Velouté (page 74)
Watercress cream (page 106)

Pasta, Pizza, Rice and Hot Eggs

Cooked eggs

Allemande (page 20)
Aurore (page 22)
Béchamel (page 24)
Bourguignonne (page 28)
Cheddar cheese sauce (page 31)
Chili tomato sauce (page 32)
Cream sauce (page 36)
Curry cream sauce (page 40)
Curry sauce (page 40)
Deviled cream (page 41)
Fines herbes (page 48)
Fondue (page 49)
Garlic fondue (page 49)
Mornay (page 58)
Soufflé cheese sauce (page 69)
Velouté (page 74)

Pasta

Americaine (with shrimp) (p. 20)
Anchovy butter (page 80)
Bagna cauda (page 109)

Blender tomato sauce (page 96)
Bolognese (page 27)
Carbonara (page 30)
Chasseur (page 31)
Cheddar cheese sauce (page 31)
Clam sauce (page 33)
Crab sauce (page 36)
Cream sauce (page 36)
Crème des foies (page 85)
Creole sauce (page 37)
Dolcelatte (page 41)
Emergency tomato sauces
    (page 44)
Five-minute pasta sauce (page 48)
Kidney and red wine sauce (p. 52)
Lemony chicken sauce (page 54)
Lentil sauce (page 54)
Maître d'hôtel butter (page 91)
Marinara (page 56)
Mornay (page 58)
Mushroom sauce (page 59)
Pesto (page 95)
Poulette (page 64)
Raw tomato sauce (page 96)
Shrimp sauce (page 68)
Springtime green sauce (page 70)

Sugo (page 70)
Tomato amatriciana (page 72)
Tomato sauce (page 73)
Winter tomato sauce (page 76)

Pizza

Blender tomato sauce (page 96)
Five-minute pasta sauce (page 48)
Raw tomato sauce (page 96)
Tomato amatriciana (page 72)
Tomato sauce (page 73)
Winter tomato sauce (page 76)

Rice

Apricot and lamb tagine (page 22)
Bolognese (page 27)
Creole sauce (page 37)
Curry sauce (page 40)
Gumbo (page 51)
Kidney and red wine sauce
    (page 52)
Korma curry sauce (page 53)
Lemony chicken sauce (page 54)
Marinara (page 56)
Tomato amatriciana (page 72)
Vindaloo curry sauce (page 74)

Cold Food

Beef, venison and hare
Anchoïade (page 109)
Cucumber relish (page 86)
Damson cheese (page 87)
Demi glace (page 40)
Last-minute chutney (page 90)
Parsley jelly (page 93)
Raita (page 96)
Ravigote (page 122)
Rémoulade (page 97)

Chicken
Cashew cream (page 81)
Chaudfroid (page 82)
Cocktail sauce (page 83)
Coronation sauce (page 83)
Creamy tomato (page 84)
Herby yogurt dressing (page 117)
Jellied mayonnaise (page 90)
Lemon mayonnaise (page 92)
Peach purée (page 122)
Peanut cream (page 100)
Ravigote (page 122)
Russian dressing (page 123)
Sauce verte (page 100)
Tarator (page 105)
Tofu dip or salad dressing
   (page 125)
Tomato sour cream sauce (page 85)
Watercress cream (page 106)

Duck, turkey, goose and game birds
Apple mayonnaise (page 80)
Aspic (page 79)

Cranberry spicy jelly (page 84)
Cranberry whole berry sauce
   (page 84)
Orange pickle (page 94)
Piquant mayonnaise (page 92)

Ham, tongue and headcheese
Cambridge sauce (page 81)
Chaudfroid (page 82)
Cumberland sauce (page 86)
Green-green dressing (page 116)
Orange pickle (page 94)
Peach purée (page 122)
Ravigote (page 122)
Rémoulade (page 97)
Russian dressing (page 123)

Hard-cooked eggs
Anchoïade (page 109)
Basil and tomato sauce (page 109)
Creamy tomato sauce (page 84)
Cucumber cream (page 85)
Curry mayonnaise (page 92)
Eggless thick dressing (page 113)
Green goddess dressing (p. 113)
Mayonnaise (page 92)
Raw tomato sauce (page 96)
Salad cream (page 123)
Tahini cream (page 104)
Tomato aspic (page 105)
Tomato dressing (page 125)
Tomato sour cream sauce (page 85)
Watercress cream (page 106)

Lamb
Aspic (page 79)
Chantilly mint sauce (page 82)

Chaudfroid (page 82)
Cucumber and yogurt dip (page 86)
Herby aspic (page 79)
Mint jelly (page 93)
Mint sauce (page 93)
Rosemary jelly (page 93)
Soubise (page 68)

Pork and rabbit
Apple mayonnaise (page 80)
Apple sauce, Normandy-style
   (page 130)
Banana raita (page 81)
Chaudfroid (page 82)
Cucumber and yogurt dip (page 86)
Damson cheese (page 87)
Last-minute chutney (page 90)
Orange pickle (page 94)
Rémoulade (page 97)
Spicy tomato sauce (page 73)
Tomato aspic (page 105)

Veal
Apple horseradish (page 80)
Aspic (page 79)
Blender tomato sauce (page 96)
Chaudfroid (page 82)
Cranberry spicy jelly (page 84)
Cumberland sauce (page 86)
Damson cheese (page 87)
Green-green dressing (page 116)
Last-minute chutney (page 90)
Piquant mayonnaise (page 92)
Ravigote (page 122)
Tuna mayonnaise (page 106)

Reheating Leftovers

Beef and lamb
Beef stock gravy (page 25)
Brown sauce (page 29)
Emergency tomato sauces
   (page 44)
Five-minute pasta sauce (page 48)
Lyonnaise (page 55)
Sweet and sour, Chinese style
   (page 71)
Tomato sauce (page 73)

Chicken and turkey
Celery sauce (page 31)
Creole sauce (page 37)
Curry sauce (page 40)
Deviled cream (page 41)
Emergency tomato sauces (p. 44)
Five-minute pasta sauce (page 48)
à la King (page 53)
Lyonnaise (page 55)
Mushroom and wine cream (p. 59)
Orange sauce (page 62)
Paprika sauce (page 62)
Sweet and sour, Chinese style (71)
Tomato amatriciana (page 72)

Pork, ham and veal
Cider sauce (page 33)
Creole sauce (page 37)
Cumberland sauce (page 86)
Curry sauce (page 40)
à la King (page 53)
Korma curry sauce (page 53)
Mushroom sauce (page 59)
Mushroom and wine cream (p. 59)
Orange sauce (page 62)
Paprika sauce (page 62)
Piquant brown sauce (page 63)
Tomato amatriciana (page 72)

Hot Fish and Shellfish

Crêpes, patty shells and pastry cases
Crab sauce (page 36)
Nantua (page 60)
Newburg sauce (with shrimp) (page 61)
Shrimp sauce (page 68)

Deep-fried fish and shellfish
Chili tomato sauce (page 32)
Colbert butter (page 91)
Rémoulade (page 97)
Skordalia (page 101)
Tartare (page 105)

Fried and broiled fish and shellfish
Anchovy butter (page 80)
Aurore (page 22)
Beurre blanc (page 26)
Browned butter (page 26)
Cream cheese sauce (page 36)
Creole sauce (page 37)
Devil sauce (page 41)
Fennel and Pernod sauce (page 45)
Gooseberry sauce (page 49)
Green peppercorn butter (page 91)
Hot tomato sauce (page 89)
Lemon marinade (page 91)
Maître d'hôtel butter (page 91)
Montpellier butter (page 94)
Mushroom sauce (page 59)
Mustard butter (page 91)
Red wine sauce (page 66)
Rémoulade (page 97)

Rusty sauce (page 97)
Skordalia (page 101)
Snail butter (page 101)
Tartare (page 105)
Teriyaki sauce (page 72)
Tomato sauce (page 73)
Watercress sauce (page 75)

Mousses, timbales and quenelles
Crab sauce (page 36)
Foaming wine sauce (page 48)
Green fields sauce (page 50)
Hollandaise (page 52)
Mousseline (page 59)
Nantua (page 60)

Poached fish
Allemande (page 20)
Anchovy butter (page 80)
Béchamel 2 (page 25)
Bercy (page 25)
Caper sauce (page 30)
Cheddar cheese sauce (page 31)
Chive sauce (page 63)
Court bouillon for fish (page 12)
Crab sauce (page 36)
Cream sauce (page 36)
Creole sauce (page 37)
Cucumber cream (page 85)
Curry cream sauce (page 40)
Egg sauce (page 44)
Egg and lemon sauce (page 44)
Fish fumet (page 12)
Fish glaze (page 12)
Foaming wine sauce (page 48)
Grape cream (page 50)
Green butter (page 87)
Green peppercorn sauce (page 50)

Hazelnut and almond sauce (page 88)
Hollandaise (page 52)
Korma curry sauce (page 53)
Maître d'hôtel butter (page 91)
Maltaise (page 55)
Mock hollandaise (page 58)
Mornay (page 58)
Mushroom sauce (page 59)
Mustard sauce (page 60)
Nantua (page 60)
Parsley sauce (page 63)
Pimiento cream (page 95)
Quick court bouillon (page 12)
Saffron cream (page 67)
Shellfish butter (page 100)
Shrimp sauce (page 68)
Soufflé cheese sauce (page 69)
Suprême (page 71)
Velouté (page 74)
Whiskey cream (page 75)
White wine sauce (page 76)

Shellfish
Americaine (page 20)
Beurre blanc (page 26)
Creole sauce (page 37)
Curry cream sauce (page 40)
Hazelnut and almond sauce (p. 88)
Korma curry sauce (page 53)
Maltaise (page 55)
Newburg sauce (page 61)
Orange cream (page 61)
Poulette (page 64)
Saffron cream (page 67)
Shellfish butter (page 100)
Snail butter (page 101)
Tartare (page 105)

Cold Fish and Shellfish

Poached white fish
Aïoli (page 80)
Basil and tomato sauce (page 109)
Crème frappé (page 85)
Dill and mustard cream (page 112)
Dill and sour cream sauces (page 87)
Green goddess dressing (page 113)
Green-green dressing (page 116)
Mayonnaise (page 92)

Mustard chantilly (page 94)
Ravigote (page 122)
Raw tomato sauce (page 96)
Sauce gribiche (page 97)
Sauce verte (page 100)
Watercress cream (page 106)

Shellfish
Blender tomato sauce (page 96)
Cocktail sauce (page 83)
Coronation sauce (page 83)
Creamy tomato sauce (page 84)

Dill and sour cream sauces (p. 87)
Green goddess dressing (page 113)
Green-green dressing (page 116)
Hot tomato sauce (page 89)
Mayonnaise (page 92)
Mustard chantilly (page 94)
Raw tomato sauce (page 96)
Russian dressing (page 123)
Sauce gribiche (page 97)
Thousand island dressing (page 125)
Tomato aspic (page 105)
Tuna mayonnaise (page 106)

Hot Vegetables

Asparagus and artichoke hearts
Beurre blanc (page 26)
Beurre noisette (page 26)
Hollandaise (page 52)
Maître d'hôtel butter (page 91)
Mousseline (page 59)
Snail butter (page 101)

Baked potatoes and vegetables baked in foil
Aïoli (page 80)
Maître d'hôtel butter (page 91)
Pesto (page 95)
Pimiento cream (page 95)
Snail butter (page 101)

Beans and chick-peas
Aïoli (page 80)
Anchovy butter (page 80)
Bolognese (page 27)
Creole sauce (page 37)
Five-minute pasta sauce (page 48)
Pesto (page 95)
Rusty sauce (page 97)
Skordalia (page 101)
Sugo (page 70)
Tomato amatriciana (page 72)
Vindaloo curry sauce (page 74)

Boiled and steamed vegetables
Aïoli (page 80)
Allemande (page 20)
Béchamel (pages 24–25)
Cream sauce (page 36)
Egg and lemon sauce (page 44)

Hollandaise (page 52)
Maître d'hôtel butter (page 91)
Mock hollandaise (page 58)
Parsley sauce (page 63)
Poulette (page 64)
Soufflé cheese sauce (page 69)
Tarragon sauce (page 72)
Tomato sauce (page 73)
Velouté (page 74)
Winter tomato sauce (page 76)

Broiled and deep-fried vegetables
Chili dip (page 82)
Creole sauce (page 37)
Montpellier butter (page 94)
Rusty sauce (page 97)
Skordalia (page 101)
Tomato amatriciana (page 72)

Cabbage and Brussels sprouts
Buttered almond sauce (page 29)
Buttered crumbs à la polonaise (page 29)
Stir-fry Chinese sauce (page 70)

Cauliflower and broccoli
Beurre blanc (page 26)
Beurre noisette (page 26)
Buttered almond sauce (page 29)
Buttered crumbs (page 29)
Curry cream sauce (page 40)
Hollandaise (page 52)
Tomato and coriander bouillon (page 72)

Gratins
Béchamel (page 24)
Cheddar cheese sauce (page 31)

Cream sauce (page 36)
Mornay (page 58)
Soufflé cheese sauce (page 69)

Green beans
Dolcelatte (page 41)
Emergency tomato sauces (page 44)
Green butter (page 87)
Tomato sauce (page 73)

Mousses
Cream sauce (page 36)
Curry cream sauce (page 40)
Foaming wine sauce (page 48)
Mushroom sauce (page 59)
Suprême (page 71)
White wine sauce (page 76)

Peas
Browned butter (page 26)
Chantilly mint sauce (page 82)
Hollandaise (page 52)
Mint butter (page 57)

Roast vegetables and fritters
Chili dip (page 82)
Emergency tomato sauces (page 44)
Snail butter (page 101)
Tomato sauce (page 73)
Winter tomato sauce (page 76)
Yogurt dressing (page 106)

Zucchini and leeks
Beurre blanc (page 26)
Fines herbes (page 48)
Sweet and sour, Italian style (p. 71)
Tomato and coriander bouillon (page 72)

Salmon or other whole fish
Aspic (page 79)
Chaudfroid (page 82)
Crème frappé (page 85)
Cucumber cream (page 85)
Jellied mayonnaise (page 90)
Tarator (page 105)

Smoked fish
Cossack dressing (page 123)
Crème frappé (page 85)
Horseradish cream (page 89)

Salads

Coleslaw
Apple mayonnaise (page 80)
Caraway dressing (page 110)
Coleslaw dressing (page 111)
Creamy mayonnaise (page 92)
Dairy cheese dressing (page 112)
Dill and mustard cream (page 112)
Dill and sour cream sauces (page 87)
Eggless thick dressing (page 113)

Green pepper cream (page 116)
Mock mayonnaise (page 121)
Peanut cream (page 100)
Raita (page 96)
Sour cream dressing (page 124)
Tahini cream (page 104)
Tomato dressing (page 125)
Tuna mayonnaise (page 106)
Watercress cream (page 106)
Yogurt dressing (page 106)

Continued overleaf

Salads (from previous page)

Cooked, cold vegetables

Aïoli (page 80)
Basil and tomato sauce (page 109)
Butler's dressing (page 110)
Buttermilk dressing (page 110)
Cashew cream (page 81)
Chiffonade dressing (page 111)
Cocktail sauce (page 83)
Coleslaw dressing (page 111)
Cottage cheese dressing (page 112)
Creamy tomato sauce (page 84)
Cucumber cream (page 85)
Dairy cheese dressing (page 112)
Eggless thick dressing (page 113)
Green pepper cream (page 116)
Herb dressing in one minute (p. 116)
Honey sweet and sour dressing
   (page 117)
Ketchup pour over (page 120)
Onion vinaigrette (page 126)
Ravigote (page 122)
Sesame seed dressing (page 124)
Tofu dip or salad dressing (p. 125)
Tomato aspic (page 105)
Tomato and coriander bouillon
   (page 72)
Watercress cream (page 106)
Yogurt dressing (page 106)

Dips for raw vegetables

Aïoli (page 80)
Anchoïade (page 109)
Bagna cauda (page 109)
Cashew cream (page 81)
Chantilly mint sauce (page 82)
Cocktail sauce (page 83)
Coconut sambal (page 83)
Crème des foies (page 85)
Cottage cheese dressing (page 112)
Curry mayonnaise (page 92)
Guacamole (page 88)
Herby garlic mayonnaise (page 92)
Hummus (page 90)
Mem sahib's dressing (page 121)
Peanut cream (page 100)
Pimiento cream (page 95)
Poor man's caviar (page 96)
Raita (page 96)
Tuna mayonnaise (page 106)

Dried legumes

Aïoli (page 80)

Anchoïade (page 109)
Bagna cauda (page 109)
Basil and honey vinaigrette (p. 109)
Basil and tomato sauce (page 109)
Celery seed dressing (page 111)
Curry mayonnaise (page 92)
Green goddess dressing (page 113)
Herb dressing in one minute
   (page 116)
Herby garlic mayonnaise (page 92)
Honey and yogurt dressing
   (page 117)
Ketchup pour over (page 120)
Lemon cream dressing (page 126)
Mustard vinaigrette (page 126)
Onion vinaigrette (page 126)
Sweet vinaigrette (page 126)
Tuna mayonnaise (page 106)

Fruit appetizers

Celery seed dressing (page 111)
Creamy lemon dressing (page 126)
Curry vinaigrette (page 112)
Dairy cheese dressing (page 112)
Lime or lemon dressing (page 120)
Mayonnaise (page 92)
Mem sahib's dressing (page 121)
Roquefort cream (page 123)
Salad cream (page 123)
Sour cream dressing (page 124)

Green salads

Butler's dressing (page 110)
Buttermilk dressing (page 110)
Caesar dressing (page 110)
Chapons (page 108)
Chiffonade dressing (page 111)
Cottage cheese dressing (page 112)
Croûtons (page 120)
Dairy cheese dressing (page 112)
Egg vinaigrette (page 113)
Herb dressing in one minute (p. 116)
Honey sweet and sour dressing
   (page 117)
Italian dressing with croûtons
   (page 120)
Lime or lemon dressing (page 120)
Low calorie dressing (page 121)
Parmesan dressing (page 122)
Soy salad dressing (page 121)
Sydney Smith's salad dressing
   (page 124)
Tarragon dressing (page 124)

Thousand island dressing
   (page 125)
Tofu dip or salad dressing
   (page 125)
Vinaigrette (page 126)
Walnut oil vinaigrette (page 126)
Yogurt dressing (page 106)

Potato salad

Apple mayonnaise (page 80)
Basil and tomato sauce (page 109)
Butler's dressing (page 110)
Cambridge sauce (page 81)
Chiffonade dressing (page 111)
Cocktail sauce (page 83)
Creamy mayonnaise (page 92)
Creamy tomato sauce (page 84)
Dill and sour cream sauces
   (page 87)
Egg vinaigrette (page 113)
Green goddess dressing (page 113)
Herb dressing in one minute (p. 116)
Herby garlic mayonnaise (page 92)
Hot bacon dressing (page 117)
Ravigote (page 122)
Sauce verte (page 100)
Thousand island dressing (p. 125)
Vinaigrette (page 126)

Spreads for bread, crackers

Anchoïade (page 109)
Anchovy butter (page 80)
Garlic butter (page 101)
Maître d'hôtel butter (page 91)
Pimiento cream (page 95)
Roquefort cream (page 123)
Sardine butter (page 80)
Snail butter (page 101)

Tomato salad

Aïoli (page 80)
Anchoïade (page 109)
Basil and honey vinaigrette (p. 109)
Curry vinaigrette (page 112)
Eggless thick dressing (page 113)
Green-green dressing (page 116)
Green pepper cream (page 116)
Honey and yogurt dressing (p. 117)
Mem sahib's dressing (page 121)
Minty vinaigrette (page 116)
Salad cream (page 123)
Soy salad dressing (page 121)
Watercress cream (page 106)

Hot Fruit Desserts

Baked apples, bananas, etc
Ali baba sauce (page 130)
Burnt honey cream (page 133)
Butterscotch syrup (page 133)
Caramel syrup (page 134)
Chantilly cream (page 134)
Hard sauce (page 143)
Rum and raisin sauce (page 153)
Sabayon (page 156)
Sauternes sauce (page 156)
Walnut butterscotch syrup (p. 133)

Charlottes and bread puddings
Banana frappé (page 161)
Burnt honey cream (page 133)
Cinnamon frappé (page 136)
Crème anglaise (page 137)
Crème fraîche (page 138)
Foaming butter sauce (page 139)
Fruity fondue (page 141)

Hard sauce (page 143)
Orange yogurt (page 148)
Sabayon (page 156)
Sauternes sauce (page 156)

Compotes, stewed fruit, purées
Chantilly cream (page 134)
Cinnamon frappé (page 136)
Crème fraîche (page 138)
Mock cream (page 148)
Orange yogurt (page 148)
Sour cream sauce (page 157)
Vanilla foam (page 160)

Fritters and deep-fried fruit
Apricot liqueur sauce (page 130)
Cocoa sauce (page 136)
Dunking syrup (page 129)
Pineapple orange sauce (page 141)
Pineapple sauce (page 149)
Rum and raisin sauce (page 153)
Sabayon (page 156)
Suzette sauce (page 160)

Vanilla sugar (page 128)

Pies
Banana frappé (page 161)
Burnt honey cream (page 133)
Crème anglaise (page 137)
Fluffy butter sauce (page 139)
Foaming butter sauce (page 139)
Sour cream sauce (page 157)
Vanilla foam (page 160)
Vanilla sugar (page 128)

Poached pears, peaches, etc
Caramel syrup (page 134)
Cinnamon frappé (page 136)
Cocoa sauce (page 136)
Green peppercorn syrup (page 142)
Orange yogurt (page 148)
Red wine syrup (page 152)
Sauternes sauce (page 156)
Sugar syrup (page 129)
Vanilla foam (page 160)
Wine foam (page 161)

Hot Desserts

Chocolate and coffee desserts
Apricot liqueur sauce (p. 130)
Chocolate sauce Belle Hélène (page 135)
Cocoa sauce (page 136)
Coffee liqueur sauce (page 137)
Instant coffee cream (page 144)
Maple cream (page 145)
Mocha mousseline (page 145)
Pineapple sauce (page 149)

Crêpes, pancakes, waffles
Apple and date sauce (page 130)
Black currant purée (page 131)
Blueberry sauce (page 132)
Brandy cream (page 132)
Burnt honey cream (page 133)
Butterscotch syrup (page 133)
Caramel syrup (page 134)
Cherry jubilee (page 134)
Chocolate fudge sauce (page 141)
Coffee liqueur sauce (page 137)
Cranberry spicy jelly (page 84)
Crème au beurre (page 138)
Egg nog sauce (page 139)

Fluffy butter sauce (page 139)
Frangipane (page 140)
Fudgy cream (page 141)
Jammy jammy (page 144)
Maple cream (page 145)
Maple, orange pancake sauce (page 145)
Suzette sauce (page 160)

Fritters and beignets
Apple and walnut sauce (page 130)
Dunking syrup (page 129)
Pineapple orange sauce (page 141)
Pineapple sauce (page 149)
Rose-water syrup (page 153)
Rum and raisin sauce (page 153)
Sabayon (page 156)

Milky grain puddings
Ali baba sauce (page 130)
Apricot liqueur sauce (page 130)
Blackberry kir (page 131)
Blueberry sauce (page 132)
Cherry sauce (page 32)
Fudgy cream (page 141)

Plum pudding, mince pies
Brandy butter (page 132)
Brandy cream (page 132)

Foaming butter sauce (page 139)
Hard sauce (page 143)

Soufflés and omelettes
Apricot liqueur sauce (page 130)
Butterscotch syrup (page 133)
Cherry sauce (page 32)
Cinnamon apple sauce (page 130)
Pineapple sauce (page 149)

Sponge, batter, suet puddings
Apple sauce, Normandy-style (130)
Blueberry sauce (page 132)
Butterscotch syrup (page 133)
Cherry sauce (page 32)
Cocoa sauce (page 136)
Crème anglaise (page 137)
Egg nog sauce (page 139)
Fluffy butter sauce (page 139)
Foaming butter sauce (page 139)
Gingered honey (page 142)
Golden lemon sauce (page 142)
Lemon 'n' lime sauce (page 142)
Jammy jammy (page 144)
Orange yogurt (page 148)
Port wine plum sauce (page 149)
Rhubarb sauce (page 49)
Sabayon (page 156)

Chilled Fruit

Apricots and peaches
Apple and sour cream sauce
(page 130)
Fruit foam (page 157)
Melba sauce (page 145)
Rich rum cream (page 153)
Strawberry cream (page 160)
Syllabub (page 160)
Whipped banana topping
(page 161)

Banana splits
Blueberry sauce (page 132)
Heady cherry sauce (page 143)
Melba sauce (page 145)
Rum and raisin sauce (page 153)

Blackberries, black currants and blueberries
Chantilly cream (page 134)
Cinnamon frappé (page 136)
Crème anglaise (page 137)

Dried fruit compotes
Apple and sour cream sauce (p. 130)
Burnt honey cream (page 133)
Citrus fluff (page 136)
Coconut cream (page 136)
Crème anglaise (page 137)
Gingered honey (page 142)
Orange yogurt (page 148)

Fruit salad
Brittle topping (page 132)

Burnt honey cream (page 133)
Caramel syrup (page 134)
Chantilly cream (page 134)
Citrus fluff (page 136)
Coconut cream (page 136)
Crème fraîche (page 138)
Fruity cream cheese (page 140)
Fruit foam (page 157)
Mock cream (page 148)
Orange yogurt (page 148)
Praline (page 152)
Sour cream sauce (page 157)
Strawberry cream (page 160)
Syllabub (page 160)
Vanilla foam (page 160)
Wine foam (page 161)

Mousses and purées
Chantilly cream (page 134)
Chocolate marquise (page 135)
Citrus fluff (page 136)
Crème fraîche (page 138)
Fruity cream cheese (page 140)
Fruit foam (page 157)
Orange yogurt (page 148)
Praline (page 152)
Vanilla foam (page 160)

Oranges and pineapples
Brittle topping (page 132)
Caramel syrup (page 134)
Coconut cream (page 136)
Coconut lime or lemon sauce (137)
Crème anglaise (page 137)
Ginger syrup sauce (page 142)
Orange yogurt (page 148)

Stewed and poached fruit
Chantilly cream (page 134)
Cinnamon frappé (page 136)
Crème anglaise (page 137)
Sour cream sauce (page 157)
Wine foam (page 161)

Strawberries and raspberries
Chantilly cream (page 134)
Chocolate marquise (page 135)
Citrus fluff (page 136)
Crème anglaise (page 137)
Ganache (page 141)
Hazelnut cream (page 143)
Melba sauce (page 145)
Orange yogurt (page 148)
Sherry custard (page 156)
Sour cream sauce (page 157)
Syllabub (page 160)
Whipped banana topping (p. 161)
Wine foam (page 161)

Tarts and flans
Apricot glaze (page 21)
Chantilly cream (page 134)
Crème anglaise (page 137)
Crème fraîche (page 138)
Crème pâtissière (page 138)
Frangipane (page 140)
Italian meringue (page 144)
Mock cream (page 148)
Rich rum cream (page 153)
Sherry custard (page 156)
Sour cream sauce (page 157)
Strawberry cream (page 160)
Syllabub (page 160)
Wine foam (page 161)

Ice Creams

Apple and date sauce (page 130)
Apple sauce, Normandy-style (130)
Apple and walnut sauce (page 130)
Blackberry kir (page 131)
Black currant purée (page 131)
Brittle topping (page 132)
Cherry jubilee (page 134)
Chocolate marquise (page 135)
Chocolate fudge sauce (page 141)

Chocolate sauce Belle Hélène
(page 135)
Cinnamon apple sauce (page 130)
Coffee liqueur sauce (page 137)
Coffee and nut sauce (page 144)
Cranberry whole berry sauce (p. 84)
Fruit sundae sauce (page 140)
Fudgy cream (page 141)
Ganache (page 141)
Heady cherry sauce (page 143)
Hot caramel sauce (page 133)
Instant coffee cream (page 144)

Maple cream (page 145)
Melba sauce (page 145)
Molasses cream (page 145)
Nectarine sauce (page 149)
Nutty fudge sauce (page 141)
Peach sauce (page 149)
Port wine plum sauce (page 149)
Praline (page 152)
Raisin fudge sauce (page 141)
Redberry sauce (page 152)
Suzette sauce (page 160)
Treacle cream (page 145)

Cakes, Cheesecakes and Meringues

Angel cakes
Apricot nectar (page 131)
Cherry sauce (page 32)
Cranberry spicy jelly (page 84)
Damson cheese (page 87)
Fruit sundae sauce (page 140)
Heady cherry sauce (page 143)
Italian meringue (page 144)
Pineapple sauce (page 149)
Redberry sauce (page 152)
Rich rum cream (page 153)
Rum and raisin sauce (page 153)
Sauternes sauce (page 156)
Sherry custard (page 156)
Spiced mango sauce (page 157)
Strawberry cream (page 160)
Whipped banana topping
  (page 161)
Wine foam (page 161)

Cheesecakes
Black currant purée (page 131)
Blueberry sauce (page 132)
Cherry sauce (page 32)

Cold Desserts

Chocolate and coffee desserts
Apple and walnut sauce (page 130)
Brandy cream (page 132)
Chocolate custard (page 135)
Hazelnut cream (page 143)
Heady cherry sauce (page 143)
Rich rum cream (page 153)

Cookies and tartlets
Cranberry spicy jelly (page 84)
Cumberland rum butter (p. 132)
Damson cheese (page 87)
Fluffy butter sauce (page 139)
Fruity cream cheese (page 140)
Hard sauce (page 143)

Cream cheese desserts
Ali baba sauce (page 130)
Apple and walnut sauce (page 130)

Heady cherry sauce (page 143)
Redberry sauce (page 152)

Cream puffs, éclairs and sweet rolls
Apricot nectar (page 131)
Chantilly cream (page 134)
Chocolate marquise (page 135)
Crème au beurre (page 138)
Crème pâtissière (page 138)
Crème St Honoré (page 139)
Frangipane (page 140)
Hard sauce (page 143)
Hazelnut cream (page 143)
Pâtissier's lemon sauce (page 148)
Praline (page 152)

Flaky and puff pastry
Chantilly cream (page 134)
Crème au beurre (page 138)
Crème pâtissière (page 138)
Frangipane (page 140)
Hazelnut cream (page 143)
Pâtissier's lemon sauce (page 148)
Praline (with cream) (page 152)
Rose-water syrup (page 153)
Walnut cream (page 161)

Meringues, tortes and nut layers
Apricot nectar (page 131)

Apricot nectar (page 131)
Cherry sauce (page 32)
Cranberry spicy jelly (page 84)
Damson cheese (page 87)
Melba sauce (page 145)
Peach sauce (page 149)
Redberry sauce (page 152)
Spiced mango sauce (page 157)

Milky grain puddings
Ali baba sauce (page 130)
Blackberry kir (page 131)
Cherry sauce (page 32)
Cranberry whole berry sauce
  (page 84)
Redberry sauce (page 152)
Spiced mango sauce (page 157)

Mousses and cold puddings
Apple sauce, Normandy-style
  (page 130)
Apricot liqueur sauce (page 130)

Black currant purée (page 131)
Chantilly cream (page 134)
Chocolate marquise (page 135)
Crème au beurre (page 138)
Hazelnut cream (page 143)
Italian meringue (page 144)
Praline buttercream (page 138)
Walnut cream (page 161)

Savarins and babas
Blueberry sauce (page 132)
Cherry sauce (page 32)
Fruit sundae sauce (page 140)
Heady cherry sauce (page 143)
Savarin rum syrup (page 156)

Sponge cake layers
Apricot nectar (page 131)
Chantilly cream (page 134)
Chocolate marquise (page 135)
Crème au beurre (page 138)
Crème pâtissière (page 138)
Frangipane (page 140)
Hard sauce (page 143)
Italian meringue (page 144)
Pâtissier's lemon sauce (page 148)
Praline (with cream) (page 152)
Whipped banana topping
  (page 161)

Blackberry kir (page 131)
Black currant purée (page 131)
Blueberry sauce (page 132)
Fruit sundae sauce (page 140)
Heady cherry sauce (page 143)
Redberry sauce (page 152)
Melba sauce (page 145)
Strawberry cream (page 160)

Yogurt and baked custard
Apple and date sauce (page 130)
Apricot liqueur sauce (page 130)
Blackberry kir (page 131)
Black currant purée (page 131)
Blueberry sauce (page 132)
Cherry sauce (page 32)
Gingered honey (page 142)
Port wine plum sauce (page 149)
Redberry sauce (page 152)
Rose-water syrup (page 153)
Spiced mango sauce (page 157)

INDEX